VOLUME NINETY EIGHT

ADVANCES IN
COMPUTERS

VOLUME NINETY EIGHT

Advances in
COMPUTERS

Edited by

ALI R. HURSON

*Missouri University of Science and Technology Rolla,
MO, USA*

AMSTERDAM • BOSTON • HEIDELBERG • LONDON
NEW YORK • OXFORD • PARIS • SAN DIEGO
SAN FRANCISCO • SINGAPORE • SYDNEY • TOKYO
Academic Press is an imprint of Elsevier

Academic Press is an imprint of Elsevier
225 Wyman Street, Waltham, MA 02451, USA
525 B Street, Suite 1800, San Diego, CA 92101-4495, USA
125 London Wall, London, EC2Y 5AS, UK
The Boulevard, Langford Lane, Kidlington, Oxford OX5 1GB, UK

First edition 2015

Notices
Knowledge and best practice in this field are constantly changing. As new research and experience broaden our understanding, changes in research methods, professional practices, or medical treatment may become necessary.

Practitioners and researchers must always rely on their own experience and knowledge in evaluating and using any information, methods, compounds, or experiments described herein. In using such information or methods they should be mindful of their own safety and the safety of others, including parties for whom they have a professional responsibility.

To the fullest extent of the law, neither the Publisher nor the authors, contributors, or editors, assume any liability for any injury and/or damage to persons or property as a matter of products liability, negligence or otherwise, or from any use or operation of any methods, products, instructions, or ideas contained in the material herein.

ISBN: 978-0-12-802132-3
ISSN: 0065-2458

For information on all Academic Press publications
visit our web site at store.elsevier.com

Working together
to grow libraries in
developing countries

www.elsevier.com • www.bookaid.org

CONTENTS

PREFACE

Traditionally, *Advances in Computers*, the oldest series to chronicle the rapid evolution of computing, annually publishes four volumes, each typically comprised of four to eight chapters, describing new developments in the theory and applications of computing. The theme of this 98th volume is inspired by the advances in information technology. Within the spectrum of information technology, this volume touches a variety of topics ranging from computer architecture and energy-efficient design techniques, cyber-physical critical infrastructure systems, model-based testing, and multi-objective optimization methods. The volume is a collection of four chapters that were solicited from authorities in the field, each of whom brings to bear a unique perspective on the topic.

In Chapter 1, "An Overview of Architecture-Level Power- and Energy-Efficient Design Techniques," Ratković *et al.* articulate the holistic consideration of power and energy consumption of computer systems at all design levels without sacrificing the processing power. Several circuit and architectural metrics are defined, the notion of dynamic and static energy is discussed, distinction between power and energy is articulated, and metrics such as "Energy-Delay Product" and "Energy per Instruction" are introduced. The Chapter then classifies, surveys, and analyzes, in detail, recent power- and energy-efficient optimization techniques such as dynamic voltage and frequency scaling (DVFS), power gating, and clock gating, as advanced in the literature.

In Chapter 2, "A Survey of Research on Data Corruption in Cyber-Physical Critical Infrastructure Systems," Woodard *et al.* emphasize the effect of data corruption, either intentional (i.e., cyber, physical, or cyber-physical attacks) or unintentional (i.e., failures in sensors, processors, storage, or communication hardware), within the scope of critical cyber-physical systems (i.e., power grids, intelligent water distribution networks, smart transportation systems). It presents a comprehensive analysis of various data corruption and mitigation techniques. Finally, a number of studies on the negative effects of system execution on corrupted data are presented.

In Chapter 3, "A Research Overview of Tool-Supported Model-Based Testing of Requirements-Based Designs," Marinescu *et al.* address software testing objectives as a means to gain confidence in software products through fault detection, by observing the differences between the behavior of the implementation and the expected behavior described in the specification. The Chapter presents an overview of and classifies the state of the art in tool-supported model-based testing with an eye toward gaining insight into the gaps in the current tools used by industry and academia. Four representative tools (i.e., ProTest, UPPAAL Cover, MaTeLo, and CompleteTest) are chosen to show the differences in modeling notations, test-case generation methods, and the produced test cases.

Finally, in Chapter 4, "Preference Incorporation in Evolutionary Multiobjective Optimization: A Survey of the State of the Art," Bechikh *et al.* emphasize on the application of evolutionary algorithms as a means for multiobjective optimization. A classification of preference-based Multi-objective Optimization Evolutionary Algorithms based on the structure of the decision maker's preference information is presented and several approaches are discussed and analyzed. Finally, the future trends in this research area and some possible paths for future research are outlined.

I hope that you find these articles of interest, and useful in your teaching, research, and other professional activities. I welcome feedback on the volume and suggestions for future volumes.

ALI R. HURSON
Missouri University of Science and Technology
Rolla, MO, USA

CHAPTER ONE

An Overview of Architecture-Level Power- and Energy-Efficient Design Techniques

Ivan Ratković[*,†], Nikola Bežanić[‡], Osman S. Ünsal[*], Adrian Cristal[*,†,§], Veljko Milutinović[‡]

[*]Barcelona Supercomputing Center, Barcelona, Spain
[†]Polytechnic University of Catalonia, Barcelona, Spain
[‡]School of Electrical Engineering, University of Belgrade, Belgrade, Serbia
[§]CSIC-IIIA, Barcelona, Spain

Contents

Abstract

Power dissipation and energy consumption became the primary design constraint for almost all computer systems in the last 15 years. Both computer architects and circuit designers intent to reduce power and energy (without a performance

Advances in Computers, Volume 98
ISSN 0065-2458
http://dx.doi.org/10.1016/bs.adcom.2015.04.001

1

degradation) at all design levels, as it is currently the main obstacle to continue with further scaling according to Moore's law. The aim of this survey is to provide a comprehensive overview of power- and energy-efficient "state-of-the-art" techniques. We classify techniques by component where they apply to, which is the most natural way from a designer point of view. We further divide the techniques by the component of power/energy they optimize (static or dynamic), covering in that way complete low-power design flow at the architectural level. At the end, we conclude that only a holistic approach that assumes optimizations at all design levels can lead to significant savings.

ABBREVIATIONS

A Switching Activity Factor
ABB Adaptive Body Biasing
BHB Block History Buffer
C Capacitance
CMP Chip-Multiprocessor
CPI Cycles per Instruction
CU Control Unit
d Delay
DCG Deterministic Clock Gating
DVFS Dynamic Voltage and Frequency Scaling
DVS Dynamic Voltage Scaling
E Energy
EDP Energy-Delay Product
E^iD^jP Energy^i-Delay^j Product
EPI Energy-per-Instruction
FP Floating Point
FU Functional Unit
GALS Globally Asynchronous Locally Synchronous
IQ Instruction Queue
IPC Instructions Per Cycle
LSQ Load/Store Queue
LUT Look-up Table
MCD Multiple-Clock-Domain
MFLOPS Millions of Floating point Operations Per Second
MILP Mixed-Integer Linear Programming
MIPS Millions of Instructions Per Second
NEMS Nanoelectromechanical Systems
P Power
PCPG Per-Core Power Gating
RBB Reverse Body Biasing
RDO Runtime DVFS Optimizer
RF Register File
ROB Reorder Buffer
SIMD Single Instruction, Multiple Data
UC Micro-Operation Cache

1. INTRODUCTION

After the technology switch from bipolar to CMOS, in the 1980s and early 1990s, digital processor designers had high performance as the primary design goal. At that time, power and area remained to be secondary goals. Power started to become a growing design concern when, in the mid- to late-1990s, it became obvious that further technology feature size scaling according to Moore's law [1] would lead to a higher power density, which could became extremely difficult or almost impossible to cool.

While, during the 1990s, the main way to reduce microprocessor power dissipation was to reduce dynamic power, by the end of the twentieth century the leakage (static) power became a significant problem. In the mid-2000s, rapidly growing static power in microprocessors approaches to its dynamic power dissipation [2]. The leakage current of a MOSFET increases exponentially with a reduction in the threshold voltage. Static power dissipation, a problem that had gone away with the introduction of CMOS, became a forefront issue again.

Different computer systems have different design goals. In high-performance systems, we care more about power dissipation than energy consumption; however, in mobile systems, the situation is reverse. In battery-operated devices, the time between charges is the most important factor; thus, lowering the microprocessor energy as much as possible, without spoiling performance, is the main design goal. Unfortunately, the evolution of the battery capacity is much slower than the electronics one.

Power density limits have already been spoiling planned speed-ups by Moore's law, and this computation acceleration degradation trend is still growing. As technology feature size scaling goes further and further, power density is getting higher and higher. Therefore, it is likely that, very soon, majority of the chip's area is going to be powered off; thus, we will have "dark silicon." Dark silicon (the term was coined by ARM) is defined as the fraction of die area that goes unused due to power, parallelism, or other constraints.

Due to the above described facts, power and energy consumption are currently one of the most important issues faced by computer architecture community and have to be reduced at all possible levels. Thus, there is a need to collect all efficient power/energy optimization techniques in a unified, coherent manner.

This comprehensive survey of architectural-level energy- and power-efficient optimization techniques for microprocessor's cores aims to help low-power designer (especially computer architects) to find appropriate techniques in order to optimize their design. In contrast with the other low-power survey papers [3–5], the classification here is done in a way that processor designers could utilize in a straightforward manner—by component (Section 3). The presentation of the techniques (Section 4) was done by putting the emphasis on newer techniques rather than older ones. The metrics of interest for this survey are presented in Section 2 which help reading for audience with less circuit-level background. Future trends are important in the long-term projects as CMOS scaling will reach its end in a few years. Current state of microprocessor scaling and a short insight of novel technologies are presented in Section 5. At the end, in Section 6 we conclude this chapter and a short review of the current low-power problems.

2. METRICS OF INTEREST

Here we present the metrics of interest as a foundation for later sections. We present both circuit- and architectural-level metrics.

2.1 Circuit-Level Metrics

We can define two types of metrics which are used in digital design—basic and derived metrics. The first one is well-known, while the latter is used in order to provide a better insight into the design trade-offs.

2.1.1 Basic Metrics

Delay (d) Propagation delay, or gate delay, is the essential performance metric, and it is defined as the length of time starting from when the input to a logic gate becomes stable and valid, to the time that the output of that logic gate is stable and valid. There are several exact definitions of delay but it usually refers to the time required for the output to reach from 10% to 90% of its final output level when the input changes. For modules with multiple inputs and outputs, we typically define the propagation delay as the worst-case delay over all possible scenarios.

Capacitance (C) is the ability of a body to hold an electrical charge, and its unit according to IS is the *Farad (F)*. Capacitance can also be defined as a measure of the amount of electrical energy stored (or separated) for a given electric potential. For our purpose more appropriate is the last definition.

Switching Activity Factor (A) of a circuit node is the probability the given node will change its state from 1 to 0 or vice versa at a given clock tick. Activity factor is a function of the circuit topology and the activity of the input signals. Knowledge of activity factor is necessary in order to analytically compute—estimate dynamic power dissipation of a circuit and it is sometimes indirectly expressed in the formulas as $C_{switched}$, which is the product of activity factor and load capacitance of a node C_L. In some literature, symbol α is used instead of A.

Energy (E) is generally defined as the ability of a physical system to perform a work on other physical systems and its SI unit is the *Joule (J)*. The total energy consumption of a digital circuit can be expressed as the sum of two components: dynamic energy (E_{dyn}) and static energy (E_{stat}).

Dynamic energy has three components which are results of the next three sources: charging/discharging capacitances, short-circuit currents, and glitches. For digital circuits analysis, the most relevant energy is one which is needed to charge a capacitor (transition 0→1), as the other components are parasitic; thus, we cannot affect them significantly with architectural-level low-power techniques. For that reason, in the rest of this chapter, the term dynamic energy is referred to the energy spent on charging/discharging capacitances. According to the general energy definition, dynamic energy in digital circuits can be interpreted as: When a transition in a digital circuit occurs (a node changes its state from 0 to 1 or from 1 to 0), some amount of electrical work is done; thus, some amount of electrical energy is spent. In order to obtain analytical expression of dynamic energy, a network node can be modeled as a capacitor C_L which is charged by voltage source V_{DD} through a circuit with resistance R. In this case, the total energy consumed to charge the capacitor C_L is:

$$E = C_L V_{DD}^2 \qquad (1)$$

where the half of the energy is dissipated on R and half is saved in C_L,

$$E_C = E_R = \frac{C V_{DD}^2}{2}. \qquad (2)$$

The total static energy consumption of a digital network is the result of leakage and static currents. Leakage current I_{leak} consists of drain leakage, junction leakage, and gate leakage current, while static current I_{DC} is DC bias current which is needed by some circuits for their correct work. Static energy at a time moment $t(t > 0)$ is given as follows:

$$E(t) = \int_0^t V_{DD}(I_{leak} + I_{DC})\mathrm{d}\tau = V_{DD}(I_{DC} + I_{leak})t. \tag{3}$$

As CMOS technology advances into sub-100 nm, leakage energy is becoming as important as dynamic energy (or even more important).

Power (P) is the rate at which work is performed or energy is converted, and its SI unit is the *Watt (W)*. Average power (which is, for our purpose, more important than instantaneous power) is given with the formula: $P = \frac{\Delta E}{\Delta t}$, in which ΔE is amount of energy consumed in time period Δt. Power dissipation sources in digital circuits can be divided into two major classes: dynamic and static. The difference between the two is that the former is proportional to the activity in the network and the switching frequency, whereas the latter is independent of both.

Dynamic power dissipation, like dynamic energy consumption, has several sources in digital circuits. The most important one is charging/discharging capacitances in a digital network and it is given as:

$$P_{dyn} = AC_L V_{DD}^2 f, \tag{4}$$

in which f is the switching frequency, while A, C_L, and V_{DD} were defined before. The other sources are results of short-circuit currents and glitches, and they are not going to be discussed due to the above-mentioned reasons.

Static power in CMOS digital circuits is a result of leakage and static currents (the same sources which cause static energy). Static power formula is given as follows:

$$P_{stat} = V_{DD}(I_{DC} + I_{leak}). \tag{5}$$

Another related metric is surface power density, which is defined as power per unit area and its unit is $\frac{W}{m^2}$. This metric is the crucial one for thermal studies and cooling system selection and design, as it is related with the temperature of the given surface by *Stefan–Boltzmann law* [6].

2.1.2 Derived Metrics
In today's design environment where both delay and energy play an almost equal role, the basic design metrics may not be sufficient. Hence, some other metrics of potential interest have been defined.

Energy-Delay Product (EDP) Low power often used to be viewed as synonymous with lower performance that, however, in many cases, application runtime is of significant relevance to energy- or power-constrained systems. With the dual goals of low energy and fast runtimes in mind,

EDP was proposed as a useful metric [7]. *EDP* offers equal "weight" to energy and performance degradation. If either energy or delay increases, the *EDP* will increase. Thus, lower *EDP* values are desirable.

Energy^i-Delay^j Product (E^iD^jP) *EDP* shows how close the design is to a perfect balance between performance and energy efficiency. Sometimes, achieving that balance may not necessarily be of interest. Therefore, typically one metric is assigned greater weight, for example, energy is minimized for a given maximum delay or delay is minimized for a given maximum energy. In order to achieve that, we need to adjust exponents i and j in E^iD^jP. In high-performance arena, where performance improvements may matter more than energy savings, we need a metric which has $i < j$, while in low-power design we need one with $i > j$.

2.2 Architectural-Level Metrics

$\frac{MIPS}{Watt}$ Millions of Instructions Per Second (MIPS) per Watt is the most common (and perhaps obvious) metric to characterize the power-performance efficiency of a microprocessor. This metric attempts to quantify efficiency by projecting the performance achieved or gained (measured in MIPS) for every watt of power consumed. Clearly, the higher the number, the "better" the machine is.

$\frac{MIPS^i}{Watt}$ While the previous approach seems a reasonable choice for some purposes, there are strong arguments against it in many cases, especially when it comes to characterizing high-end processors. Specifically, a design team may well choose a higher frequency design point (which meets maximum power budget constraints) even if it operates at a much lower $\frac{MIPS}{W}$ efficiency compared to one that operates at better efficiency but at a lower performance level. As such, $\frac{MIPS^2}{Watt}$ or even $\frac{MIPS^3}{Watt}$ may be appropriate metric of choice. On the other hand, at the lowest end (low-power case), designers may want to put an even greater weight on the power aspect than the simplest MIPS/Watt metric. That is, they may just be interested in minimizing the power for a given workload run, irrespective of the execution time performance, provided the latter does not exceed some specified upper limit.

Energy-per-Instruction (EPI) One more way of expressing the relation between performance (expressed in number of instructions) and power/energy.

$\frac{MFLOPS^i}{Watt}$ While aforementioned metrics are used for all computer systems in general, when we consider scientific and supercomputing, $\frac{MFLOPS^i}{Watt}$ is the most common metric for power-performance efficiency, where Millions of Floating point Operations Per Second (MFLOPS) is a metric for floating point performance.

3. CLASSIFICATION OF SELECTED ARCHITECTURE-LEVEL TECHNIQUES

This section presents a classification of existing examples of architectural-level power and energy-efficient techniques. In the first section, the classification criteria are given. The classification criteria were chosen to reflect the essence of the basic viewpoint of this research. Afterward, the classification tree was obtained by application of the chosen criteria. The leaves of the classification are the classes of examples (techniques). The list of the most relevant examples for each class is given in the second section.

3.1 Criteria

The classification criteria of interest for this research as well as the thereof are given in Table 1. All selected classification criteria are explained in the caption of Table 1 and elaborated as follows:

C1 Criterion C1 is the top criterion and divides the techniques by level at which they can be applied, core- or core blocks level. Here, the term "Core" implies processor's core without L1 cache.

C2 This criterion divides core blocks into front- and back-end of the pipeline. By front-end, we assume control units and RF, while back-end assumes functional units. Where an optimization technique optimizes both front- and back-end, we group them together and call them only *pipeline*.

Table 1 Classification Criteria (C1, C2, C3): Hierarchical Level, Core Block Type, and Type of Power/Energy Being Optimized

C1: Hierarchical level	– Core – Functional blocks
C2: Core block type	– Front-end – Back-end
C3: Type of power/energy being optimized	– Dynamic – Static

C1 is a binary criterion (core, functional blocks); C2 is also binary criterion (functional units, control units, and RF); and C3 is, like the previous two criteria, is binary (dynamic, static).

C3 Application of the last criterion gave us the component of the metric (power or energy) that we optimize.

The full classification tree, derived from the above introduced classification criteria, is presented in Fig. 1. Each leaf of the classification tree is given a name. Names on the figure are short form of the full names as it is presented in Table 2.

3.2 List of Selected Examples

For each class (leaf of the classification), the list of the most relevant existing techniques (examples) is given in Table 3. For each selected technique, the past work is listed in Table 3. The techniques are selected using two criteria. The first criterion by which we chose the most important works is the number of citation. In order to obtain this number, Google Scholar [8] was used. Important practical reasons for this are that Google Scholar is freely available to anyone with an Internet connection, has better citation indexing and

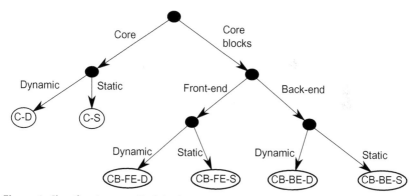

Figure 1 Classification tree. Each leaf represents a class derived by criteria application.

Table 2 Class Short Names Explanations and Class Domains

Short Name	Full Name	Covered Hardware
C-D	Core-Dynamic	Whole core
C-S	Core-Static	
CB-FE-D	Core Blocks-FE-Dynamic	Front-end
CB-FE-S	Core Blocks-FE-Static	
CB-BE-D	Core Blocks-BE-Dynamic	Back-end
CB-BE-S	Core Blocks-BE-Static	

Table 3 List of Presented Solutions
Core-Dynamic

Dynamic Voltage and Frequency Scaling (DVFS)
"Scheduling for reduced CPU energy," M. Weiser, B. Welch, A. J. Demers, and S. Shenker [11]
"Automatic performance setting for dynamic voltage scaling," K. Flautner, S. Reinhardt, and T. Mudge [12]
"The design, implementation, and evaluation of a compiler algorithm for CPU energy reduction," C. Hsu and U. Kremer [13]
"Energy-conscious compilation based on voltage scaling," H. Saputra, M. Kandemir, N. Vijaykrishnan, M. Irwin, J. Hu, C.-H. Hsu, and U. Kremer [14]
"Compile-time dynamic voltage scaling settings: opportunities and limits," F. Xie, M. Martonosi, and S. Malik [15]
"Intraprogram dynamic voltage scaling: bounding opportunities with analytic modeling," F. Xie, M. Martonosi, and S. Malik [16]
"A dynamic compilation framework for controlling microprocessor energy and performance," Q. Wu, V. J. Reddi, Y. Wu, J. Lee, D. Connors, D. Brooks, M. Martonosi, and D. W. Clark [17]
"Identifying program power phase behavior using power vectors," C. Isci and M. Martonosi [18]
"Live, runtime phase monitoring and prediction on real systems with application to dynamic power management," C. Isci, G. Contreras, and M. Martonosi [19]
"Power and performance evaluation of globally asynchronous locally synchronous processors," A. Iyer and D. Marculescu [20]
"Toward a multiple clock/voltage island design style for power-aware processors," E. Talpes and D. Marculescu [21]
"Dynamic frequency and voltage control for a multiple clock domain microarchitecture," G. Semeraro, D. H. Albonesi, S. G. Dropsho, G. Magklis, S. Dwarkadas, and M. L. Scott [22]
"Formal online methods for voltage/frequency control in multiple clock domain microprocessors," Q. Wu, P. Juang, M. Martonosi, and D. W. Clark [23]
"Energy-efficient processor design using multiple clock domains with dynamic voltage and frequency scaling," G. Semeraro, G. Magklis, R. Balasubramonian, D. H. Albonesi, S. Dwarkadas, and M. L. Scott [24]

Table 3 List of Presented Solutions—cont'd
Core-Dynamic

Optimizing Issue Width

"Power and energy reduction via pipeline balancing," R. I. Bahar and S. Manne [25]

Dynamic Work Steering

"Slack: maximizing performance under technological constraints," B. Fields, R. Bodik, and M. D. Hill [26]

Core-Static(+Dynamic)

Combined Adaptive Body Biasing (ABB) and DVFS

"Impact of scaling on the effectiveness of dynamic power reduction schemes," D. Duarte, N. Vijaykrishnan, M. J. Irwin, H.-S. Kim, and G. McFarland [27]

"Combined dynamic voltage scaling and adaptive body biasing for lower power microprocessors under dynamic workloads," S. M. Martin, K. Flautner, T. Mudge, and D. Blaauw [28]

"Joint dynamic voltage scaling and adaptive body biasing for heterogeneous distributed real-time embedded systems," L. Yan, J. Luo, and N. K. Jha [29]

Core Blocks-Pipeline-Dynamic

Clock Gating

"Deterministic clock gating for microprocessor power reduction," H. Li, S. Bhunia, Y. Chen, T. N. Vijaykumar, and K. Roy [30]

"Pipeline gating: speculation control for energy reduction," S. Manne, A. Klauser, and D. Grunwald [31]

"Power-aware control speculation through selective throttling," J. L. Aragon, J. Gonzalez, and A. Gonzalez [32]

Significance Compression

"Very low power pipelines using significance compression," R. Canal, A. Gonzalez, and J. E. Smith [33]

Work Reuse

"Dynamic instruction reuse," A. Sodani and G. S. Sohi [34]

"Exploiting basic block value locality with block reuse," J. Huang and D. J. Lilja [35]

"Trace-level reuse," A. Gonzalez, J. Tubella, and C. Molina [36]

"Dynamic tolerance region computing for multimedia," C. Alvarez, J. Corbal, and M. Valero [37]

Continued

Table 3 List of Presented Solutions—cont'd
Core Blocks-FE-Dynamic

Exploiting Narrow–Width Operands

"Register packing: exploiting narrow-width operands for reducing register file pressure. Proc. 37th Annual IEEE/ACM Int. Symp. Microarchitecture (MICRO-37)," O. Ergin, D. Balkan, K. Ghose, and D. Ponomarev

Instruction Queue (IQ) resizing

"A circuit level implementation of an adaptive issue queue for power-aware microprocessors," A. Buyuktosunoglu, D. Albonesi, S. Schuster, D. Brooks, P. Bose, and P. Cook [38]

"Reducing power requirements of instruction scheduling through dynamic allocation of multiple datapath resources," D. Ponomarev, G. Kucuk, and K. Ghose [39]

"Energy-effective issue logic," D. Folegnani and A. Gonzalez [40]

Loop Cache

"Energy and performance improvements in microprocessor design using a loop cache," N. Bellas, I. Hajj, C. Polychronopoulos, and G. Stamoulis [41]

"Instruction fetch energy reduction using loop caches for embedded applications with small tight loops," L. H. Lee, B. Moyer, and J. Arends [42]

"Using dynamic cache management techniques to reduce energy in a high-performance processor," N. Bellas, I. Hajj, and C. Polychronopoulos [43]

"HotSpot cache: joint temporal and spatial locality exploitation for I-cache energy reduction," C. Yang and C.H. Lee [44]

Trace Cache

"Micro-operation cache: a power aware frontend for variable instruction length ISA," B. Solomon, A. Mendelson, D. Orenstien, Y. Almog, and R. Ronen [45]

Core Blocks-FE-Static

Idle Register Dynamic Voltage Scaling (DVS)

"Saving register-file static power by monitoring short-lived temporary-values in ROB," W.-Y. Shieh and H.-D. Chen [46]

Register File Access Optimization

"Dynamic register-renaming scheme for reducing power-density and temperature," J. Kim, S. T. Jhang, and C. S. Jhon [47]

Table 3 List of Presented Solutions—cont'd
Core Blocks-BE-Dynamic

Exploiting Narrow-Width Operands

"Minimizing floating-point power dissipation via bit-width reduction," Y. Tong, R. Rutenbar, and D. Nagle [48]

"Dynamically exploiting narrow width operands to improve processor power and performance," D. Brooks and M. Martonosi [49]

"Value-based clock gating and operation packing: dynamic strategies for improving processor power and performance," D. Brooks and M. Martonosi [50]

Work Reuse

"Accelerating multi-media processing by implementing memoing in multiplication and division units," D. Citron, D. Feitelson, and L. Rudolph [51]

"Fuzzy memoization for floating-point multimedia applications," C. Alvarez, J. Corbal, and M. Valero [52]

Core Blocks-BE-Static

Power Gating

"Microarchitectural techniques for power gating of execution units," Z. Hu, A. Buyuktosunoglu, V. Srinivasan, V. Zyuban, H. Jacobson, and P. Bose [53]

Dual V_t

"Managing static leakage energy in microprocessor functional units," S. Dropsho, V. Kursun, D. H. Albonesi, S. Dwarkadas, and E. G. Friedman [54]

For each solution, the name and the authors are given.

multidisciplinary coverage than other similar search engines [9], and is generally praised for its speed [10]. The second criterion is the date in a sense that newer works have an advantage over the old ones. For the most recent papers, an additional criterion will be the authors' judgment.

3.3 Postclassification Conclusion

In conclusion, we would like to stress the following:

- The classification of power- and energy-efficient techniques is systematically done by the component.
- As noted earlier, a technique that tackles both control and functional units is referred as technique that optimizes pipeline. For example, *work*

reuse technique is present in two classes, in *Core-BE-Dynamic* and in *Core-Pipeline-Dynamic*. The first one reduces the BE power, while the second one reduces the power of both BE and FE.

- Although DVFS (and DVS as special case of DVFS where $f = const.$) is often considered as dynamic energy/power optimization technique, it is static power/energy optimization technique as well. According to (3) and (5), static energy/power is linearly/quadratically proportional to voltage supply ($E_{stat} \propto V_{DD}, P_{stat} \propto V_{DD}^2$); thus, when we scale voltage supply, we also conserve static components of energy and power.

4. PRESENTATION OF SELECTED ARCHITECTURE-LEVEL TECHNIQUES

In this section, the techniques which list is given in the previous section are presented. For each technique, a set of solutions is given. Recently done solutions are elaborated in detail than older ones.

4.1 Core

Core-level low-power techniques initially were mainly proposed for dynamic power and energy reduction. However, in the last few years, low-power research is mainly focused on the reduction of the static component of power and energy.

4.1.1 Dynamic

Here, we mostly play with voltage and frequencies in order to reduce dynamic power and energy components.

DVFS

DVFS proposals mainly differ in area of their scope (e.g., core, functional units) and in their control management (e.g., OS level). Usefulness of DVFS in modern low-power system is discussed in Section 4.5.

OS Level   One of the first applications of the core-level DVFS was proposed by Weiser *et al.* [11]. They noticed that during idle time system actually wastes energy. Considering the case where the processor has to finish all its work in a given time slot, we often have idle time in which processor does nothing useful but waste energy and dissipate power. By stretching work as much as possible and lowering voltage supply to the minimum acceptable level, according to Formulas (1) and (4), we lower energy quadratically and power cubically.

With this motivation, Weiser *et al.* propose three interval-based scheduling algorithms, called OPT, FUTURE, and PAST, aiming to eliminate the idle time. Their work specifically targets idle time as it is experienced in the operating system, i.e., the time taken by the idle loop or I/O waiting time. Of course, in case of very long idle periods (e.g., periods measured in seconds), the best policy is to shut down all components (since the display and disk surpass the processor in power consumption).

The scheduling algorithms are supposed to be implemented on a system that contains short burst and idle activity. Instead of actually implementing these algorithms in a real system, Weiser *et al.* collect traces and use them to model the effects on the total power consumption of the processor. The traces are taken from workstations running a variety of different workloads that contain timestamps of context switches, entering and exiting the system idle loop, process creation and destruction, and waiting or waking up on events. To prevent whole system shut-down (processor, display, and disk), any period of 30 s or longer with a load below 10% is excluded from consideration. Traces are divided into fixed-length intervals, and the proportion of time that the CPU is active within each interval is computed individually. At the end of each interval, the speed of the processor for the upcoming interval is decided. If the processor does not finish its work within the time slot, work spills over to the next time slot.

Among the three aforementioned scheduling algorithms, the first two are impractical since they can look into the future of the trace data, while the third is a plausible candidate for the implementation. First scheduling algorithm is a simplified Oracle algorithm that perfectly eliminates idle time in every time slot by stretching the run times in a trace. It can look arbitrarily far into the future. FUTURE is a simple modification of OPT that can only look into the subsequent interval. For long intervals, FUTURE approaches OPT in terms of energy savings, while for smaller intervals it falls behind. The only run-time implementable algorithm, the PAST algorithm, looks into the past in order to predict the future. The speed setting policy increases the speed if the current interval is busier than idle and lowers speed if idle time exceeds some percentage of the time slot.

There is a trade-off between the number of missed deadlines and energy savings which depends on interval size. If the interval is smaller, there are fewer missed deadlines because speed can be adjusted at a finer time resolution. However, energy savings are smaller due to frequent switching between high and low speeds. In contrast, with long intervals, better energy savings can be achieved at the expense of more missed deadlines, more work spilled-over, and a decreased response time for the workload. Regarding actual results, Weiser *et al.* conclude that, for their setup, the optimal interval size ranges between 20 and 30 ms yielding power savings between 5% and 75%.

Flautner *et al.* [12] look into a more general problem on how to reduce frequency and voltage without missing deadlines. They consider various classes of machines with emphasis on general-purpose processors with deadline strongly dependent on the user perception—soft real-time systems.

The approach derives deadlines by examining communication patterns from within the OS kernel. Application interaction with the OS kernel reveals the, so-called, execution episodes corresponding to different communication patterns. This allows the classification of tasks into interactive, periodic producer, and periodic consumer. Depending on the classification of each task, deadlines are established for their execution episodes. In particular, the execution episodes of interactive tasks are assigned deadlines corresponding to the user-perception threshold, which is in the range of 50–100 ms. Periodic producer and consumer tasks are assigned deadlines corresponding to their periodicity. All this happens within the kernel without requiring modification of the applications. By having a set of deadlines for the interactive and the periodic tasks, frequency and voltage settings are then derived so that the execution episodes finish within their assigned deadlines. The approach can result in energy savings of 75% without altering the user experience.

After OS-based DVFS, one step deeper is the program and program phase-level DVFSs. Those groups of techniques involve compiler-based analysis (both off- and online) and phase-based techniques.

Compiler Analysis-Based DVFS There are off-line and online approaches.

Off-line Approach. The basic idea of application compiler off-line analysis to achieve DVFS in a system is based on identifying regions of code where voltage and frequency adjustments could be helpful. Of course, those regions have to be enough large to amortize the overheads of DVFS adjustment.

Hsu and Kremer [13] propose a heuristic technique that lowers the voltage for memory-bound sections. This compiler algorithm is based on heuristics and profiling information to solve a minimization problem. The idea is to slow down microprocessor during memory-bound parts of the code. The techniques are implemented within the SUIF2 source-to-source compiler infrastructure (gcc compilers were used to generate object code).

The goal is to, for a given program P, find a program region R and frequency f (lower than the maximum frequency f_{max}) such that if R is executed at the reduced frequency f and with reduced voltage supply, the total execution time (including the voltage/frequency scaling overhead) is not increased more than a small factor over the original execution time. The factor should be small enough in order to achieve the total energy savings.

For the measurement, in Ref. [13] they use laptops with Linux and GNU compilers and digital ampere-meter. The program is annotated with mode-set instructions, which select DVFS settings on AMD mobile Athlon 4 and Transmeta Crusoe processors. They report energy savings of up to 28% with performance degradation of less than 5% for the SPECfp95 benchmarks.

While heuristic techniques offer some benefits, subsequent work seeks to refine these techniques toward optimal or bounded-near-optimal solutions. For example, research done by Saputra *et al.* provides an exact *Mixed-Integer Linear Programming (MILP)* technique that can determine the appropriate (V, f) setting for each loop nest [14]. An MILP approach is required because discrete (V, f) settings lead to a nonconvex optimization space. Their technique reports improvements in energy savings compared to prior work. However, it does not account for the energy penalties incurred by mode switching. Furthermore, the long runtimes of straightforward MILP approaches make their integration into a compiler somewhat undesirable.

Work by Xie *et al.* expand on these ideas in several ways [15, 16]. First, they expand the MILP approach by including energy penalties for mode switches, providing a much finer grain of program control, and enabling the use of multiple input data categories to determine optimal settings. In addition, they determine efficient methods for solving the MILP optimization problem with boundable distance from the true optimal solution. Time and energy savings offered by the MILP approach vary heavily depending on the application performance goal and the (V, f) settings available. In some case, $2 \times$ improvements are available.

Online Approach. The problem with off-line compiler analysis is the absence of knowledge of data inputs which can affect the program behavior. Online dynamic compiler analysis aims to determine efficiently where to place DVFS adjustments.

Wu *et al.* [17] study methods using dynamic compilation techniques to analyze program behavior and also to dynamically insert DVFS adjustments

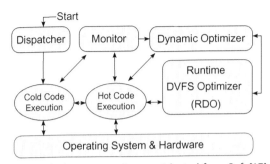

Figure 2 Dynamic compilation system. *Source: Adapted from Ref. [17].*

at the locations determined to be most fruitful. They implement a proto-type of this *Runtime DVFS Optimizer (RDO)* and integrate it into an industrial-strength dynamic optimization system. Their methodology is depicted in Fig. 2.

Often executable code is considered as hot and is analyzed in order to determine whether it is memory or CPU bound. In the first case, the code is considered for DVFS. If it cannot be determined if some code is memory or CPU bound, and the region of code is large enough, it is divided up into smaller regions and the algorithm repeats for each of the smaller regions. The flowchart of RDO is shown in Fig. 3.

Power measurements are taken on an actual system using RDO on a variety of benchmarks. On average, their results achieve an EDP improvement (over non-DVFS approaches) of 22.4% for SPEC95 FP, 21.5% for SPEC2K FP, 6.0% for SPEC2K INT, and 22.7% for Olden benchmarks. The results are three to five times better than a baseline approach based on static DVFS decisions.

Power Phase Analysis-Based DVFS Above proposed online and off-line compiler analysis-based DVFSs have significant monitoring overhead. In most of the general purpose processors, we have user-readable hardware performance counters which can be used to build up a history of program behavior from seeing aggregate event counts.

Isci *et al.* show aggregate power data from different counters to identify program phase behavior [18]. In their later work [19], they elaborate on their technique by including a predictor table that can predict future power behavior based on recently observed values.

They make a "history table" similar to hardware branch predictors. The difference is that these tables are implemented in software by OS. Like a

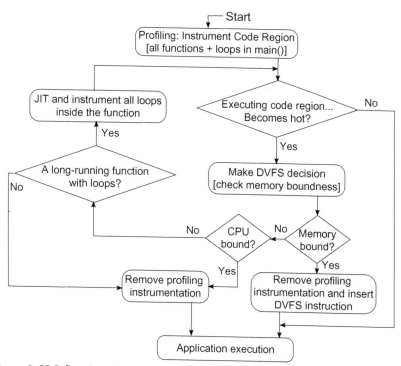

Figure 3 RDO flowchart. *Source: Adapted from Ref. [17].*

branch predictor, it stores a history table of recently measured application metrics that are predictive of proper DVFS adjustments. Applying this technique, they achieve EDP improvement of 34% for variety of workloads.

DVFS for Multiple Clock Domain Processors *Multiple-Clock-Domain (MCD)* processors are inherently suitable for DVFS application. In the *Globally Asynchronous Locally Synchronous (GALS)* approach, a processor core is divided into synchronous islands, each of which is then interconnected asynchronously but with added circuitry to avoid metastability. The islands are typically intended to correspond to different functional units, such as the instruction fetch unit, the ALUs, the load–store unit, and so forth. A typical division is shown in Fig. 4.

In early work on this topic [20, 21], they consider opportunities of DVFS application to GALS. They found that GALS designs are initially less efficient than synchronous architecture but that there are internal slacks that could be exploited. For example, in some MCD designs, the floating point unit could be clocked much more slowly than the instruction fetch unit

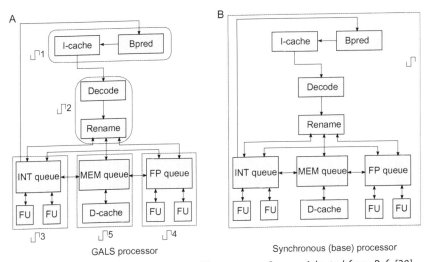

GALS processor   Synchronous (base) processor

Figure 4 GALS (A) versus synchronous (B) processor. *Source: Adapted from Ref. [20].*

because its throughput and latency demands are lower. Iyer and Marculescu [20] show that for a GALS processor with five clock domains, the drop in performance ranges between 5% and 15%, while power consumption is reduced by 10% on the average. Thus, fine-grained voltage scaling allows GALS to match or exceed the power efficiency of fully synchronous approaches.

Similar work was done by Semeraro *et al.* [22, 24] where they divide the processor into five domains: Front end, Integer, Floating point, Load/Store, and External (Main Memory) which interfaces via queues. In their first work, they use an off-line approach [24], while in the next one they apply an online approach which is more efficient [22].

In the off-line approach, they first assign adequate frequency for each instruction. Since executing each instruction at a different frequency is not practical, in the second step the results of the first phase are processed, and this aims to find a single minimum frequency per interval for each domain.

From the off-line approach analysis, Semeraro *et al.* conclude that decentralized control of the different domains is possible, and the utilization of the input queues is a good indicator for the appropriate frequency of operation. Based on those observations, they devise an online DVFS control algorithm for multiple domains called Attack/Decay. This is a decentralized, interval-based algorithm. Decisions are made independently for each domain at regular sampling intervals. The algorithm tries to react to changes in the utilization of the issue (input) queue of each domain. During sudden changes, the algorithm sets the frequency aggressively to try to match the utilization change. This is the Attack mode. If the utilization is increased by a significant amount since the last interval, the frequency is also increased by a significant factor. Conversely, when utilization suddenly drops, frequency is also decreased. In the absence of any significant change in the issue queue, frequency is slowly decreased by a small factor. This is the Decay mode.

Their algorithm achieve a 19% reduction on average (from a non-DVFS baseline) in energy per instruction across a wide range of MediaBench, Olden, and Spec2000 benchmarks and a 16.7% improvement in EDP. The approach incurred a modest 3.2% increase in Cycles per Instruction (CPI). Interestingly, their online control-theoretic approach is able to achieve a full 85.5% of the EDP improvement offered by the prior off-line scheduling approach. Wu *et al.* [23] extend the online approach using formal control theory and a dynamic stochastic model based on input-queue occupancy for the MCDs.

Dynamic Work Steering

Apart from having various processor domains clocked with different frequencies, another approach to exploit internal core slack is to have multiple instances of component that does the same function, but at a different speed, thus with different power dissipation. It is interesting especially today with new nanometer feature sizes when we care about power dissipation more than area.

Fields *et al.* [26] propose a work steering technique which dispatches instructions to functional units with appropriate speed in order to exploit instruction-level slack (Fig. 5). They find that there are instructions that

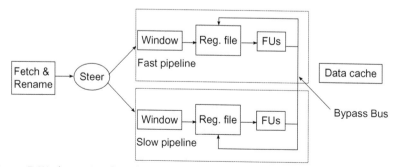

Figure 5 Work steering for a fast and a slow pipeline. *Source: Adapted from Ref. [26].*

could be delayed without significant impact on the performance. In order to locate instructions, they use off- and online approaches. In the first one, they make dependency graphs to find instructions that produce slack, and they achieve promising results. Even better results they achieve with the online approach where they dynamically predict slack in hardware. Online control policies discussed previously for DVFS in MCD processors cannot treat each instruction individually. There is simply no possibility of dynamically changing the frequency of execution individually for each instruction; instead, the frequency of each domain is adjusted according to the aggregate behavior of all the instructions processed in this domain over the course of a sampling interval. According to Ref. [26], for 68% of the static instructions, 90% of their dynamic instances have enough slack to double their latency. This slack locality allows slack prediction to be based on sparsely sampling dynamic instructions and determining their slack. Their results show that a control policy based on slack prediction is second best, in terms of performance, only to the ideal case of having two fast pipelines instead of a fast and a slow pipeline.

Optimizing Issue Width

One more approach to make balanced low-power core which will consume just necessary energy for its work is to adapt its "working capacity" to its actual workload. Out-of-order processors are known as power hungry solutions and they are suitable for application of aforementioned kinds of techniques. Bahar and Manne [25] propose a dynamic change of the width of an 8-issue processor to 6-issue or 4-issue when the application cannot take advantage of the additional width. They model their target processor after an 8-issue Alpha 21264 [55], comprising two 4-issue clusters (Fig. 6). To switch the processor to 6-issue, one-half of one of the clusters is disabled. To switch to the 4-issue, one whole cluster is disabled.

To disable half or a whole cluster, the appropriate functional units are clock gated. In addition to disabling functional units, part of the instruction queue hardware is also disabled, thus realizing additional power benefits. Decisions are made at the end of a sampling window assuming that the behavior of the program in the last window is a good indicator for the next. This technique can save up to 20% (10%) power from the execution units, 35% (17%) from the instruction queue, and 12% (6%) in total, in the 4-issue (6-issue) low-power mode. However, the power savings for the whole processor are not as dramatic, and Bahar and Manne finally conclude that a single technique alone cannot solve the power consumption problem.

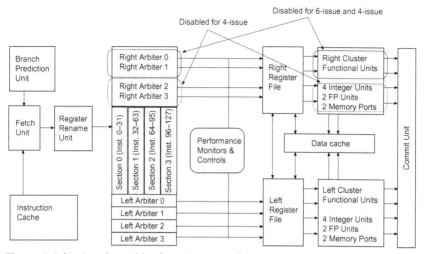

Figure 6 Adjusting the width of an 8-issue machine to 6- or 4-issue. *Source: Adapted from Ref. [56].*

4.1.2 Static and Dynamic

In order to significantly reduce static power/energy, existing DVFS techniques are augmented with adaptive body bias (ABB) techniques.

Combined ABB and DVFS

Reverse Body Biasing (RBB) technique increases the threshold voltage and thus brings an exponential reduction in leakage power. However, the increase in threshold voltage reduces gate overdrive ($V_{DD} - V_t$), reducing circuit's performance (V_{DD} is voltage of the power supply and V_t threshold voltage). Either scaling V_{DD} or increasing V_t slows down switching. Considering dynamic or leakage power independently, the performance can be traded for power by scaling either V_{DD} or V_t. As in both cases, performance degradation is linear to the scaling of the V_{DD} or V_t, whereas power savings are either quadratic or exponential, the resulting improvement in EDP is substantial.

In case that we want to optimize total power ($E_{stat} + E_{dyn}$), the best approach depends on static/dynamic power ratio. In older technologies, like 70 nm, where dynamic power component is still the dominant one, V_{DD} scaling gives better results. On the contrary, while considering more recent technologies, like 35 nm, RBB provides better savings. DVS/RBB balance is shown in Fig. 7. The balance of dynamic and leakage power shifts across

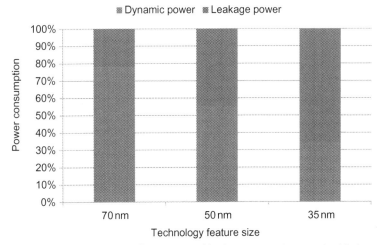

Figure 7 Relative contribution of dynamic and leakage power in an embedded processor. *Source: Adapted from Ref. [29].*

technologies and among different implementations in the same technologies. Additionally, the leakage also changes dynamically as a function of temperature. This aspect, however, has not been researched adequately.

For a given frequency and switching delay, the best possible power savings come from carefully adjusting both V_{DD} and V_t, depending on the balance of dynamic versus leakage power at that point. While the $V_{DD} - V_t$ difference determines switching speed, maximum gains in power consumption come from a combined adjustment of the two. Three independent studies came to the same conclusion.

The work of Duarte *et al.* [27] studied the impact of scaling on a number of approaches for dynamic power reduction. Among their experiments, they simultaneously scale the supply voltage (V_{DD}) and the body-to-source bias voltage (V_{bs}), i.e., they simultaneously perform DVS and ABB. Their study is not constrained in any variable, meaning that they examine a wide spectrum of possible values for the two quantities. Their results show a clear advantage over DVS alone.

Martin *et al.* [28] combine DVS and ABB to lower both dynamic and static power of a microprocessor during execution. They derive closed-form formulas the total power dissipation and the frequency, expressing them as a function of V_{DD} and V_{bs}. The system-level technique of automatic performance setting was used. In this technique, deadlines are derived from monitoring system calls and interprocess communication. The performance setting algorithm sets the processor frequency for the executing workload so it does not disturb its real-time behavior. Solving the system of the two mentioned equations for a given performance setting, Martin *et al.* are able to estimate the most profitable combination of V_{DD} and V_{bs} to maximize power dissipation savings. The approach can deliver savings over DVS alone of 23% in a 180 nm process and 39% in a (predicted) 70 nm process.

Yan [29] studies the application of combined DVS and ABB in heterogeneous distributed real-time embedded systems. In analogy to the work of Martin *et al.*, the author determines the lowest frequency of operation that can satisfy the real-time constraints of an embedded system using the worst-case analysis. In contrast to the previous work, the deadlines are known and are hard real time. Given the required operation frequencies, Yan shows that both V_{DD} and V_t have to scale to obtain the minimum power across the range of frequencies for a 70 nm technology. They notice that for higher frequencies, when dynamic component of power is significant, V_{DD} scaling is more useful. However, for lower frequencies, where static (leakage) power starts to dominate, we should decrease V_{bs} voltage, i.e., to apply RBB, to make power dissipation lower.

4.2 Core-Pipeline

In this section, the techniques which target complete pipeline (both functional and control units) are presented.

4.2.1 Dynamic

There are three most popular approaches to reduce dynamic energy in pipeline. The first one is clock gating of large power hungry pipeline units and their accompanying latches. The second one is a result from the effort to exploit the bit redundancy in data, while the third one is based on reusing some pieces of already executed code, i.e., generating already computed outputs directly from some memory structure.

Clock Gating
Pipeline blocks are clock gated either if they are known to be idle or if they are supposed to be doing useless work. The first approach (*deterministic clock gating*) is more conservative and do not spoil performance, while the second one is more "risky" and could degrade performance with, of course, significant power savings.

Deterministic Clock Gating The idea of *Deterministic Clock Gating (DCG)* application on the pipeline is to clock gate the structures that are known to be idle, without spoiling the performance but decreasing EDP at the same time. Li *et al.* [30] give a detailed description of DCG in a super-scalar pipeline. They consider a high-performance implementation using dynamic domino logic for speed. This means that besides latches, the pipeline stages themselves must be clock gated.

The idea is to find out if a latch or pipeline stage is not going to be used. In Fig. 8 is depicted a pipeline which clock-gate-able parts are shown dark. The Fetch and Decode stages and their latches are, for example, never clock gated since instructions are needed almost every cycle, while there is completely enough time to clock gate functional units.

DCG was evaluated with Wattch [30]. By applying DCG to all the latches and stages described above, they report power savings of 21% and 19% (on average) for the SPEC2000 integer and floating point benchmarks, respectively. They found DCG more promising than pipeline balancing, another clock gating technique.

Although this work is applied to scalar architecture, it is also applicable to other kinds of architectures. An example of an efficient DCG application on functional units for energy-efficient vector architectures can be found in Ref. [57].

Improving Energy Efficiency of Speculative Execution Although they are necessary in order to keep functional units busy and to have high Instructions Per Cycle (IPC), branch predictors and speculative activity approach are fairly power hungry. Besides the actual power consumption

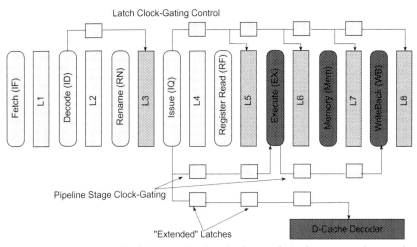

Figure 8 Deterministic Clock Gating. Pipeline latches and pipeline stages that can be clock gated are shown shaded. *Source: Adapted from Ref. [56].*

overhead of supporting branch prediction and speculative execution (e.g., prediction structures, support for check pointing, increased run-time state), there is also the issue of incorrect execution.

Manne *et al.* [31] try to solve this energy inefficiency of speculative activity proposing approach which is named *pipeline gating*. The idea is to gate and stall the whole pipeline when the processor threads down to very uncertain (execution) paths. Since pipeline gating refrains from executing when confidence in branch prediction is low, it can hardly hurt performance. There are two cases when it does: when execution would eventually turn out to be correct and is stalled, or when incorrect execution had a positive effect on the overall performance (e.g., because of prefetching). On the other hand, it can effectively avoid a considerable amount of incorrect execution and save the corresponding power.

The confidence of branch prediction in Ref. [31] is determined in two ways: counting the number of mispredicted branches that can be detected as low confidence, and the number of low-confidence branch predictions that are turn out to be wrong. They find out that if more than one low-confident branch enters the pipeline, then the chances of going down the wrong path increase significantly. They propose several confidence estimators which details could be found in Ref. [31]. In their test, authors show that certain estimators used for gshare and McFarling application with a gating threshold of 2 (number of low-confident branches), a significant part of incorrect execution, can be eliminated without perceptible impact on performance. Of course, the earlier the pipeline is gated, the more incorrect work is saved. However, this assumes larger penalty of stalling correct execution.

Aragón *et al.* [32] did similar work but with slightly different approach. Instead of having a single mechanism to stall execution as Manne *et al.*, Aragón *et al.* examine a range of throttling mechanisms: fetch throttling, decode throttling, and selection-logic throttling. As throttling is performed deeper in the pipeline, its impact on execution is diminished. Thus, fetch throttling at the start of the pipeline is the most aggressive in disrupting execution, starving the whole pipeline from instructions, while decode or selection-logic throttling deeper in the pipeline is progressively less aggressive. This is exploited in relation to branch confidence: the lower the confidence of a branch prediction, the more aggressively the pipeline is throttled. The overall technique is called "selective throttling."

Pipeline gating, being an all-or-nothing mechanism, is much more sensitive to the quality of the confidence estimator. This is due to the severe impact on performance when the confidence estimation is wrong. Selective throttling, on the other hand, is able to better balance confidence estimation with performance impact and power savings, yielding a better EDP for representative SPEC 2000 and SPEC 95 benchmarks.

Significance Compression

Slightly different approach than previous one is proposed by Canal *et al.* [33]. The idea is to compress nonsignificant bits (strings of zeros or ones) anywhere they appear in the full width of an operand. Each 32-bit word is augmented with a 3-bit tag describing the significance of each of its four bytes. A byte can be either significant or a sign extension of its preceding byte (i.e., just a string of zeros or ones). The authors report that the majority of values (87%) in SPECint and Mediabench benchmarks can be compressed with significance compression. A good 75% of all values is narrow-width using above-mentioned 16-bit definition (i.e., only the first and possibly second bytes are significant).

Canal *et al.* propose three kinds of pipeline adapted to work with compressed data. The first one is named *byte-serial pipeline* where only significant bytes flow through the pipeline and are operated. The rest is carried and stored via their tags. This opens up the possibility of a very low-power byte-serial operation. If more than one significant byte needs to be processed at a pipeline stage, then this stage simply repeats for the significant bytes. However, although activity savings range from 30% to 40% for the various pipeline stages, performance is substantially reduced; CPI increases 79% over a full-width (32-bit) pipeline.

Another, faster, approach is to double pipeline width (byte-parallel pipeline), and this results with 24% performance losses while retaining 30–40% activity savings. Increasing the pipeline width to four bytes (byte-parallel pipeline) and enabling only the parts that correspond to the significant bytes of a word retain most of the activity savings and further improves performance, bringing it very close (6–2% slowdown depending on optimizations) to a full pipeline operating on uncompressed operands.

Work Reuse

Pipeline-level work reuse can be implemented at instruction level or block of instructions (basic block) level.

Instruction-Level Reuse The work reuse approach can be even more efficient if we reuse the whole instructions, or set of instructions, instead of operations only (Section 4.4.1). Early work on this topic is done by Sodani and Sohi who propose dynamic instruction reuse [34]. The motivation for their work is a discovery that execution in a mispredicted path converges with execution in the correct path resulting in some of the instructions beyond the point of convergence being executed twice, verbatim, in the case of a misprediction. Furthermore, the iterative nature of programs in conjunction with the way code is written modularly to operate on different input results in significant repetition of the same inputs for the same instructions. The results of such instructions can be saved and simply reused when needed rather than reexecuting the computation. Sodani and Sohi claim that in some cases, over 50% of the instructions can be reused in this way. They do not evaluate power saving of their proposals, but their work was actually a step forward to more general and more energy-efficient approach—basic block reuse.

Basic Block-Level Reuse   The basic block reuse is done by Huang and Lilja [35]. Their observations concern whole basic blocks for which they find that their inputs and outputs can be quite regular and predictable. Their study shows, for the SPEC95 benchmarks, a vast majority of basic blocks (90%) have few input and output registers (up to four and five, respectively) and only read and write few memory locations (up to four and two, respectively). A *Block History Buffer (BHB)* stores inputs and outputs of basic blocks and provides reuse at the basic block level. The increased number of inputs that must match for the result to be determinable means that basic block reuse is not as prevalent as instruction reuse. However, when reuse succeeds, it does not only avoids the execution of the individual instructions in the basic block but also breaks the dependence chains in it, returning results in a single cycle. In addition to the energy saved by not executing instructions in functional units, considerable energy can be also saved because all the bookkeeping activities in the processor (instruction pointer update, instruction fetch, decode, rename, issue, etc.) during the execution of a basic block are eliminated. Depending of the chosen buffer, sometimes, it is more expensive to access and match entries in the buffer since each entry consists of arrays of values and valid bits.

Trace-Level Reuse   One more work reuse approach is proposed by Gonzalez *et al.* [36]. Traces are groups of consecutive instructions reflecting not their position in the static code layout but their order in dynamic execution. A trace may span more than one basic block by allowing executed branches (taken or nontaken) in the middle of the trace. Similarly to basic blocks, a trace too can start with the same inputs, read the same values from memory, and produce the same results and side effects (e.g., memory writes). Trace-level reuse has analogous problems and benefits with basic block reuse. The problems are actually amplified as the traces can be longer.

Region Reuse Region reuse stands for exploiting the value locality exhibited by sets of instructions inside a program. These sets of instructions may have different granularity: basic blocks, traces, or even whole functions can be selected as candidates for computation reuse. The classical region reuse mechanism is showed in Fig. 9. The design consists of three different boxes: an input logic box, a reuse table, and a reuse check logic box.

We can obtain more power/energy efficiency when we introduce some acceptable error—*tolerant region reuse*. Tolerant region reuse improves classical region reuse with significant EDP reduction gains (from 13% to 24%) and consistently reduces both time and energy consumption for the whole span of media applications studied. These gains come at the cost of minor degradation of the output of the applications (noise introduced always bounded to an SNR of 30 dB) which make it ideal for the portable domain where quality vs. form-factor/battery life is a worthy trade-off. The main

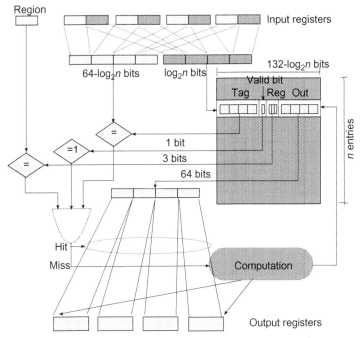

Figure 9 Classical region reuse mechanism. *Source: Adapted from Ref. [37].*

drawback of tolerant region reuse is the strong reliance on application profiling, the need for careful tuning from the application developer, and the inability of the technique to adapt to the variability of the media contents being used as inputs. To address that inflexibility, Alvarez *et al.* [37] introduce *dynamic tolerant region reuse*.

This technique overcomes the drawbacks of tolerant region reuse by allowing the hardware to study the precision quality of the region reuse output. The proposed mechanism allows the programmer to grant a minimum threshold on SNR (signal-to-noise ratio) while letting the technique adapt to the characteristics of the specific application and workload in order to minimize time and energy consumption. This leads to greater energy–delay savings while keeps output error below noticeable levels, avoiding at the same time the need of profiling.

They applied the idea to a set of three different processors, simulated by Simplescalar and Wattch, from low to high end. The used applications are JPEG, H263, and GSM. Alvarez *et al.* show their technique leads to consistent performance improvements in all of our benchmark programs while reducing energy consumption and EDP savings up to 30%.

4.3 Core-Front-End

Control unit is an unavoidable part of every processor and the key part of out-of-order processors. As out-of-order processors tend to have pretty high EDP factor, there is a lot of room for energy-efficiency improvement.

4.3.1 Dynamic

Beside clock gating, as the most popular dynamic power/energy optimization mechanism, here caching takes a part as well.

Exploiting Narrow-Width Operands

Although low–power research that focus on narrow–width operands exploitation mostly target functional units, this approach can also apply on RFs, and it is done by Ergin *et al.* [58]. The intent is not so much to reduce power consumption, but to alleviate register pressure by making better use of the available physical registers. Similarly to packing two narrow values in the inputs of functional units or packing compressed lines in caches, multiple narrow values are packed in registers.

A number of these values can be packed in a register either "conservatively" or "speculatively." Conservatively means that a value is packed only after it is classified as narrow. This happens after a value is created by a functional unit. When a narrow value is packed in a different register than the one it was destined for, the register mapping for the packed value is updated in all the in-flight instructions. In contrast, "speculative packing" takes place in the register renaming stage, without certain knowledge of the width of the packed value. Packing and physical register assignment are performed by predicting the output width of instructions. The prediction history (per instruction) is kept in the instruction cache. The technique works well for performance—increases IPC by 15%.

Instruction Queue Resizing

On-demand issue queue resizing, from the power efficiency point of view, was first proposed by Buyuktosunoglu et al. [38]. They propose circuit-level design of an issue queue that uses transmission gate insertion to provide dynamic low cost configurability of size and speed. The idea is to dynamically gather statistics of issue queue activity over intervals of instruction execution. Later on, they use mentioned statistics to change the size of an issue queue organization on the fly to improve issue queue energy and performance.

The design of the IQ is a mixed CAM/SRAM design where each entry has both CAM and SRAM fields. The SRAM fields hold instruction information (such as opcode, destination register, status) and the CAM fields constitute the wakeup logic for the particular entry holding the input operand tags. Results coming from functional units match the operand tags in the CAM fields and select the SRAM part of entry for further action. When an instruction matches both its operands, it becomes "ready" to issue and waits to be picked by the scheduler.

The IQ is divided into large chunks with transmission gates placed at regular intervals on its CAM and SRAM bitlines. The tag match in the CAM fields is enabled by dedicated taglines. Partitioning of the IQ in chunks is controlled by enabling or disabling the transmission gates in the bitlines and the corresponding taglines. The design is depicted in Fig. 10.

Buyuktosunoglu et al. achieve power savings for the IQ 35% (on average) with an IPC degradation of just over 4%, for some of the integer SPEC2000 benchmarks, on a simulated 4-issue processor with a 32-entry issue queue.

Ponomarev et al. go one step further, making the problem more generalized by examining total power of main three structures of instruction scheduling mechanisms: IQ, Load/Store Queue (LSQ), and Reorder Buffer (ROB) [39]. They notice that IPC-based feedback control proposed by Ref. [38] does not really reflect the true needs of the program but actually depend

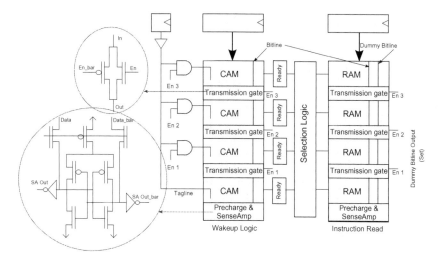

Figure 10 Adaptive CAM/SRAM structure. *Source: Adapted from Ref. [38].*

on many other factors: cache miss rates, branch misprediction rates, amount of instruction-level parallelism, occupancy, etc. Hence, they considered occupancy of a structure as the appropriate feedback control mechanism for resizing.

The proposed feedback scheme measures occupancy of each of three main structures and makes decisions at the end of the sample period. The mechanism allows on-demand resizing IQ, LSQ, and ROB, by increasing/decreasing their size according to the actual state. In simulations for a 4-issue processor, this method yields power savings for the three structures in excess of 50% with a performance loss of less than 5%.

A different approach to the same goal (dynamically IQ adaption for power savings) is proposed by Folegnani *et al.* [40]. Instead of disabling large chunks at a time, they disable individual IQ entries. Another difference to the previous two approaches is that IQ is not limited physically but logically. Actually, they organized IQ as FIFO buffer with its head and tail pointers (Fig. 11). Novelty is the introduction of a new pointer, called the *limit pointer* which always moves at a fixed offset from the head pointer. This pointer limits the logical size of the instruction queue by excluding the entries between the head pointer and itself from being allocated.

They resize the IQ to fit program needs. Unused part is disabled in a sense that empty entries need not participate in the tag match; thus, significant power savings are possible. The feedback control is done using a heuristic with empirically chosen parameters. The IQ is logically divided into

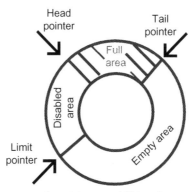

Figure 11 Instruction queue with resizing capabilities. *Source: Adapted from Ref. [40].*

16 partitions. The idea for the heuristic is to measure the contribution to performance from the youngest partition of the IQ which is the partition allocated most recently at the tail pointer. The contribution of a partition is measured in terms of issued instructions from this partition within a time window. If that contribution is below some empirically chosen threshold, then the effective size of the IQ is reduced by expanding the disabled area. The effective IQ size is periodically increased (by contracting the disabled area). This simple scheme increases the energy savings to about 91% with a modest 1.7% IPC loss.

Loop Cache

The loop cache is designed to hold small loops commonly found in media and DSP workloads [41, 43]. It is typically just a piece of SRAM that is software or compiler controlled. A small loop is loaded in the loop buffer under program control and execution resumes, fetching instructions from the loop buffer rather than from the usual fetch path. The loop buffer being a tiny piece of RAM is very efficient in supplying instructions, avoiding the accesses to the much more power-consuming instruction L1. Because the loop buffer caches a small block of consecutive instructions, no tags and no tag comparisons are needed for addressing its contents. Instead, only relative addressing from the start of the loop is enough to generate an index in order to correctly access all the loop instructions in the buffer. Lack of tags and tag comparisons makes the loop buffer far more efficient than a typical cache.

Fully automatic loop caches, which detect small loops at run-time and install them in the loop cache dynamically, are also proposed in Refs.

[42–44]. However, such dynamic proposals, although they enhance the generality of the loop cache at the expense of additional hardware, are not critical for the DSP and embedded world where loop buffers have been successfully deployed. Nevertheless, the fully automatic loop buffer appears in Intel's Core 2 architecture [59].

Trace Cache

Due to CISC nature of the IA-32 (x86) instruction set processors, that translate the IA-32 instructions into RISC-like instructions called uops, the work required in such a control unit is tremendous, and this is reflected in the large percentage (28%) of the total power devoted to the control unit. To address this problem, Solomon *et al.* [45] describe a trace cache that can eliminate the repeated work of fetching, decoding, and translating the same instructions over and over again. Called the Micro-Operation Cache (UC), the concept was implemented as the trace cache of the Pentium-4 [60]. The reason why it works so well in this environment is that traces are created after the IA-32 instructions are decoded and translated in uops. Traces are uop sequences and are directly issued as such.

The Micro-Operation Cache concept is depicted in Fig. 12. The UC fill part starts after the instruction decode. A fill buffer is filled with uops until the first branch is encountered. In this respect, the UC is more a basic BHB than a trace cache, but this is not an inherent limitation in the designs; it was so chosen just to make it as efficient as possible. Another interesting characteristic of the UC design is that, although a hit can be determined in the UC during the first pipeline stage, the uops are not delivered to the issue stage until after four more cycles (stages). This ensures that there is no bubble in the pipeline switching back and forth from streaming uops out of the

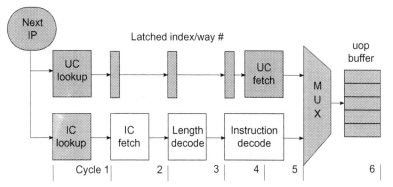

Figure 12 Control unit of the pipeline with uop cache. *Source: Adapted from Ref. [45].*

Control Unit (CU) to fetching IA-32 instructions from the instruction cache and decoding them.

The benefits for often repeating traces, of course, are significant. Solomon *et al.* report that 75% of all instruction decoding (hence, uop translation) is eliminated using a moderately sized micro-operation cache. This is translated to a 10% reduction of the processor's total power for the Intel's P6 architecture[61]. The Pentium-4 trace cache is a prime example of a power-saving technique eliminating repetitive and cacheable computation (decoding).

4.3.2 Static

The ROB and the RF are the two critical components to enhance a processor's ILP but, unfortunately, they have serious static power, especially occurred in a large RF which in average consumes around 20% of the processor's power budget. The RF shows the highest power density as it has a severe access frequency and occupies a relatively small area. As a result, due to high areal power density, the RF is known to the hottest unit in the microprocessor [62].

Idle Register File DVS

During program execution, RF dissipates two types of static power. First, between the instruction issue stage and commit stage, the register does not store useful values, but waits for instruction commitment, thus waste static energy/power. The second type occurs when a register stores a temporary value which is no longer to be used or may be referenced again but after a long time. In this case, because most consumer instructions nearby the producer have already read out that value from the ROB, it is possible that the register keeps a useless value for a long time without any references. In some cases, the short-lived values even let allocated registers never be referenced once after the instruction issue stage. In Ref. [46], they find that more than 70% values in a program are short lived.

To address mentioned RF inefficiency problem, Shieh and Chen [46] proposed monitoring mechanism in the datapath and ROB to find out which temporary values possibly make registers have more static power. To prevent the first type of mentioned static power components, the mechanism identifies that a register will temporarily become idle after the instruction issue stage. Because the allocated register will not be referenced during instruction execution until the commit stage, the monitoring mechanism has the ability to monitor each register's usage along pipeline stages.

To prevent the second-type static power, identify that a register possibly stores a "seldom-used" temporary value. They added a simple indicator in each ROB entry to monitor, for each temporary value, how many consumer instructions have appeared before commitment. If a temporary value has many consumers appearing before commitment, the probability that this value becomes "seldom-used" after commitment will become very large.

Their monitoring mechanism cooperates with the DVS mechanism. When it identifies that a register is idle, it triggers the DVS mechanism to power down that register's supply voltage to lower voltage levels. If the monitoring mechanism finds that a register will be accessed soon (e.g., at the stage just before instruction reference or commitment), it early alerts the DVS mechanism to power on that register's supply voltage to the normal voltage level. They assumed that each register has three voltage levels: active (1 V), drowsy (0.3 V), and destroy (0 V).

Simulation results show that through ROB monitoring, a RF can save at least 50% static power consumption with almost negligible performance loss.

Register File Access Optimization

A problem with RF accesses is that they are not spread through the whole RF, but clustered on one of its side (Fig. 13).

Kim *et al.* [47] proposed an idea that evenly redistributes accesses to the full range of the RF through the improvement of the traditional renaming unit. By uniformly distributing writing accesses to the RF, the power density decreases and the possibility of hotspots forming also reduces.

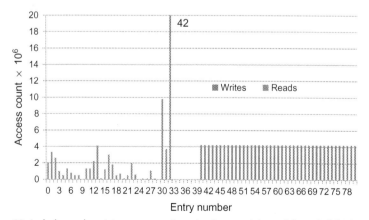

Figure 13 Imbalanced register accesses in gzip. *Source: Adapted from Ref. [47].*

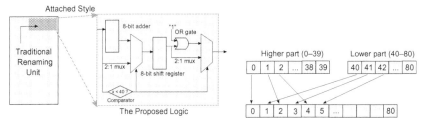

Figure 14 The proposed small logic attached to the traditional renaming unit and the mapping scenario. *Source: Adapted from Ref. [47].*

Consequently, the leakage power decreases as it is proportional to the exponential function of temperature.

The proposed is actually a remapping technique revealing that architectural registers (i.e., entry number 0–40) are relocated to the full range of entry numbers (i.e., 0–79) with only the even number allocation, and also that the assignments to physical registers (i.e., 40–80) are also repositioned throughout whole RF area (i.e., 1–80) with the odd number. The algorithm is realized through several steps. First, the traditional renaming unit allocates an index number of a physical register entry to an architectural register. Next, a new index number is generated by our simple algorithm; if the index number is less than 40, then a new index number will be achieved from multiplying the first index number by 2; otherwise (i.e., 40–80), we subtract 40 from the first index, multiply it by 2, and add 1. These simple algorithms can be implemented by a small logic, and the logic can be attached to the traditional renaming unit; the attached logic consists of six small components: an 8-bit adder, an 8-bit shift register, a comparator, an OR gate, and two 2:1 multiplexors (Fig. 14). The authors report notable temperature drop reaching up to 11% on average 6%, and leakage power savings reached up to 24% on average 13%.

4.4 Core-Back-End

Functional units are a fundamental part of every processor. They provide a lot of trade-off; thus, plenty of techniques for both dynamic and static power/energy components have been proposed.

4.4.1 Dynamic

The essence of almost all dynamic power/energy optimization techniques for this part of the processor is clock gating.

Exploiting Narrow-Width Operands

The first approach optimizes the integer structures and the results are still 100% accurate, while the second one optimizes Floating Point (FP) units and introduce some error.

Integers

Each processor has defined its data width, and it is one of its main characteristics. Often, applications running on a processor do not really need full data width. It has become especially evident in 64-bit processors. Brooks and Martonosi [49] notice a disproportion through a set of measurements they did for SPECint95 and MediaBench application running on 64-bit Alpha machines and find useful statistics. They find a lot of operations where the both operands have the number of significant bit of 16 and 33, respectively.

There are two ways to exploit this characteristic. One reduces power while the other improves performance. They both have the same goal—to improve energy and EDP. In the both of the cases, the first step is the same—detect narrow operands. Brooks and Martonosi [49] consider each 16-bit, or less wide, as narrow operand. They do detection dynamically by tagging ALU and memory outputs with "narrow bit" if it is narrow.

First approach is to clock gate unused part of ALU when we have two narrow operands (Fig. 15). This technique yields significant power savings for the integer unit comprising of an adder, a booth multiplier, bit-wise logic, and a shifter. Specifically, in an Alpha-class, 4-instruction-wide superscalar, the average power consumption of the integer units can be reduced by 55% and 58% for the SPECint95 and the Mediabench benchmark suites, respectively.

Another approach is to pack two narrow operands and to process it simultaneously. This is done by detecting two narrow-operand instructions which are ready to execute and shifting significant part of the one to high order part (which is "empty") of the other. The combined operations are executed in the ALU in Single Instruction, Multiple Data (SIMD) mode, similarly to SIMD multimedia extension instructions. The problem with the packing approach is overhead logic (mainly MUXs) which spoils energy savings.

However, the above-presented packing narrow-width values approach does not achieve significant speedup. The improvement of this approach is to introduce speculation in the methodology. We suppose that both operands are narrow, pack them like in the normal case, and if we find we were wrong,

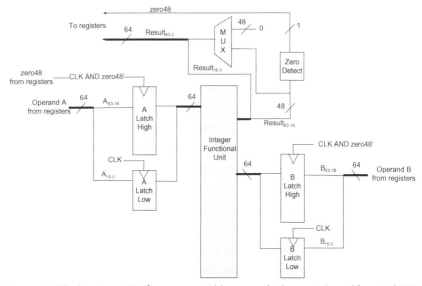

Figure 15 Clock gating ALUs for narrow-width operands. *Source: Adapted from Ref. [49].*

squash and reexecute them separately. This optimization brings the speedup of packing narrow-width operations to approximately 4% for SPECint95 and 8% for MediaBench for an Alpha-class, 4-instruction-wide, superscalar CPU. Speedup increases with the width of the machine as more instructions become available to choose from and pack together.

Floating Point

While the above exploitation of narrow operands relies on keeping accuracy, one step further to be more energy efficient is to introduce some "acceptable" error. Acceptable is a very relative term, and it strongly depends on the application's nature. Tong *et al.* [48] analyze several floating point programs that utilize low-resolution sensory data and notice that the programs suffer almost no loss of accuracy even with a significant reduction in bit-width. Figure 16A shows how program accuracy decreases when we utilize lower number on mantissa bits, while Fig. 16B shows program accuracy across various exponent bit-widths.

Tong *et al.* exploit this characteristic of applications they profiled by proposing the use of a variable bit-width floating point unit to reduce power consumption. To create hardware capable of variable bit-width multiplications (up to 24 × 24 bit), they used a 24 × 8 bit digit-serial architecture (Fig. 17). The 24 × 8 bit architecture allows performing 8, 16, and

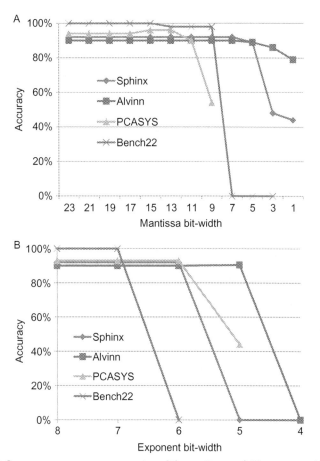

Figure 16 Program accuracy across various (A) mantissa and (B) exponent bit-widths. *Source: Adapted from Ref. [48].*

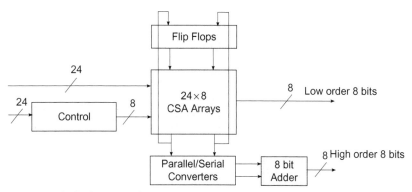

Figure 17 Block diagram of a 24 × 8 digit-serial multiplier. *Source: Adapted from Ref. [48].*

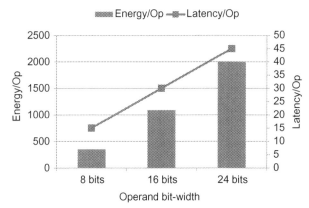

Figure 18 Power reduction using digit-serial multiplier. *Source: Adapted from Ref. [48].*

24-bit multiplication by passing the data once, twice, or three times through the serial multiplier. A finite state machine is used to control the number of iterations through the CSA array.

Proposed FP architecture was compared with widely used Wallace architecture. Figure 18 shows the potential power reduction for our three programs if we use the digit-serial multiplier as the mantissa multiplier. For 8-bit multiplication, the digit-serial multiplier consumes less than 1/3 of power than the Wallace Tree multiplier (in the case of Sphinx and ALVINN). When 9–16 bits of the mantissa are required (in the case of PCASYS and Bench22), the digit-serial multiplier still consumes 20% less power than the Wallace Tree multiplier. The digit-serial multiplier does consume 40% more power when performing 24-bit multiplication due to the power consumption of the overhead circuitry.

Work Reuse

The idea of the application of the work reuse technique on functional units is to cache the results and to reuse them later instead of recompute them. This can save considerable power if the difference in energy between accessing the cache and recomputing the results is quite large. The first work in this topic is done by Citron *et al.* [51]. This act of remembering the result of an operation in relation to its inputs they named *memoization*. A memoization cache, or Look-up Table (LUT), stores the input operands and the result of floating point operations. Upon seeing the same operands, the result is retrieved from the Memo-table and is multiplexed onto the output (Fig. 19). The Memo-table access and the floating point operation start

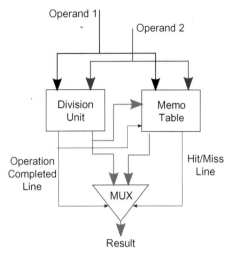

Figure 19 Operation-level memoization: The Memo-table in this particular example captures inputs and results from a division unit. When inputs previously seen are detected, the result is read from the Memo-table. *Source: Adapted from Ref. [51].*

simultaneously. However, accessing the Memo-table is much faster (single-cycle) than performing the actual multicycle operation. Since the result is available much earlier, this translates into performance benefits but also (by gating the floating point unit before it completes the operation) to power benefits. The power benefits are commensurable to the energy differential between accessing the cache and performing the operation to completion.

Although in Ref. [51] they do not perform any power analysis, they do statistics for multimedia applications (effect benchmark suite, SPEC FP95, and imaging/DSP applications) which, in conjunction with simple power models for the floating point unit and the memo-tables, can be used to derive power estimates. For their workloads, 59% of integer multiplications, 43% of FP multiplications, and 50% of FP divisions are memoizable and can be "performed" in a single cycle with small (32-entry, 4-way set-associative) LUTs.

The work from Alvarez *et al.* [52] is a kind of mixture of previous presented technique and the technique from Tong *et al.* [48]. In order to achieve more power savings from memoization (i.e., higher reuse), they play with human perception tolerance and propose technique called tolerant memoization which targets low-power embedded processors for hand-held devices with multimedia workloads. Performance and power dissipation can

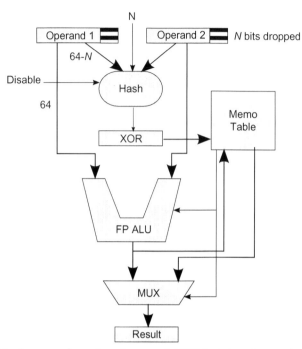

Figure 20 Hardware configuration of sequential LUT for tolerant memoization. *Source: Adapted from Ref. [52].*

be improved at the cost of small precision losses in computation. The key idea is to associate entries with the similar inputs to the same output. They targeted low-power processors for hand-held devices with multimedia workloads.

Except the ability to have a hit when the inputs are not exactly the same, the rest of the proposed hardware (Fig. 20) is more or less the same as in the previously presented technique. The additional option is a possibility to serial LUT memoization, which means that FPU waits until it is known if there is a hit in the LUT or miss. In that way, the hardware is slower but more power efficient. The results showed when only a low hit rate is achieved (classical reuse and speech), parallel configuration works better as it saves some energy but does not increase the operation latency. When the hit rate grows, serial configuration arises as the best solution because it only infrequently uses one more cycle, but often saves the entire energy of the FPU; therefore, serial configuration is the best choice for tolerant reuse.

With tolerant memoization and realistic table sizes, the reuse hit rate is raised and, as a result, considerable power and time savings are achieved (up to a 25% improvement in the EDP for some of the benchmarks) at the cost of introducing some errors in the output data that are negligible in the context of hand-held devices.

4.4.2 Static

While dynamic power/energy optimization techniques are mostly based on clock gating, here this is the case with power gating.

Power Gating

Power gating of functional units is not used to be as attractive as power gating memory cells. Due to short idle intervals, it is a question if we save anything as we spend dynamic energy to power them up or down. However, as leakage becoming dominant component of total power consumption, power gating is getting more attractive. Hu *et al.* [53] make an analysis of power gating application on functional units. They propose analytical formulas that, for a number of assumptions, yield break-even point, in cycles, for power gating functional units. To simplify the formulas, a leakage factor L is introduced, which specifies the ratio of the average leakage power to the average switching power dissipated per cycle by a functional unit.

They proposed two policies for fine grain functional unit power gating: a time-based policy (*functional unit decay*) and an event-guided policy (*event guided power-gating*).

The first policy is based on idle time detection. As soon as an idle period is detected, the functional unit is switched-off. There are three timing factors that determine the behavior of this approach:

1. the break-even point in cycles after which there are net gains in energy,
2. the time it takes for the functional unit to wake up from the moment it is needed, and
3. the decay interval, i.e., the time it takes to decide to put the functional unit in sleep mode.

The first two are technology and functional-unit specific, while the third, the decay interval, is an architectural knob that one can turn to tune the policy. Functional unit design can vary a lot, and this affects the first two of factors. Floating point functional units tend to have a wide range of idle periods (in SPEC-FP 2000). Although their short idle periods are more numerous than their longer ones, most idle cycles are due to the longer periods by virtue of their size. In this case, a long decay interval skips the short idle periods and selects only the large ones. This minimizes the number of times the functional units are unavailable because they are powered down while still benefiting by having the functional unit powered down for a significant part of the time. Overall, this technique can power down the floating point units for 28% of the time with only minimal performance penalty (less than 2%) for the SPEC FP 2000. For integers, the situation with short idle periods is even worse as the integer unit is often used by address arithmetic and longer idle periods usually occur after L2 misses.

In order to increase power savings in applications during which executions there are a lot of short idle periods, Hu *et al.* propose event-guided power gating. They used various events as L2 misses, instruction cache misses, or branch mispredictions as clues to upcoming idleness of the functional units. Upon detecting a misprediction, the functional units are put immediately into sleep mode without waiting for the normal decay interval.

This simple rule extends the powered-down time of the functional units without incurring any additional performance penalty. The use of clues increases the percentage of cycles in sleep mode for a given performance loss, or, conversely, for the same percentage of cycles in sleep mode the use of clues eases the performance impact. Similarly to branch mispredictions, other events can also provide useful hints for the idleness of the functional units but have not been studied further.

V_t-Based Technique

As the design of functional units demands maximum speed, in most cases, they are built using domino logic. The problem with domino logic, from the low power point of view, is that every cycle domino logic is charged and discharged (sometimes) by the evaluation of its inputs, thus preventing only input from switching is not enough to stop energy to drain! With respect to static power, leakage paths in dynamic domino logic depend on the state of the internal dynamic nodes. This property is exploited for the implementation of a sleep mode specific to domino logic.

The solution is to use MTCMOS approach by selectively using high V_t devices in the noncritical paths [54]. In that case, the performance is not compromised. In Fig. 21, the integration of high-VT devices (shaded transistors) in the domino-logic AND gate is showed. If either input is low, the dynamic node remains charged, resulting in a large subthreshold leakage current through the high-leakage transistors N1, N2, N3, and N4. However, when the dynamic node is discharged, the low leakage transistors P1, P2, and N5 are strongly cut-off, and the leakage in the whole circuit is dramatically reduced.

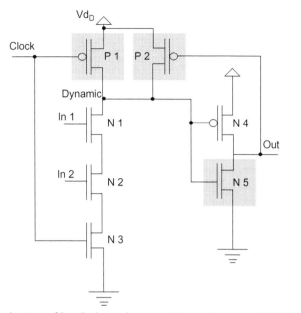

Figure 21 Realization of low leakage domino AND circuit, using MTCMOS approach. *Source: Adapted from Ref. [54].*

A step further to be more power efficient is to apply power gating on the existing low leakage domino AND circuit. The challenges are almost the same as in CMOS power gating—the short idle periods. An overly aggressive policy to enter the sleep mode is probably not optimal. For this reason, Dropsho *et al.* propose a *gradual* sleep policy that puts the functional unit in sleep mode in stages by adding additional sleep transistor to the existing low leakage asymmetric circuit (Fig. 22). The gradual sleep technique is shown in Fig. 23. The functional unit is divided into slices which are put in sleep mode consecutively as long as the functional unit remains idle. As soon as it is needed again, all slices are brought back to active mode and are precharged.

They show that the simple GradualSleep design works well across a range of technology and application parameters by amortizing the energy cost of entering the sleep mode across several cycles.

4.5 Conclusion About the Existing Solutions

From the above presented, we can conclude that only comprehensive approach to optimize the components of power/energy of microprocessors can lead to the significant savings. Thus, it is very important to consider all

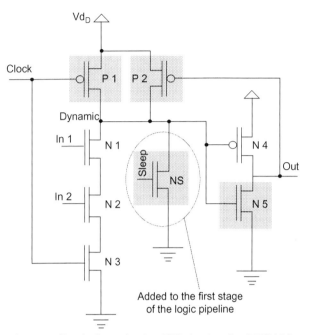

Figure 22 Realization of low leakage domino AND circuit, using MTCMOS approach and one sleep transistor. *Source: Adapted from Ref. [54].*

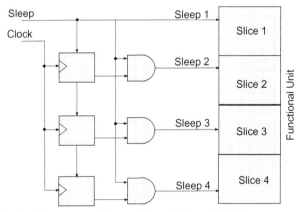

Figure 23 Gradual sleep mode. *Source: Adapted from Ref. [54].*

the possible optimization solutions during the design process. Blind DVFS application, for example, could increase total energy consumption! For instance, Miyoshi *et al.* [63] concluded that for Pentium-based system, it is energy efficient to run only at the highest frequency, while on the

PowerPC-based system, it is more energy efficient to run at the lowest frequency point.

There are a lot of possible solutions to reduce power/energy at each level; thus, there are situations when we wonder which technique to apply. For example, if we consider core-level techniques, one of the first decisions is the selection of power management: software (OS) or hardware (on-chip) one. Then we should pick adequate management strategy. There are off-line (compiler-based) and online strategies. The online strategies can be based on events or predictions. Low-power design is a process which needs a lot of time and effort, and there are a lot of questions that need to be answered. It essentially important to consider savings/overhead balance before we apply a particular technique; otherwise, we can make the system even less efficient.

Generally, it is always important to consider Amdahl's law. Before starting optimization process, we should first examine the percentage that a component being optimized takes in total power budget.

5. FUTURE TREND

It is becoming obvious that due to the "power wall" further scaling is in crisis. While sole core scaling saturated, the relief was Chip-Multiprocessor (CMP). Unfortunately, it is a matter of time when the same will happen with CMP scaling. An essential question is how much more performance can be extracted from the multicore path in the near future.

The study on this topic is performed by Esmaeilzadeh et al. [64]. The multicore designs they study include single-threaded CPU-like and massively threaded GPU-like multicore chip organizations with symmetric, asymmetric, dynamic, and composed topologies with PARSEC benchmark. Unfortunately, the results are not optimistic! Even at 22 nm, 21% of a fixed-size chip must be powered off, and at 8 nm, this number grows to more than 50%. This turned off part of the core we call "dark silicon." Through 2024, only 7.9 × average speedup is possible across commonly used parallel workloads, leaving a nearly 24-fold gap from a target of doubled performance per generation. Results for ITRS scaling are slightly better but not much. With conservative scaling, a speedup gap of at least 22 × exists at the 8 nm technology node compared to Moore's law. Assuming ITRS scaling, the gap is at least 13 × at 8 nm.

They conclude that radical microarchitectural innovations are necessary to alter the power/performance pareto frontier to deliver speedup commensurate with Moore's law. Actually, maybe the solutions are micro-electronics innovations rather than microarchitectural ones. Due to many predictions, CMOS will be replaced in next 10 years. Thus, we will again have the situation where fundamental physics and truly adventurous electrical engineering can again play a central role in the evolution of the information technology.

There are several possible MOSFET replacements. Especially interesting are Nanoelectromechanical Systems (NEMS)-based switchers that reliably open and close trillions of times and emulate closer to the ideal switch. Those devices physically move the actual gate up and down depending upon the applied gate voltage. The main characteristic of NEMS devices is their huge resistance when they are off and ultra small resistance when they are on.

6. CONCLUSION

We presented a comprehensive overview of power- and energy-efficient techniques for microprocessor architecture. The goal is to summarize the work done in low-power area. In past 20 years, low-power area evaluated from marginal topic of computer architecture community to unavoidable part of contemporary architecture research. Although today we care about power more than ever, we should keep being holistic and consider power together with other design goals as performance, reliability, design verifiability, etc.

This overview is beneficial for everyone who is interested in low-power design. Nevertheless, computer architects are the ones who should take the most benefit from this research. The presented low-power solutions are presented in a way that is the most appropriate for them. Software-oriented architects can profit from this overview too.

While dynamic power optimization techniques like DVFS have become enough mature and it is not very probable that we are going to harvest more from them in the future, reducing leakage power is currently the main "obsession" of microprocessor designers. Leakage reduction management is for sure one of the key areas of future architecture-level power research.

Power gating is still the most popular technique to reduce leakage power, especially with its latest incarnation of Per-Core Power Gating (PCPG). Unfortunately, due to growing gate leakage current, the technique is getting less efficient. The situation is currently under control due to the introduction of high-k dielectrics and the whole chip body biasing, but with further technology scaling things are going to be more complicated.

In order to keep power gating efficient, we need more efficient switchers. One of the possible solutions is NEMS-based switcher. With that kind of switcher, we could expect to have ignorable gate leakage current.

Clock gating, although already an intensively utilized approach, is still an indispensable tool to reduce switching activity. Moreover, there is still room to further reduce switching activity of energy-inefficient out-of-order logic of performance-oriented processors.

At the end, it is important to stress that only systematic and comprehensive approach including all the relevant factors can lead us to a successful low-power design. It is crucial that a microprocessor designer considers the whole processor-system power dissipation and its workload rather than a sole component. There are situations when core-only optimizations lead to the system power dissipation increase [65]. It is also very important to adapt the software to the target architecture. The code indeed affects power dissipation in some cases [66]; thus, we should follow the motto: let hardware and software work together.

It is more than obvious that CMOS scaling does not really help anymore; it even makes the problem worse. The only solution on which we could rely today in order to control energy consumption and power dissipation is to apply different techniques to all designing levels. While we do not get the new technology, we need to invent new and to improve existing techniques in order keep power dissipation and energy consumption below the purpose critical values.

REFERENCES

[1] G.E. Moore, Cramming more components onto integrated circuits, Electronics 38 (8) (1965) 114–117.
[2] G. Venkatesh, J. Sampson, N. Goulding, S. Garcia, V. Bryksin, J. Lugo-Martinez, S. Swanson, M.B. Taylor, Conservation cores: reducing the energy of mature computations, ACM SIGARCH Comput. Archit. News 38 (1) (2010) 205–218.
[3] W. Chedid, C. Yu, Survey on Power Management Techniques for Energy Efficient Computer Systems, Department of Electrical and Computer Engineering Cleveland State University, 2002.
[4] V. Venkatachalam, M. Franz, Power reduction techniques for microprocessor systems, ACM Comput. Surv. 37 (2005) 195–237.
[5] V. Venkatachalam, M. Franz, A Survey on Low Power Architecture, 2007.
[6] URL, 2013. http://en.wikipedia.org/wiki/Stefan%E2%80%93Boltzmann_law/.
[7] R. Gonzalez, M. Horowitz, Energy dissipation in general purpose microprocessors, IEEE J. Solid State Circuits 31 (9) (1996) 1277–1284.
[8] URL, 2013. http://scholar.google.com.
[9] A. Noruzi, Google Scholar: the new generation of citation indexes, Libri 55 (2005) 170–180.

[10] J. Bosman, I. van Mourik, M. Rasch, E. Sieverts, H. Verhoeff, Scopus reviewed and compared: the coverage and functionality of the citation database Scopus, including comparisons with Web of Science and Google Scholar, 2006.

[11] M. Weiser, B. Welch, A. Demers, S. Shenker, Scheduling for reduced CPU energy, in: OSDI'94, 1994.

[12] K. Flautner, S. Reinhardt, T. Mudge, Automatic performance setting for dynamic voltage scaling, Wirel. Netw. 8 (2002) 507–520.

[13] C.-H. Hsu, U. Kremer, The design, implementation, and evaluation of a compiler algorithm for CPU energy reduction, in: PLDI'03, 2003, pp. 38–48.

[14] H. Saputra, M. Kandemir, N. Vijaykrishnan, M.J. Irwin, J.S. Hu, C.-H. Hsu, U. Kremer, Energy-conscious compilation based on voltage scaling, in: LCTES/SCOPES'02, 2002, pp. 2–11.

[15] F. Xie, M. Martonosi, S. Malik, Compile-time dynamic voltage scaling settings: opportunities and limits, SIGPLAN Not. 38 (2003) 49–62.

[16] F. Xie, M. Martonosi, S. Malik, Intraprogram dynamic voltage scaling: bounding opportunities with analytic modeling, ACM Trans. Archit. Code Optim. 1 (2004) 323–367.

[17] Q. Wu, M. Martonosi, D.W. Clark, V.J. Reddi, D. Connors, Y. Wu, J. Lee, D. Brooks, A dynamic compilation framework for controlling microprocessor energy and performance, in: MICRO 38, 2005, pp. 271–282.

[18] C. Isci, M. Martonosi, Runtime power monitoring in high-end processors: methodology and empirical data, in: MICRO 36, 2003, pp. 93–104.

[19] C. Isci, G. Contreras, M. Martonosi, Live, runtime phase monitoring and prediction on real systems with application to dynamic power management, in: MICRO 39, 2006, pp. 359–370.

[20] A. Iyer, D. Marculescu, Power and performance evaluation of globally asynchronous locally synchronous processors, SIGARCH Comput. Archit. News 30 (2002) 158–168.

[21] E. Talpes, D. Marculescu, Toward a multiple clock/voltage island design style for power-aware processors, IEEE Trans. Very Large Scale Integr. Syst. 13 (2005) 591–603.

[22] G. Semeraro, D.H. Albonesi, S.G. Dropsho, G. Magklis, S. Dwarkadas, M.L. Scott, Dynamic frequency and voltage control for a multiple clock domain microarchitecture, in: MICRO 35, 2002, pp. 356–367.

[23] Q. Wu, P. Juang, M. Martonosi, D.W. Clark, Formal online methods for voltage/frequency control in multiple clock domain microprocessors, in: Proceedings of the 11th International Conference on Architectural Support for Programming Languages and Operating Systems, ASPLOS-XI, 2004, pp. 248–259.

[24] G. Semeraro, G. Magklis, R. Balasubramonian, D.H. Albonesi, S. Dwarkadas, M.L. Scott, Energy-efficient processor design using multiple clock domains with dynamic voltage and frequency scaling, in: Proceedings of the 8th International Symposium on High-Performance Computer Architecture, HPCA'02, 2002, pp. 29–42.

[25] R.I. Bahar, S. Manne, Power and energy reduction via pipeline balancing, in: ISCA'01, 2001, pp. 218–229.

[26] B. Fields, R. Bodík, M.D. Hill, Slack: maximizing performance under technological constraints, in: ISCA'02, 2002, pp. 47–58.

[27] D. Duarte, N. Vijaykrishnan, M. Irwin, H.-S. Kim, G. McFarland, Impact of scaling on the effectiveness of dynamic power reduction schemes, in: Computer Design, International Conference on, 2002, p. 382.

[28] S.M. Martin, K. Flautner, T. Mudge, D. Blaauw, Combined dynamic voltage scaling and adaptive body biasing for lower power microprocessors under dynamic workloads, in: ICCAD'02, 2002, pp. 721–725.

[29] L. Yan, Joint dynamic voltage scaling and adaptive body biasing for heterogeneous distributed real-time embedded systems, IEEE Trans. Comput. Aided Des. Integr. Circuits Syst. 24 (7) (2005) 1030–1041.

[30] H. Li, S. Bhunia, Y. Chen, T.N. Vijaykumar, K. Roy, Deterministic clock gating for microprocessor power reduction, in: HPCA'03, 2003, pp. 113–122.

[31] S. Manne, A. Klauser, D. Grunwald, Pipeline gating: speculation control for energy reduction, SIGARCH Comput. Archit. News 26 (1998) 132–141.

[32] J.L. Aragón, J. González, A. González, Power-aware control speculation through selective throttling, in: HPCA'03, 2003, pp. 103–112.

[33] R. Canal, A. González, J.E. Smith, Very low power pipelines using significance compression, in: MICRO 33, 2000, pp. 181–190.

[34] A. Sodani, G.S. Sohi, Dynamic instruction reuse, in: ISCA'97, 1997, pp. 194–205.

[35] J. Huang, D. Lilja, Exploiting basic block value locality with block reuse, in: Proceedings of the 5th International Symposium on High Performance Computer Architecture, HPCA'99, 1999.

[36] A. Gonzalez, J. Tubella, C. Molina, Trace-level reuse, in: ICPP'99, 1999, pp. 30–39.

[37] C. Alvarez, J. Corbal, M. Valero, Dynamic tolerance region computing for multimedia, IEEE Trans. Comput. 61 (5) (2012) 650–665.

[38] A. Buyuktosunoglu, D. Albonesi, S. Schuster, D. Brooks, P. Bose, P. Cook, A circuit level implementation of an adaptive issue queue for power-aware microprocessors, in: GLSVLSI'01, 2001, pp. 73–78.

[39] D. Ponomarev, G. Kucuk, K. Ghose, Reducing power requirements of instruction scheduling through dynamic allocation of multiple datapath resources, in: MICRO 34, 2001, pp. 90–101.

[40] D. Folegnani, A. González, Energy-effective issue logic, in: ISCA'01, 2001, pp. 230–239.

[41] N. Bellas, I. Hajj, C. Polychronopoulos, G. Stamoulis, Energy and performance improvements in microprocessor design using a loop cache, in: Computer Design, International Conference on, 1999, p. 378.

[42] L.H. Lee, B. Moyer, J. Arends, Instruction fetch energy reduction using loop caches for embedded applications with small tight loops, in: ISLPED'99, 1999, pp. 267–269.

[43] N. Bellas, I. Hajj, C. Polychronopoulos, Using dynamic cache management techniques to reduce energy in a high-performance processor, in: ISLPED'99, 1999, pp. 64–69.

[44] C.-L. Yang, C.-H. Lee, HotSpot cache: joint temporal and spatial locality exploitation for i-cache energy reduction, in: ISLPED'04, 2004, pp. 114–119.

[45] B. Solomon, A. Mendelson, R. Ronen, D. Orenstien, Y. Almog, Micro-operation cache: a power aware frontend for variable instruction length ISA, IEEE Trans. Very Large Scale Integr. Syst. 11 (2003) 801–811.

[46] W.-Y. Shieh, H.-D. Chen, Saving register-file static power by monitoring short-lived temporary-values in ROB, in: Computer Systems Architecture Conference, 2008, ACSAC 2008, 13th Asia-Pacific, 2008, pp. 1–8.

[47] J. Kim, S.T. Jhang, C.S. Jhon, Dynamic register-renaming scheme for reducing power-density and temperature, in: SAC'10, 2010, pp. 231–237.

[48] Y.F. Tong, R.A. Rutenbar, D.F. Nagle, Minimizing floating-point power dissipation via bit-width reduction, in: ISCA'98, 1998.

[49] D. Brooks, M. Martonosi, Dynamically exploiting narrow width operands to improve processor power and performance, in: HPCA'99, 1999, pp. 13–22.

[50] D. Brooks, M. Martonosi, Value-based clock gating and operation packing: dynamic strategies for improving processor power and performance, ACM Trans. Comput. Syst. 18 (2000) 89–126.

[51] D. Citron, D. Feitelson, L. Rudolph, Accelerating multi-media processing by implementing memoing in multiplication and division units, SIGOPS Oper. Syst. Rev. 32 (1998) 252–261.

[52] C. Alvarez, J. Corbal, M. Valero, Fuzzy memoization for floating-point multimedia applications, IEEE Trans. Comput. 54 (2005) 922–927.

[53] Z. Hu, A. Buyuktosunoglu, V. Srinivasan, V. Zyuban, H. Jacobson, P. Bose, Micro-architectural techniques for power gating of execution units, in: ISLPED'04, 2004, pp. 32–37.

[54] S. Dropsho, A. Buyuktosunoglu, R. Balasubramonian, D.H. Albonesi, S. Dwarkadas, G. Semeraro, G. Magklis, M.L. Scott, Integrating adaptive on-chip storage structures for reduced dynamic power, in: International Conference on Parallel Architectures and Compilation Techniques, 2002.

[55] M.K. Gowan, L.L. Biro, D.B. Jackson, Power considerations in the design of the Alpha 21264 microprocessor, in: DAC'98, 1998, pp. 726–731.

[56] S. Kaxiras, M. Martonosi, Computer Architecture Techniques for Power-Efficiency, Morgan & Claypool Publishers, 2008.

[57] I. Ratkovic, O. Palomar, M. Stanic, O.S. Unsal, A. Cristal, M. Valero, On the selection of adder unit in energy efficient vector processing, in: ISQED, 2013, pp. 143–150.

[58] O. Ergin, D. Balkan, K. Ghose, D. Ponomarev, Register packing: exploiting narrow-width operands for reducing register file pressure, in: MICRO 37, 2004, pp. 304–315.

[59] URL, 2015. http://en.wikipedia.org/wiki/Intel_Core_2.

[60] URL, 2015. http://en.wikipedia.org/wiki/Pentium_4.

[61] URL, 2015. http://en.wikipedia.org/wiki/P6_%28microarchitecture%29.

[62] M.R. Stan, K. Skadron, M. Barcella, W. Huang, K. Sankaranarayanan, S. Velusamy, Hotspot: a dynamic compact thermal model at the processor-architecture level, Micro-electron. J. 34 (12) (2003) 1153–1165.

[63] A. Miyoshi, C. Lefurgy, E. Van Hensbergen, R. Rajamony, R. Rajkumar, Critical power slope: understanding the runtime effects of frequency scaling, in: ICS'02, 2002, pp. 35–44.

[64] H. Esmaeilzadeh, E. Blem, R. Amant, K. Sankaralingam, D. Burger, Dark silicon and the end of multicore scaling, in: ISCA'11, 2011.

[65] Z. Herczeg, D. Schmidt, A. Kiss, N. Wehn, T. Gyimóthy, Energy simulation of embedded XScale systems with XEEMU, J. Embed. Comput. 3 (2009) 209–219.

[66] V. Tiwari, S. Malik, A. Wolfe, Power analysis of embedded software: a first step towards software power minimization, in: ICCAD'94, 1994, pp. 384–390.

ABOUT THE AUTHORS

Ivan Ratković received the BS and MS degrees in Electrical Engineering and Computer Science from the University of Belgrade, School of Electrical Engineering in 2009 and 2011, respectively. He worked as a visiting researcher at Berkeley Wireless Research Center and he is currently a PhD student at Polytechnic University of Catalonia, Department of Computer Architecture and a researcher at Barcelona Supercomputing Center. His research interests include low power design, computer architecture, vector processors, digital arithmetic, VLSI design flows, and embedded systems.

Nikola Bežanić received the BS and MS degrees in Electronics from School of Electrical Engineering, University of Belgrade, Serbia, in 2009 and 2011, respectively. In period 2009–2011, he was a member of the Microsoft Research team at Barcelona Supercomputing Center, Spain, where he did research in low-power vector processing. In 2012, he enrolled in the PhD program at the Electronics Department, School of Electrical Engineering, University of Belgrade, where he is currently working as an associate researcher. His duties include development of low-power, adaptable, multiprocessor and multi-sensor electronic systems.

Osman Sabri Ünsal is co-leader of the Architectural Support for Programming Models group at the Barcelona Supercomputing Center. In the past, Dr. Ünsal was involved with Intel Microprocessor Research Labs, BSC Microsoft Research Center, and Intel/BSC Exascale Lab.

He holds BS, MS, and PhD degrees in Electrical and Computer Engineering from Istanbul Technical University, Brown University, and University of Massachusetts, Amherst, respectively.

His research interests are in computer architecture, low-power and energy-efficient computing, fault tolerance, and transactional memory.

Adrián Cristal received the "licenciatura" in Compuer Science from Universidad de Buenos Aires (FCEN) in 1995 and the PhD degree in Computer Science in 2006, from the Universitat Politécnica de Catalunya (UPC), Spain. From 1992 to 1995, he has been lecturing in Neural Network and Compiler Design. In UPC, from 2003 to 2006 he has been lecturing on computer organization.

Currently, and since 2006, he is researcher in Computer Architecture group at Barcelona Supercomputing Center. He is currently co-manager of the "Computer Architecture for Parallel Paradigms." His research interests cover the areas of microarchitecture, multicore architectures, and programming models for multicore architectures. He has published around 60 publications in these topics and participated in several research projects with other universities and industries, in framework of the European Union programs or in direct collaboration with technology leading companies.

Veljko Milutinović received his PhD in Electrical Engineering from the University of Belgrade in 1982. During the 80s, for about a decade, he was on the faculty of Purdue University, West Lafayette, Indiana, USA, where he coauthored the architecture and design of the world's first DARPA GaAs microprocessor. Since the 90s, after returning to Serbia, he is on the faculty of the School of Electrical Engineering, University of Belgrade, where he is teaching courses related to computer engineering, sensor networks, data flow, and data mining. He has published about 50 papers in SCI journals, about 20 books with major publishers in the USA, and he has about 3000 Google Scholar Citations. Professor Milutinović is a Fellow of the IEEE and a Member of Academia Europaea.

CHAPTER TWO

A Survey of Research on Data Corruption in Cyber–Physical Critical Infrastructure Systems

Mark Woodard*, Sahra Sedigh Sarvestani*, Ali R. Hurson*

*Missouri University of Science and Technology, Rolla, Missouri, USA

Contents

Abstract

Computer systems are present in every aspect of modern life. In many of these systems, corruption of data is unavoidable as a result of both intentional and unintentional means. In many systems, this erroneous data can result in severe consequences including financial loss, injury, or death. Critical infrastructure cyber–physical systems utilize intelligent control to improve performance; however, they are heavily data dependent. These systems have the potential to propagate corrupted data, leading to failure. This chapter presents a survey of work related to the propagation of corrupted data within critical infrastructure cyber–physical systems, including the sources of corrupted data and the structure of critical infrastructure cyber–physical systems. In addition, it presents a comparative analysis of various data corruption detection and mitigation techniques. Additionally, we discuss a number of studies on the negative effects of system execution

Advances in Computers, Volume 98
ISSN 0065-2458
http://dx.doi.org/10.1016/bs.adcom.2015.03.002

59

on corrupted data. These key topics are essential to understanding how undetected corrupted data propagates through a critical infrastructure cyber–physical system.

1. INTRODUCTION

Advances in computer technology and reduced hardware cost have caused almost all modern systems to rely heavily on stored computer data. However, the corruption of data in many systems is unavoidable. Erroneous data can be created within a system through unintentional means, such as failures in sensors, processors, storage, or communication hardware, or through intentional means such as an attack. Corrupted data in many of these systems can have severe consequences. One example is the stock market and other financial systems, as described by Kirilenko *et al.* [1]. One notable example of financial computing system failure occurred in August 2012, where a software error ended up costing Knight Capital, a mid-size financial firm, $10 million/min. In addition to economic consequences, failures in other systems such as critical infrastructure and manufacturing systems could result in the loss of life.

Critical infrastructure systems have evolved from purely physical systems into critical infrastructure cyber–physical systems (CPSs) to meet performance requirements and growing demands. In a CPS, the physical infrastructure's functionality is enhanced by utilizing intelligent embedded systems, communication capabilities, distributed computing, and intelligent control [2]. Examples of these complex CPSs include smart power grids, intelligent water distribution networks, smart transportation systems, and cyber-enabled manufacturing systems. The intelligent control provided by CPSs requires access to real-time and previously recorded data from the control entities' immediate area and system-wide information to calculate optimal control settings. Drawing data from system-wide sources allows the system to avoid adverse consequences caused by localized control. An example of improved CPS control is presented by Bakken *et al.* [3], who discuss how the major challenges of power generation and distribution in the smart grid can be addressed with the use of real-time measurements. Buttyán *et al.* [4] discuss the design and protection challenges of CPS, examining the importance of fault tolerance, security, and privacy in many components of CPS required to provided real-time field data including sensor nodes, networking protocols, and operating systems. Given CPSs' reliance on real-time field data, the protection of critical infrastructures provides a fascinating application for database and sensor networks.

The motivation for the survey presented in this chapter are the numerous critical infrastructure failures in recent history. One of these failures is presented by Miller *et al.* [5]. In June 1999, Bellingham, WA, a gas pipeline ruptured and leaked 237,000 gallons of gasoline from a 16-inch pipe into a creek that flowed through Whatcom Falls Park. After 1 1/2 h, the gasoline ignited and burned approximately 1 1/2 miles of forest along the creek resulting in three deaths and eight documented injuries. The failure was exacerbated by the control systems being unable to react due to the company's practice of performing database development work on the system while it was operating, making the real-time data unavailable. Another failure of note was in Italy on September 28, 2003, which resulted in half of Italy being without power for multiple days. Berizzi [6] and Buldyrev *et al.* [7] describe in detail the cascading failure, which was triggered by a single line failure near the Swiss-Italian border. However, this local failure led to the failure of nodes in the Internet communication network, which in turn caused further breakdown of power stations. While these examples are not the result of corrupted data, they demonstrate CPSs' reliance on accurate real-time data and the need for fault-tolerant database systems.

This chapter presents a survey of research related to the propagation of corrupted data. Figure 1 is a taxonomy of the topics presented in this chapter drawn from recent papers shown in Fig. 2. This work also serves as a

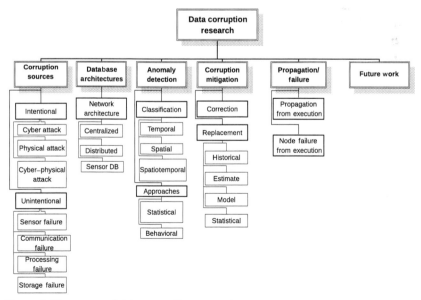

Figure 1 Taxonomy of data corruption research.

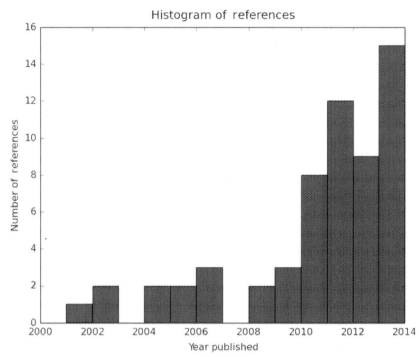

Figure 2 Histogram of papers cited.

foundation for future work in understanding and modeling the propagation of corrupted data through a CPS.

The remainder of this chapter is structured as follows. In Section 2, we address the sources of corrupted data. In Section 3, we discuss the structure of CPS and present an example application for comparison of techniques. Additionally, we discuss how data propagates through the example system, as undetected corrupted data will propagate in the same manner. In Section 4, we present a variety of data corruption detection methods that can be employed in a CPS. Section 5 is intended to address a variety of mitigation techniques that can be employed in a CPS. In Section 6, we discuss how corrupted data propagates through a system and its potential effects. Lastly, Section 7 addresses future directions for this research.

2. SOURCES OF CORRUPTED DATA

An understanding of fault tolerance and dependability is necessary in order to discuss the sources of data corruption. Avižienis *et al.* [8] define a number of terms in the field of dependability used to describe the state of a system in the presence of a disruptive event in terms of the system's ability to provide its specified service. The most general terms used to describe the threats to system operation are failure, error, and fault. A system failure occurs when the system does not comply with the system specifications. An error is a system state that may cause a subsequent failure, i.e., a failure occurs when an error alters the service. A fault is the cause of an error. Faults can be classified based on a number of factors including persistence, activity, and intent. Corrupted data can be a failure, error, or fault depending on its location in the system. Producing corrupted data in a system is a failure; processing corrupted data is a system error; corrupted data as an input to the system is a fault. Erroneous data can be created within a system in a number of different ways, both deliberate and nondeliberate.

Deliberate data corruption is the result of an attack. Attacks can be classified as cyber, physical, or cyber–physical depending on the source of the attack. Mo et al. [9] describe both purely cyber and purely physical attacks on critical infrastructure. Purely cyber attacks are attacks that remotely compromise the confidentiality, integrity, or availability of data. Cyber attacks include denial of service and malware designed to disrupt a control system. Purely physical attacks utilize physical tampering of either the system or the environment to disrupt operation. An example of this is power meter bypassing which allows a customer to steal power by bypassing the meter. Cyber–physical attacks are more complex and involve coordinated attacks on cyber and physical systems to produce undetectable adverse effects. Pasqualetti et al. [10] and Amin et al. [11] describe cyber–physical attacks on power and water critical infrastructures, respectively.

Nondeliberate data corruption is the result of corruption during communication, processing, or storage as well as inaccurate sensor readings. Aggarwal et al. [12] present the case for "data cleaning" of sensor readings. Sensor readings are often created by converting a measured quantity such as voltage into another measured quantities such as temperature. This process can produce very noisy data because it may not be precise. Other errors can be introduced by external conditions or sensor aging. Recalibrating the sensor can reduce these errors but cannot prevent these errors. Additionally, data may be incomplete due to periodic failures of sensors. Some sensor types can be even noisier than conventional sensors, for example, RFID data because of the reader-tag communication process.

Modern computer systems are composed of many potential sources of data corruption. Cebula and Young [13] provide a more detailed taxonomy of cyber and physical risks to information and technology assets. However, in many large distributed systems, the cause of the erroneous data (e.g., sensor, communication, processing, storage) is difficult to determine. Regardless of the source of the error, the corrupted data can be mitigated using the same techniques.

3. SENSOR NETWORKS: APPLICATION FOR COMPARISON

In this section, a practical CPS application will be defined. This application will be used for comparing of corrupted data detection and mitigation techniques and demonstrating the potential for propagation of corrupted data. The physical infrastructure of the practical CPS application consists of supply, transportation, and distribution. Sensors are dispersed throughout a physical infrastructure to collect information such as demand patterns, and quantity and quality of the supplied commodity. Information is critical for providing a dependable supply and is beneficial in guiding maintenance efforts and identifying vulnerable areas requiring fortification or monitoring. This information is fed to distributed algorithms running on the cyber infrastructure. These algorithms provide decision support to hardware controllers which control the commodity distribution. Figure 3 depicts a practical example CPS. This figure shows the physical infrastructure which consists of

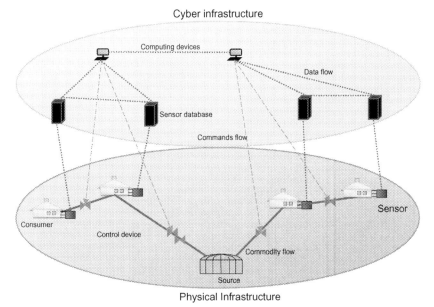

Figure 3 An intelligent water distribution network.

the commodity source, distribution, control, and consumers, as well as the networked cyber infrastructure which improves the performance of the physical infrastructure.

CPS sensor databases are designed to ensure the availability of accurate real-time data. A great deal of research has been conducted to meet the real-time data requirements of CPSs. Akyildiz et al. [14] provide surveys of sensor network systems research focusing primarily on management, storage, querying, and processing of sensor data. Diallo et al. [15] discuss real-time data storage and querying techniques in sensor database nodes and outline challenges and open issues. The major challenge of real-time database applications is the time constraints and accuracy of the result. This section discusses a number of database architectures used in sensor networks.

3.1 Sensor Network Database Requirements

In order to compare sensor database architectures for critical infrastructure use, a set of system requirements must first be established. Chen et al. [16] discuss the use of sensor and actuator network applications in critical infrastructure protection. Specifically, they propose a set of quality of service requirements for critical infrastructure systems in addition to the traditional dependability attributes which include reliability, confidentiality, availability, integrity, and safety. Their requirements are summarized here:

- Priority: Systems will have a way to assign importance levels to the data flows. For example, monitoring readings would be less important than the failure or attack notifications.
- Periodicity: Systems will be able to report periodic readings.
- Deadline: Systems will have a maximum length of time to accomplish certain tasks as certain readings may only be relevant for a specific time span.
- Maintainability: Systems must have the ability to undergo modifications and repairs.
- Energy efficiency: Systems must account for the limited power available at nodes.
- Scalability: Systems must have the ability to handle the growing size of infrastructure systems, as the scope of the monitoring network will grow.
- Bandwidth: Related to scalability, system must utilize the available bandwidth to account for a growing network as well as variations in network traffic to cope with peak resource demand.
- Responsiveness: Systems must have the ability to quickly adapt to changes in topology, i.e., as nodes fail and are repaired.

- Fault recovery: Systems must have the ability to recover from a failure in one or more nodes.
- Latency: Systems must minimize packet delivery latency as much as possible.
- Variation in delay: Systems must minimize variation in packet delivery to allow for synchronization of readings.
- Packet loss and error ratio: Systems must minimize packet loss and error rate specifically in wireless connections.

These requirements are very qualitative and system dependent; however, they provide a means for comparing sensor database system architectures.

3.2 Sensor Network Architectures

Sensor database architectures are classified based on where the data is stored, ranging from traditional sensor databases where data is stored in a centralized database to a distributed database where every sensor node has its own database.

3.2.1 Centralized

Traditional sensor networks described by Akyildiz *et al.* [14] utilize a centralized database. The network functions as a data collection system, moving all raw data to the centralized database for processing and storage, similar to a thin client/server platform. In this type of system, all sensor nodes transmit their readings to a single base station using a best-effort data collection protocol. The sensor nodes are relativity "dumb" consisting of only a sensor and minimum hardware required for collection and communication. The base station is a very powerful system responsible for all storage query processing and communication services.

The centralized sensor network architecture meets a limited number of requirements of a critical infrastructure system. The responsiveness, fault recovery, and maintainability are decent with regard to sensor node failure; however, any failure in the base station will result in total system failure. The architecture's ability to meet the periodicity requirement is adequate but requires periodic updating from every sensor nodes directly to the base station. The bottleneck associated with communicating with a single base station and the limited capability of the sensor nodes minimizes the system's ability to address priority, latency, variation in delay, bandwidth, and deadline. As a result, the architecture scales poorly due to the large number of devices and the large volume of raw data transferred regardless of the submitted query. The packet loss and error ratio are dictated by the latest advances in network communication and the distance between sensor and database. Additionally, the energy efficiency of the system is very low due to the amount of communication and processing at a single point.

3.2.2 Distributed

Another sensor network architecture is the distributed sensor database systems which provide databases closer to the controller and sensor nodes. This architecture can be thought of as a data logging network. In this type of sensor network, all sensors send all sensed data to secondary storage which can be retrieved in bulk. This architecture allows for duplication of stored data to improve performance. Distributed database architectures are not specific to sensor networks. Many approaches to distributed databases are summarized by Hurson and Jiao [17] including federated and multi-databases which address issues such as data distribution and transparency as well as query and transaction processing.

Two examples of sensor database systems which have been developed to utilize more distributed architectures are COUGAR and TinyDB. Fung et al. [18] and Bonnet et al. [19] discuss the COUGAR system in which a sink node provides a database-like frontend for filtering the current sensor values from a data collection network. COUGAR uses a two-level hierarchical architecture. The lowest level is the QueryProxy, a small database component that runs near the sensor nodes to interpret and execute queries. The next level is the Frontend component, which is more powerful than the QueryProxy and permits connections to resources outside of the sensor network. Another similar system is the TinyDB system discussed by Madden et al. [20]. TinyDB is a database system for extracting information from a network of TinyOS sensors. It provides an SQL-like interface to specify the requested data and allows for additional parameters, including the rate of extraction. The TinyDB system collects the requested data from the sensor nodes filters, aggregates it, and routes it to the requester.

The distributed database system addresses most of the requirements of a critical infrastructure sensor database system. Energy efficiency, bandwidth, and scalability are addressed by in-network processing algorithms which limit communication of raw data and distribution of processing. Periodicity is addressed by specifying the extraction rate in queries. Deadlines and variations in delay are addressed by processing being performed closer to the sensor nodes. However, maintainability and fault recovery become more complicated: as the number of processing nodes is increased, more nodes need to be updated. The limitation of this architecture for CPS applications is latency.

The next evolution of distributed sensor network architectures is the sensor database model. In this architecture, each sensor node holds a database that can be dynamically queried. Tsiftes and Dunkels [21] discuss this sensor network architecture and propose a database management system called Antelope which is designed to be dynamic, energy-efficient, and tailored for resource-constrained sensor nodes. In addition to the raw data stored in the distributed sensor database, the database can store run-time information and maintain a history of performance statistics. The sensor database architecture also allows for duplication of sensor data at multiple nodes, improving performance.

The sensor database architecture addresses all of the requirements of a critical infrastructure sensor database system. Periodicity, deadline, latency, and variation in delay are addressed by storing the data at the sensor nodes. Additionally, by limiting the communication of raw data, the sensor database model improves energy efficiency, bandwidth, and scalability. The architecture improves maintainability and fault recovery by storing performance data at the sensor nodes. However, this architecture has challenges including the system updates and database management due to its distributed nature.

The three database architecture discussed in this section are summarized in Table 1. In the practical CPS application, the database in every sensor node architecture is used. Each sensor node maintains a database of its collected data as well as aggregated data from neighboring sensors.

3.3 Sensor Network Data Propagation

Many algorithms exist for propagating and replicating data across sensor networks. Chatzigiannakis et al. [22] define the propagation problem as follows: a single sensor senses a local event. How can that sensor, via cooperation with other sensors in the network, propagate information about that event to the base station? Incel et al. [23] aim to maximize sensor network throughput by constraining the network topology to a tree which reduces routing algorithm complexity. Data propagates up the tree to the root node. A time division multiple access protocol is used to prevent wireless network collisions in communication. This type of routing is capable of delivering both raw sensor data and aggregate (e.g., minimum, maximum, average) information to the network sink. However, due to the tree architecture, it is very sensitive to network link failures.

Resilient routing algorithms are studied by Liu et al. [24]. The authors determine that in real-world applications, network topology is difficult to know a priori. Instead, they call for routing algorithms to be dynamically

Table 1 Summary of Database Architectures

Database Architecture	Description
Centralized	Centralized sensor databases function as a data collection system. Simple sensor nodes consisting of a sensor and minimum networking hardware send data to a centralized database for processing and storage
Distributed	Distributed sensor databases utilize multiple databases for distributed processing and storage. Sensor nodes have minimal functionality but data storage and processing is closer to sensor nodes
Sensor database	Sensor database systems add more processing power and a database to sensor nodes. This allows for local processing and storage at nodes

configured once the nodes are placed in the environment. In their case study they observe that once a network architecture is configured, the routes through it change very little. As such, a static routing algorithm that is updated whenever large-scale network events occur may allow the network to scale much larger without requiring the higher processing overhead of a dynamic routing algorithm.

Two algorithms for dense and sparse networks are outlined in Ref. [25]. Local Target Protocol routes packets toward nodes that are closer to the network sink. This simple greedy algorithm performs well on dense networks with high link redundancy. Its biggest advantage is that it is completely distributed; no global structures are maintained and no communication between non-neighboring nodes is needed. Probabilistic Forwarding Protocol solves the issues faced by the Local Target Protocol by probabilistically forwarding toward nodes closer to the network sink. It gives some allowance for backtracking (forwarding away from the sink), allowing it to recover from link failures and to route through sparser networks where optimal paths are less obvious. Like Local Target, Probabilistic Forwarding is completely distributed, giving it a low network overhead.

A hybrid algorithm that performs both anomaly detection and data propagation is developed by Jiang *et al.* [26]. The network of sensors is divided into clusters, each of which has a head. Linear prediction is used to estimate sensor values. Each cluster determines whether or not to use prediction based on the trade-off between the power consumption of computing predictions and the power consumption of transmitting anomalous data.

Data collection can either be aggregated from cluster heads or cluster heads can route raw sensor data to the network sink.

A different approach is to route data to maximize energy efficiency. Ehsan and Hamdaoui [27] provide a survey of energy-efficient routing algorithms, the simplest of which is Energy-Balanced Routing presented by Ren et al. [28]. Here, data is routed through nodes with more remaining battery life, allowing for a more even depletion of node batteries across the network. The network is modeled as a potential energy field with the network sink at the center having the highest potential. Node potential energy is calculated based on their proximity to the sink and their remaining power. Packets are routed through the node in such a fashion that their potential constantly increases. The net result is that battery consumption is evened out across the network.

Another approach is to route data to maximize security and dependability. Wang et al. [29] provide a survey of security-focused data distribution and storage. One approach to address security issues in network routing is proposed by Shu et al. [30]. Data packets are fragmented and encrypted, so interception of one packet does not result in even one sensor value being disclosed. Paths through the network are randomized for each packet, so a compromised sensor node cannot reveal how essential data is routed. Finally, each packet fragment is routed through a different random path, increasing the difficulty of intercepting all the fragments required to reconstruct a packet.

While not applicable to CPSs, other routing algorithms are designed for mobile elements. Di et al. [31] provide a survey of routing algorithms for wireless sensor networks. One example is presented by Saleem et al. [32] which is based on swarm intelligence. This type of routing is for self-organizing sensor networks.

Sensor network propagation algorithm development is an active field; maximizing the trade-offs between network throughput, latency, power consumption, security, and ease of use is a difficult problem that must be solved for each application of a CPS.

4. DETECTION OF CORRUPTED DATA

As stated in Section 2, corrupted data can be produced by a number of sources including miscalibrated or faulty sensor hardware and errors in processing, storage, and communication. Corrupted data can be detected by locating anomalies in the system. Rajasegarar et al. [33] discuss the importance and challenges of anomaly detection in sensor networks as it pertains to fault diagnosis, intrusion detection, and monitoring applications. The main challenge in anomaly detection algorithm development is that sensor networks are highly application and domain dependent. Two domain-specific techniques are proposed by Yin *et al.* [34] who model wind turbine data and Freeman *et al.* [35] who model aircraft pilot-static probe data. Both of these examples propose anomaly detection techniques for data with a nonlinear and unknown distribution and significant measurement noise. However, these techniques are not suitable for other domains and do not scale to CPSs. Another challenge in anomaly detection for CPS is sensor node storage and processing limitations. Anomaly detection that does not hinder normal operation must be employed. Corrupted data is detected and mitigated while the data is still viable with minimal energy consumption.

4.1 Statistical Detection

Corrupted data can be detected by locating data anomalies or statistical irregularities in the data. While faulty sensors typically report easily distinguishable extreme or unrealistic values, not all data anomalies are the result of data corruption. Extreme environmental variations can produce data anomalies that must be distinguished from corruption.

4.1.1 Types of Data Anomalies

Jurdak *et al.* [36] classify data anomalies into three broad categories: temporal, spatial, and spatiotemporal. Temporal data anomalies are local to one node and can be detected by observing sensor values over time that have one of the following attributes: high variability in subsequent sensor readings, lack of change in sensor readings, gradual reading skews, or out-of-bound readings. Examples of failures that result in this type of anomaly are as follows. A sensor may fail into a locked state or fail to obtain new samples making the sensor reading remain the same over long periods of time. As a sensor loses calibration, its data values drift away from the true value. A major malfunction of the sensor could produce out-of-bound readings that are physically not possible. And lastly, high variability in sensor readings could arise from sensor voltage fluctuations but could also signify major changes in the sensed environment. The detection process requires the data stream from a single node as well as stored historical data. The process can be conducted locally at the node, provided the node is cable of storage and processing, or by a centralized process on either a sink node or a base station.

Spatial data anomalies occur when one sensor's data readings are significantly different from surrounding nodes' readings. Detecting this type of anomaly requires a network-aware algorithm and is thus usually performed by a sink node or base station. Data redundancy between sensors is exploited to determine which sensors may have faulty readings. This type of detection is only possible for certain types of data with low spatial variation, such as air temperature or humidity. In this type of data, a change in one area will affect the surrounding sensors' readings. Networks with high spatial variation, especially video and audio data, are usually incapable of detecting such anomalies.

Spatiotemporal anomalies combine attributes of both temporal and spatial anomalies. These anomalies are somewhat rare but also more difficult to detect. For example, a storm progressively moving through an area causing sensor nodes to fail would be a spatiotemporal anomaly. As with spatial anomalies, spatiotemporal anomalies require a network-wide detection algorithm.

4.1.2 Statistical Detection Approaches

A variety of techniques are employed to detect each of these classes of data anomaly. Statistical approaches assume or estimate some statistical distribution model which captures the distribution of the data and detects anomalies by checking how well the data fits the model. Statistical approaches can be further classified as rule based, estimation based, or learning based. Zhang *et al.* [37], Chandola *et al.* [38], and Fang and Dobson [39] provide comprehensive overviews of statistical anomaly detection techniques. Below is a

Table 2 Summary of Data Anomaly Types

Type of Data Anomaly	Description
Temporal	Temporal anomalies in sensor readings exhibit high variability in subsequent sensor readings, lack of change in sensor readings, gradual reading skews, or out-of-bound readings
Spatial	Spatial anomalies in sensor readings are significantly different from surrounding nodes' readings
Spatiotemporal	Spatiotemporal anomalies exhibit a combination of temporal and spatial anomaly attributes. These are rare but difficult to detect

summary of these approaches and recent advances in anomaly detection and a discussion of their applicability to CPSs.

Rule-based statistical approaches are the simplest form of anomaly detection. An acceptable lower and upper limit for the data is set and any value outside of this range is an anomaly. This technique requires only the definition of an outlier to be set, making it inflexible and resulting in many false positives or undetected anomalies if the tolerance is set too low or high. The benefits of this technique are that it is fast, requires no additional storage capability, and can be implemented in few lines of code making it ideal for sensor nodes.

Another simple rule-based statistical approach to anomaly detection is statistical inference using the mean and variance of a data set. Ngai et al. [40] use a chi-square test performed over a sliding window. In this example, the system determines that at least one value in the sliding window is anomalous if the chi-square value falls outside of some range specified by the user. The acceptable level must be configured prior to operation. This node-local approach can detect temporal-type anomalies of a single sensor while imposing no additional network overhead. However, each sensor will require more storage, depending on the window size, and processing power to carry out the statistical analysis. Statistical inference techniques cannot adapt to changing ranges, which are very common in long-term wireless sensor network installations. Panda and Khilar [41] propose another very simple rule-based statistical anomaly detection method which calculates the mean and variance of a set of neighboring sensors to determine if a sensor is faulty. This approach can detect spatial anomalies in a set of neighboring sensors. Rule-based statistical methods can be implemented on minimal hardware and detect anomalies very quickly, provided the data is well behaved and the rules are set appropriately. As such, other approaches have been developed that do not rely on user-set parameters.

Estimation-based statistical approaches use probability distribution models of the data to detect anomalous values. Probability distribution models can be parametric or nonparametric based [37]. Parametric models assume knowledge of the data distribution, i.e., Gaussian-based model. Nonparametric models, such as histograms and kernel density estimators, do not assume knowledge of the data distribution. Histogram models estimate the probability of data occurrences by counting the frequency of occurrence and detect anomalies by comparing the new data with each of the categories in the histogram. Kernel density estimators estimate the probability distribution function (pdf) for some normal data. An anomaly is detected if new data lies in the low probability region of the pdf. Fang and Dobson [42] propose an energy-efficient detection method using an ARIMA model. The ARIMA model is a statistical model used in time series analysis. It has three terms, autoregression (AR), integration (I), and moving average (MA) to represent the data. The autoregression term compares the new value to historical data using linear regression. The integration term differences the original data series to make the process stationary. And the moving average term captures the influence of extreme values. Each sensor node maintains a matrix of all maximum and minimum differences between itself and its neighbors. Then, using a voting mechanism, values are marked as valid or erroneous.

Estimation-based approaches are mathematically proven to detect anomalies if a correct probability distribution model is used. However, knowledge of the probability distribution is not available in many real-world applications, making nonparametric approaches more useful. However, these approaches require additional hardware and storage but execute very quickly to detect anomalies.

Learning-based statistical approaches utilize data mining clustering and classification algorithms to group data with similar behaviors [39]. An anomaly is detected when data does not belong to a group. These techniques have very high detection rates but require additional processing and storage hardware.

A decentralized clustering approach to anomaly detection is set forth by Rajasegarar et al. [43]. This approach was designed specifically for hierarchical (tree-based) networks. Leaf nodes take sensor readings and cluster them into fixed-width clusters. Each nonleaf node in the tree takes clusters from its children and merges them together. Anomaly detection is performed at the root node by finding clusters that are further away from other clusters by more than one standard deviation above the average cluster distance. Chang et al. [44] use an Echo State Network (ESN), a neural network in which all neurons are connected to each other, to perform anomaly detection. The ESNs are trained before the nodes are deployed, so they are not very flexible. They operate in a similar fashion to Bayesian networks where the sensor's value is compared to the value predicted by the ESN. The advantage of using a neural net in this case is that it has much lower CPU and RAM requirements than a Bayesian network. An improvement to this approach is put forth by Obst [45]. Instead of building recurrent neural networks beforehand, each node communicates with its immediate neighbors to build a model of its sensors' values. This model is then used to estimate anomalies in the readings.

Classification approaches use a learned model to organize data into a class: in this case, normal or anomalous. One classification approach uses Bayesian networks to model sensor values and predict when values are anomalous [39]. Mayfield *et al.* [46] have developed a tool called ERACER that uses Relational Dependency Networks to correct anomalous data and fill in missing data. The tool runs on the base station and develops linear models of sensor data, taking into account readings from other sensors at that node and readings from neighbor nodes. Another example of Bayesian networks is Ref. [47], where the concentration of various gases in a mine's atmosphere is monitored. The network models sensor values over time as well as physical relationships between sensors. The system learns a baseline for the mine's concentrations that adapts to the natural fluctuations in gas concentration. It can detect both single-sensor anomalies and multi-node anomalies and events.

Ni and Pottie [48] propose using a hierarchical Bayesian space–time model to detect trustworthy sensors. The disadvantage of this technique is the amount of work required to set up the model. This technique results in excellent anomaly detection if the model accurately represents the data. However, as with all models, if the model is poorly matched to the data, the system performance degrades. A more advanced classification approach is the nearest neighbor approach. This approach uses a distance metric, for example, Euclidean distance, to determine how similar a value is to its neighbors. An anomaly is detected if the distance between neighbors is more than a user-specified threshold. Expanding on this approach, Branch *et al.* [49] use a distributed algorithm to detect outliers as data propagates through the sensor network. In this approach, each node maintains a set of outlier data points from itself and its neighbors. A ranking function is used to map data values to non-negative real numbers which indicate the degree to which the data value can be regarded as an outlier with respect to the data set. Nodes transmit data they suspect will cause the outlier set of their neighbors to change. This is similar to a distributed *k*-nearest-neighbor classification approach. This technique is flexible with respect to the outlier definition, allowing for dynamic updating and in-network detection, reducing bandwidth and energy consumption.

A method to improve the performance of learning-based approaches uses principal component analysis (PCA) to reduce the dimensionality of a data. PCA is a technique that uses spectral decomposition to find normal behavior in a data set. PCA is used to reduce dimensionality before detection by finding a subset of data which captures the behavior of the data, allowing for the detection of temporal, spatial, and spatiotemporal data anomalies. Chitradevi *et al.* [50] propose a two-step algorithm. First, a PCA model is built that can be used for fault detection. Second, the Mahalanobis distance is used to determine the similarity between the current sensor readings against the developed sensor data model. However, conventional PCA approaches are sensitive to data anomaly frequency in collected data and fail to detect slow and long-duration anomalies. Xie *et al.* [51] address this problem by using a multi-scale principal component analysis (MSPCA) to detect anomalies and extract and interpret information. MSPCA uses both wavelet analysis and PCA. The time–frequency information of the data is captured using wavelet analysis, while PCA is used to detect data anomalies. This technique allows for detecting gradual and persistent anomalies with different time–frequency features.

Lastly, a hybrid approach is proposed by Warriach *et al.* [52] to detect data anomalies based on the three methods. By combining rule-based, estimation-based, and learning-based methods, they are able to leverage domain and expert knowledge, sensor spatial and temporal correlations, and inferred models from training data to detect faulty sensor readings. This approach has the benefits of the above approaches but also requires more processing capability and power at sensor nodes.

One major issue in CPS data corruption detection is determining when anomalous data is corrupted. Tang *et al.* [53] investigate the trustworthiness of sensor data and propose a method called Tru-Alarm to eliminate false alarms by filtering out noise and false information. Tru-Alarm is able to estimate the source of alarm by constructing an alarm graph and conducting trustworthiness inference based on the graph links.

4.2 Behavioral Approaches

Behavioral approaches have also been implemented to detect the anomalous behavior of a system rather than the data produced. Many of these approaches are part of intrusion detection system (IDS). Liao *et al.* [54] provide a comprehensive overview of IDS approaches for general computing, classifying them as signature-based detection, anomaly-based detection, and stateful protocol analysis. Signature-based detection, also known as knowledge-based detection, detects a pattern or string that corresponds to a known attack. This technique is limited to detecting known attacks. Anomaly-based detection determines the normal behavior of the system and detects anomalies by comparing the current behavior with the normal

Table 3 Summary of Statistical Anomaly Detection Approaches

Statistical Detection Approaches	Description
Rule based	Rule-based detection approaches set acceptable limits for data values. These limits can be determined from an outlier set or using statistical inference. This approach requires minimal hardware to implement
Estimation based	Estimation-based detection approaches use probability distribution models of the data to detect anomalous values. These approaches require knowledge of the data distribution or the use of histograms or kernel density estimators to assume a distribution. They are mathematically proven to detect anomalies if the correct distribution model is used
Learning based	Learning-based detection approaches utilize data mining, clustering, and classification algorithms to group data. Anomalies are detected when new data does not belong to a group. These approaches require more hardware to implement and can be time consuming

behavior model. Anomaly-based detection can monitor any type of activity, including network connections, number and type of system calls, failed login attempts, processor usage, number of e-mails sent, etc. This approach can detect both known and unknown attacks. Lastly, stateful protocol analysis, also known as specification-based detection, compares a vendor-developed profile of specific protocols to current behavior. An example would be monitoring protocol states such as pairing requests and replies. Modi *et al.* [55] provide a survey of IDS techniques used for cloud computing. Many of the approaches use techniques similar to statistical anomaly detection, as well as neural networks and fuzzy logic. While some of these techniques are very computationally intensive, they can be implemented on sensor nodes without hindering the real-time access to data.

CPS-specific IDS approaches have also been developed. Buttyán *et al.* [4] discuss the WSAN4CIP Project which investigated a number of attack detection methods to determine if a sensor node is compromised. The project included intrusion detection and prevention techniques that were adapted to the wireless environment. A microkernel in the sensor node operating system supports multiple levels of security and determines if the code deployed on a sensor node is unchanged. Mitchell and Chen [56] provide a detailed review of CPS-related IDS research. In addition to

IDS, for traditional networked computing systems, CPS IDS monitors both the embedded components and the physical environment, which under attack may exhibit abnormal properties and behavior. However, this is complicated by legacy technology still used in many CPS. Some legacy components are based on mechanical or hydraulic control with no cyber component, making them difficult to modify or access. Thus, CPS IDS must define acceptable component behavior based on sensor readings of the physical environment.

5. MITIGATION OF DATA CORRUPTION

Detected corrupted or missing data can be mitigated in a number of ways depending on the criticality and valid time interval of the data. Mitigation can be accomplished by correcting, replacing, or ignoring the corrupted data. In many CPS applications, the useful life of a single piece of data is very short, making some correction or replacement techniques inappropriate. Additionally, many correction and mitigation techniques require a great deal of computation, making the energy consumption prohibitive. However, in other applications, missing and corrupted data minimizes the quality of information, and ignoring these errors may cause a serious effect in data analysis. Gantayat et al. [57] provide a review of research on missing or incomplete data. A variety of techniques are used to generate predicted values. Many of these approaches are very similar to the anomaly detection techniques discussed in Section 4. The following are approaches for mitigating missing and corrupted data:

- Imputation: This technique replaces missing data values with an estimation based on the data stream's probabilistic model.
- Predicted value imputation: This technique replaces missing data with estimated values based on the data set. The estimation methods vary in complexity from mean or mode values to more complex estimates from training data.
- Distribution-based imputation: This technique replaces missing data using a classification algorithm. A set of pseudo-instances is created when a missing value is encountered. Each pseudo-instance is tested. The replacement value is selected using a weighted comparison.
- Unique value imputation: This technique replaces the missing value using simple substitution from historic information.
- Replacing missing data: This technique replaces the missing data with a value from a test case that resembles the current data set.

- Rough sets: This technique uses lower and upper approximations to determine a replacement value. The benefit of this technique is that there is no need for preliminary or additional information about the data. A number of extensions to rough set have been proposed including tolerance relation, nonsymmetric relation, and valued tolerance relation.
- Similarity relation: This technique replaces the missing data after making a generalized decisions based on the entire data set.

Each of these mitigation techniques can be deployed on the sensor nodes of a CPS depending on the storage and processing limitations of the sensor node. These techniques can be employed to replace corrupted or missing data allowing for correct execution.

6. PROPAGATION OF CORRUPTED DATA

The creation of corrupted data is unavoidable in many sensor networks. Additionally, no detection algorithm is perfect making understanding the effect of corrupted data essential to designing safe and reliable CPS. Tseng *et al.* [58] assess the security and reliability of microprocessor-based sensor systems in CPS using a software-implemented fault injection technique to test if the system will have a cascading and catastrophic impact on the control system of the infrastructure as a whole. Specifically, investigating the effects of faults injected into the data aggregator of a power substation which is part of the essential communication bridge between the control center and the substation. The study determined that a fault in a Distributed Network Protocol 3 Client or Server can cause a control center operator to lose control of the substation with a 13% and 7% chance, respectively. Lost control of a substation can potentially result in a cascading failure leading to a blackout.

6.1 Propagation from Execution

Ayatolahi *et al.* [59] experimentally study the effects of single- and double-bit errors in instruction set architecture registers and main memory using fault injection. Fault injection is a method to test and assess the dependability (availability, reliability, and maintainability) and performance of fault-tolerant and fail-safe systems. One of its uses is benchmarking the error sensitivity of a system when it experiences hardware faults in the processor or main memory. To measure the error sensitivity, bit-flip errors are injected in the main memory and Instruction Set Architecture registers. The experiment consisted of nine campaigns of the single bit-flip and double bit-flip models, each with 12,000 trial runs on 13 test programs. Each run was categorized as one of the following categories:

- No impact: The program terminates normally and the error does not affect the output of the program.
- Hardware exception: The processor detects an error by raising a hardware exception.
- Timeout: The program fails to terminate within a predefined time.
- Silent data corruption: The program terminates normally, but the output is erroneous and there is no indication of failure.

This experiment demonstrates the error sensitivity of different registers and memory locations. Their results showed that the most common effect of both single- and double-bit errors is a hardware exception, with double-bit errors resulting in more than single bit. Both single- and double-bit errors produced corrupted results roughly 30% of the time. Timeout errors were rarely encountered. Overall, double-bit errors have more impact on results. Obviously, the error sensitivity varies depending on bit positions, registers, and the software tested. This study was conducted on a diverse set of programs, with various implementation sizes, input types and sizes, and functionalities. While none of the programs tested were CPS control systems, the results give estimates of the probability of correct incomplete, or corrupted results based on corrupted input.

In an attempt to improve a program's sensitivity to corrupted data, Sangchoolie *et al.* [60] study the impact of compiler optimizations on various programs. The study provides insight into the impact of different levels of GNU Compiler Collection compiler optimizations (-O1, -O2, -O3, -Os) on the corrupted data sensitivity of programs using 12 benchmark programs. These optimizations can be used to improve the performance of the compiled program. However, the results of the experiment show that the data corruption sensitivity of the optimized programs is only marginally lower than the nonoptimized programs.

6.2 Corrupted Data in a Sensor Node

The propagation of corrupted data in the sensor nodes of a CPS is shown in Fig. 4. Initially, corrupted data enters the node from sensors, neighboring nodes, or local storage. Corrupted data can be either erroneous or missing. Next, the corruption detection technique is employed. If corrupted data is detected, mitigation is attempted; otherwise, a node fault occurs. If the mitigation is successful, the node has recovered and regular execution takes

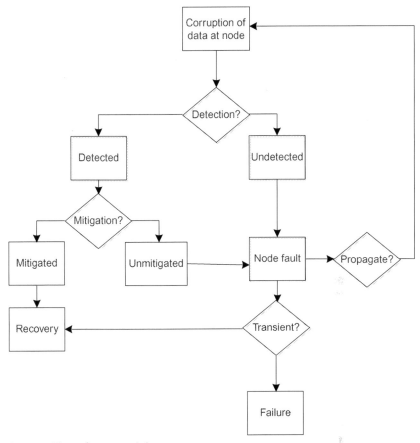

Figure 4 Flow of corrupted data.

place. However, if the corrupted data is not detected or mitigation fails, a node fault occurs.

The node executes on corrupted data if a node fault occurs with the potential of node failure and the propagation of corrupted data. As discussed earlier in Section 6, execution can result in no impact with correct data produced. In this case, the fault can be persistent leading to a node failure or transient leading to recovery. Alternatively, if execution results in a hardware exception or timeout, then both missing data is propagated to neighboring nodes and node failure. If execution produces corrupted results, then corrupted data propagates to neighboring nodes. Again this fault can be persistent leading to a node failure or transient leading to recovery.

The propagation of corrupted data in the system may be limited if the corruption is detected by its neighbors. However, understanding the extent to which the corruption has propagated is essential in designing fault-tolerant and reliable systems.

7. CONCLUSION AND FUTURE DIRECTION

Modern critical infrastructure cyber–physical systems are designed using more and more sophisticated intelligent autonomous control systems which greatly improve the performance of the system but also add complexity. Therefore, it is crucial to understand the potential for fault propagation within CPSs. In this survey, we discussed the sources of corrupted data, the structure of CPS, and compared data corruption detection and mitigation techniques. Additionally, we discussed a number of studies on the effects of execution on corrupted data. These key topics are essential to understanding how undetected corrupted data propagates through a CPS. We are working to model the extent to which corrupted data propagates, specifically looking at the cluster size of corrupted nodes. This information will be essential to designing robust CPS.

GLOSSARY
CPS critical infrastructure cyber–physical systems
ESN Echo State Network
IDS intrusion detection system
MSPCA multi-scale principal component analysis
PCA principal component analysis
pdf probability distribution function

REFERENCES
[1] A.A. Kirilenko, A.W. Lo, Moore's law versus Murphy's law: algorithmic trading and its discontents, J. Econ. Perspect. 27 (2) (2013) 51–72.
[2] P. Derler, E. Lee, A. Vincentelli, Modeling cyber physical systems, Proc. IEEE 100 (1) (2012) 13–28.
[3] D.E. Bakken, A. Bose, C.H. Hauser, D.E. Whitehead, G.C. Zweigle, Smart generation and transmission with coherent, real-time data, Proc. IEEE 99 (6) (2011) 928–951.
[4] L. Buttyán, D. Gessner, A. Hessler, P. Langendoerfer, Application of wireless sensor networks in critical infrastructure protection: challenges and design options [security and privacy in emerging wireless networks], IEEE Wirel. Commun. 17 (5) (2010) 44–49.
[5] B. Miller, D. Rowe, A survey of SCADA and critical infrastructure incidents, in: Proceedings of the 1st Annual Conference on Research in Information Technology, RIIT'12, ACM, New York, 2012, pp. 51–56.
[6] A. Berizzi, The Italian 2003 blackout, in: IEEE Power Engineering Society General Meeting, 2004, IEEE, 2004, pp. 1673–1679.

[7] S.V. Buldyrev, R. Parshani, G. Paul, H.E. Stanley, S. Havlin, Catastrophic cascade of failures in interdependent networks, Nature 464 (7291) (2010) 1025–1028.

[8] A. Aviźienis, J.C. Laprie, B. Randell, C. Landwehr, Basic concepts and taxonomy of dependable and secure computing, IEEE Trans. Dependable Secure Comput. 1 (1) (2004) 11–33.

[9] Y. Mo, T.H.-H. Kim, K. Brancik, D. Dickinson, H. Lee, A. Perrig, B. Sinopoli, Cyber-physical security of a smart grid infrastructure, Proc. IEEE 100 (1) (2012) 195–209.

[10] F. Pasqualetti, F. Dorfler, F. Bullo, Cyber-physical attacks in power networks: models, fundamental limitations and monitor design, in: 2011 50th IEEE Conference on Decision and Control and European Control Conference (CDC-ECC), IEEE, 2011, pp. 2195–2201.

[11] S. Amin, X. Litrico, S.S. Sastry, A.M. Bayen, Stealthy deception attacks on water SCADA systems, in: Proceedings of the 13th ACM International Conference on Hybrid Systems: Computation and Control, ACM, 2010, pp. 161–170.

[12] C.C. Aggarwal, N. Ashish, A. Sheth, The Internet of things: a survey from the data-centric perspective, in: Managing and Mining Sensor Data, Springer, US, 2013, pp. 383–428.

[13] J.L. Cebula, L.R. Young, A taxonomy of operational cyber security risks, 2010, Tech. Rep. DTIC Document.

[14] I. Akyildiz, W. Su, Y. Sankarasubramaniam, E. Cayirci, A survey on sensor networks, IEEE Commun. Mag. 40 (8) (2002) 102–114.

[15] O. Diallo, J.J. Rodrigues, M. Sene, Real-time data management on wireless sensor networks: a survey, J. Netw. Comput. Appl. 35 (3) (2012) 1013–1021.

[16] J. Chen, M. Díaz, L. Llopis, B. Rubio, J.M. Troya, A survey on quality of service support in wireless sensor and actor networks: requirements and challenges in the context of critical infrastructure protection, J. Netw. Comput. Appl. 34 (4) (2011) 1225–1239.

[17] A.R. Hurson, Y. Jiao, Database system architecture—a walk through time: from centralized platform to mobile computing—keynote address, in: Advanced Distributed Systems, Springer, Heidelberg, 2005, pp. 1–9.

[18] W.F. Fung, D. Sun, J. Gehrke, Cougar: the network is the database, in: Proceedings of the 2002 ACM SIGMOD International Conference on Management of Data, ACM, 2002, p. 621.

[19] P. Bonnet, J. Gehrke, P. Seshadri, Towards sensor database systems, in: Mobile Data Management, Springer-Verlag, London, UK, 2001, pp. 3–14.

[20] S.R. Madden, M.J. Franklin, J.M. Hellerstein, W. Hong, TinyDB: an acquisitional query processing system for sensor networks, ACM Trans. Database Syst. 30 (1) (2005) 122–173.

[21] N. Tsiftes, A. Dunkels, A database in every sensor, in: Proceedings of the 9th ACM Conference on Embedded Networked Sensor Systems, ACM, New York, 2011, pp. 316–332.

[22] I. Chatzigiannakis, T. Dimitriou, S. Nikoletseas, P. Spirakis, A probabilistic algorithm for efficient and robust data propagation in wireless sensor networks, Ad Hoc Netw. 4 (5) (2006) 621–635.

[23] O.D. Incel, A. Ghosh, B. Krishnamachari, K. Chintalapudi, Fast data collection in tree-based wireless sensor networks, IEEE Trans. Mob. Comput. 11 (1) (2012) 86–99.

[24] Y. Liu, Y. He, M. Li, J. Wang, K. Liu, X. Li, Does wireless sensor network scale? A measurement study on GreenOrbs, IEEE Trans. Parallel Distrib. Syst. 24 (10) (2013) 1983–1993.

[25] K. Nikitha, D.R. Lakshmi, A. Damodaram, Effective connectivity for sparse and dense wireless sensor networks, Inf. Technol. J. 12 (11) (2013).

[26] H. Jiang, S. Jin, C. Wang, Prediction or not? An energy-efficient framework for clustering-based data collection in wireless sensor networks, IEEE Trans. Parallel Distrib. Syst. 22 (6) (2011) 1064–1071.

[27] S. Ehsan, B. Hamdaoui, A survey on energy-efficient routing techniques with QoS assurances for wireless multimedia sensor networks, IEEE Commun. Surv. Tutorials 14 (2) (2012) 265–278.

[28] F. Ren, J. Zhang, T. He, C. Lin, S.K. Ren, EBRP: energy-balanced routing protocol for data gathering in wireless sensor networks, IEEE Trans. Parallel Distrib. Syst. 22 (12) (2011) 2108–2125.

[29] Q. Wang, K. Ren, S. Yu, W. Lou, Dependable and secure sensor data storage with dynamic integrity assurance, ACM Trans. Sensor Netw. 8 (1) (2011) 9.

[30] T. Shu, M. Krunz, S. Liu, Secure data collection in wireless sensor networks using randomized dispersive routes, IEEE Trans. Mob. Comput. 9 (7) (2010) 941–954.

[31] M. Di Francesco, S.K. Das, G. Anastasi, Data collection in wireless sensor networks with mobile elements: a survey, ACM Trans. Sensor Netw. 8 (1) (2011) 7.

[32] M. Saleem, G.A. Di Caro, M. Farooq, Swarm intelligence based routing protocol for wireless sensor networks: survey and future directions, Inform. Sci. 181 (20) (2011) 4597–4624.

[33] S. Rajasegarar, C. Leckie, M. Palaniswami, Anomaly detection in wireless sensor networks, IEEE Wirel. Commun. 15 (4) (2008) 34–40.

[34] S. Yin, G. Wang, H.R. Karimi, Data-driven design of robust fault detection system for wind turbines, Mechatronics 24 (4) (2014) 298–306.

[35] P. Freeman, P. Seiler, G.J. Balas, Air data system fault modeling and detection, Control Eng. Pract. 21 (10) (2013) 1290–1301.

[36] R. Jurdak, X.R. Wang, O. Obst, P. Valencia, Wireless sensor network anomalies: diagnosis and detection strategies, in: Intelligence-Based Systems Engineering, Springer, Heidelberg, 2011, pp. 309–325.

[37] Y. Zhang, N. Meratnia, P. Havinga, Outlier detection techniques for wireless sensor networks: a survey, IEEE Commun. Surv. Tutorials 12 (2) (2010) 159–170.

[38] V. Chandola, A. Banerjee, V. Kumar, Anomaly detection: a survey, ACM Comput. Surv. 41 (3) (2009) 15.

[39] L. Fang, S. Dobson, In-network sensor data modelling methods for fault detection, in: Evolving Ambient Intelligence, Springer, Switzerland, 2013, pp. 176–189.

[40] E.-H. Ngai, J. Liu, M. Lyu, On the intruder detection for sinkhole attack in wireless sensor networks, in: IEEE International Conference on Communications, 2006, ICC '06, vol. 8, 2006, pp. 3383–3389.

[41] M. Panda, P.M. Khilar, An efficient fault detection algorithm in wireless sensor network, in: Contemporary Computing, Springer, Heidelberg, 2011, pp. 279–288.

[42] L. Fang, S. Dobson, Unifying sensor fault detection with energy conservation, in: Self-Organizing Systems, Springer, Heidelberg, 2014, pp. 176–181.

[43] S. Rajasegarar, C. Leckie, M. Palaniswami, J.C. Bezdek, Distributed anomaly detection in wireless sensor networks, in: 10th IEEE Singapore International Conference on Communication Systems, 2006. ICCS 2006, IEEE, 2006, pp. 1–5.

[44] M. Chang, A. Terzis, P. Bonnet, Mote-based online anomaly detection using echo state networks, in: Distributed Computing in Sensor Systems, Springer, Heidelberg, 2009, pp. 72–86.

[45] O. Obst, Distributed backpropagation-decorrelation learning, in: NIPS Workshop: Large-Scale Machine Learning: Parallelism and Massive Datasets, 2009.

[46] C. Mayfield, J. Neville, S. Prabhakar, ERACER: a database approach for statistical inference and data cleaning, in: Proceedings of the 2010 ACM SIGMOD International Conference on Management of Data, ACM, 2010, pp. 75–86.

[47] X.R. Wang, J.T. Lizier, O. Obst, M. Prokopenko, P. Wang, Spatiotemporal anomaly detection in gas monitoring sensor networks, in: R. Verdone (Ed.), EWSN 2008. LNCS, vol. 4913, Springer, Heidelberg, 2008, pp. 90–105.

[48] K. Ni, G. Pottie, Sensor network data fault detection with maximum a posteriori selection and Bayesian modeling, ACM Trans. Sensor Netw. 8 (3) (2012) 23.

[49] J.W. Branch, C. Giannella, B. Szymanski, R. Wolff, H. Kargupta, In-network outlier detection in wireless sensor networks, Knowl. Inf. Syst. 34 (1) (2013) 23–54.

[50] N. Chitradevi, V. Palanisamy, K. Baskaran, U.B. Nisha, Outlier aware data aggregation in distributed wireless sensor network using robust principal component analysis, in: 2010 International Conference on Computing Communication and Networking Technologies (ICCCNT), IEEE, 2010, pp. 1–9.

[51] X. Ying-xin, C. Xiang-guang, Z. Jun, Data fault detection for wireless sensor networks using multi-scale PCA method, in: 2nd International Conference on Artificial Intelligence, Management Science and Electronic Commerce (AIMSEC), 2011, IEEE, 2011, pp. 7035–7038.

[52] E.U. Warriach, T.A. Nguyen, M. Aiello, K. Tei, A hybrid fault detection approach for context-aware wireless sensor networks, in: IEEE 9th International Conference on Mobile Adhoc and Sensor Systems (MASS), 2012, IEEE, 2012, pp. 281–289.

[53] L.-A. Tang, X. Yu, S. Kim, Q. Gu, J. Han, A. Leung, T. La Porta, Trustworthiness analysis of sensor data in cyber-physical systems, J. Comput. Syst. Sci. 79 (3) (2013) 383–401.

[54] H.-J. Liao, C.-H. Richard Lin, Y.-C. Lin, K.-Y. Tung, Intrusion detection system: a comprehensive review, J. Netw. Comput. Appl. 36 (1) (2013) 16–24.

[55] C. Modi, D. Patel, B. Borisaniya, H. Patel, A. Patel, M. Rajarajan, A survey of intrusion detection techniques in cloud, J. Netw. Comput. Appl. 36 (1) (2013) 42–57.

[56] R. Mitchell, I.-R. Chen, A survey of intrusion detection techniques for cyber-physical systems, ACM Comput. Surv. 46 (4) (2014) 55.

[57] S. Gantayat, A. Misra, B. Panda, A study of incomplete data—a review, in: Proceedings of the International Conference on Frontiers of Intelligent Computing: Theory and Applications (FICTA) 2013, Springer, 2014, pp. 401–408.

[58] K.-Y. Tseng, D. Chen, Z. Kalbarczyk, R.K. Iyer, Characterization of the error resiliency of power grid substation devices, in: 42nd Annual IEEE/IFIP International Conference on Dependable Systems and Networks (DSN), 2012, IEEE, 2012, pp. 1–8.

[59] F. Ayatolahi, B. Sangchoolie, R. Johansson, J. Karlsson, A study of the impact of single bit-flip and double bit-flip errors on program execution, in: Computer Safety, Reliability, and Security, Springer, 2013, pp. 265–276.

[60] B. Sangchoolie, F. Ayatolahi, R. Johansson, J. Karlsson, A study of the impact of bit-flip errors on programs compiled with different optimization levels, in: Tenth European Dependable Computing Conference (EDCC), 2014, IEEE, 2014, pp. 146–157.

ABOUT THE AUTHORS

Mark Woodard received a B.S. degree in Electrical and Computer Engineering from the Virginia Military Institute in 2008. He is currently a Ph.D. candidate in Computer Engineering at the Missouri University of Science and Technology, where he is a GAANN Fellow. His research interests include data interdependence, survivability, and modeling critical infrastructure cyber-physical systems. Mark is a member of IEEE and Tau Beta Pi.

Sahra Sedigh Sarvestani received the B.S. E.E. degree from Sharif University of Technology in 1995, and the M.S.E.E. and Ph.D. degrees from Purdue University, in 1998 and 2003, respectively. She subsequently joined the Missouri University of Science and Technology, where she is currently an Associate Professor of Electrical and Computer Engineering. Her research centers on development and modeling of dependable networks and systems, with focus on critical infrastructure. She is a Fellow of the National Academy of Engineering's Frontiers of Engineering Education Program and held a Purdue Research Foundation Fellowship from 1996 to 2000. She is a member of HKN and ACM and a senior member of the IEEE.

Ali R. Hurson received the B.S. degree in Physics from the University of Tehran in 1970, the M.S. degree in Computer Science from the University of Iowa in 1978, and the Ph.D. from the University of Central Florida in 1980. He was a Professor of Computer Science at the Pennsylvania State University until 2008, when he joined the Missouri University of Science and Technology. He has published over 300 technical papers in areas including multidatabases, global information sharing and processing, computer architecture and cache memory, and mobile and pervasive computing. He serves as an ACM distinguished speaker, area editor of the *CSI Journal of Computer Science and Engineering*, and Co-Editor-in-Chief of *Advances in Computers*. He is a senior member of the IEEE.

CHAPTER THREE

A Research Overview of Tool-Supported Model-based Testing of Requirements-based Designs

Raluca Marinescu*, Cristina Seceleanu*, Hèléne Le Guen†, Paul Pettersson*

*Mälardalen Real-Time Research Centre, Mälardalen University, Västerås, Sweden
†ALL4TEC, Laval, France

Contents

Advances in Computers, Volume 98
ISSN 0065-2458
http://dx.doi.org/10.1016/bs.adcom.2015.03.003

Abstract

Software testing aims at gaining confidence in software products through fault detection, by observing the differences between the behavior of the implementation and the expected behavior described in the specification. Nowadays, testing is the main verification technique used in industry, being a time and resource consuming activity. This has boosted the development of potentially more efficient testing techniques, like model-based testing, where test creation and execution can be automated, using an abstract system model as input. In this chapter, we provide an overview of the state-of-the-art in tool-supported model-based testing that starts from requirements-based models, by presenting and classifying some of the most mature tools available at this moment. Our goal is to get a deeper insight into the state-of-the-art in this area, as well as to form a position with respect to possible needs and gaps in the current tools used by industry and academia, which need to be addressed in order to enhance the applicability of model-based testing techniques. To achieve this, we extend an existing taxonomy with: (i) the test artifact, representing the type of information encoded in the model for the purpose of testing (i.e., functional behavior, extra-functional behavior, or the architectural description), and (ii) the mapping of test cases, which describes ways of using the generated test cases on the actual system under test. To provide further evidence of the inner-workings of different model-based testing tools, we select four representative tools (i.e, ProTest, UPPAAL Cover, MaTeLo, and CompleteTest) that we apply on a simple yet illustrative Coffee/Tea Vending Machine example, to show the differences in modeling notations, test case generation methods, and the produced test-cases.

ABBREVIATIONS

ADM architecture description language
ASM abstract state machine
AsmL abstract state machine language
DNF disjunctive normal form
EFSM extended finite state machine
FBD function block diagram
FSM finite state machine
I/O input/output
JML java modeling language
LGT LEIRIOS test generator

LTS labeled transition system
OCL object constraint language
PVS-SL prototype verification system's specification language
SUT system under test
SXM stream X-machine
TA timed automata
UIO unique input output
UML unified modeling language
VDM vienna development method

1. INTRODUCTION

Testing software systems is one of the most demanding, yet essential activities of developing computer-controlled systems. The tester's mission is to ensure that there are no dormant bugs in the system, so the test-cases that one develops must be able to exercise the software in such a way as to uncover all the potential anomalies in the system. Besides requiring highly specialized skills, traditional testing techniques are merely *ad hoc*, relying heavily on the tester's expertise and knowledge. Consequently, such techniques can be error-prone and could benefit from complementary methods such as *model-based testing*, which is a black-box testing technique that attempts to automate the generation and execution of test-cases based on an abstract system model. Model-based testing has therefore a high degree of automation [1] and can generate test-cases that would hopefully lead to early fault detection [2]. The research in his area has attracted much attention in recent years as part of an increasing general interest in formal and semi-formal approaches to testing [3]. This attention can be attributed to the fact that generating software tests is an important issue, primarily in industry, where manually written tests can be incomplete and time consuming.

The tools that support model-based testing have different characteristics that ideally should help one understand their advantages and limitations, respectively, provided that one would want to involve and integrate a particular model-based testing tool into the software development process. Practitioners have argued that adopting research prototypes by industry depends first on whether the information presented in research papers answers relevant questions such as "What domain can a particular method/tool be used in?", "How expressive are the notations and methods employed in the research?", or "What type of information do the results contain?", [1] etc. These arguments have motivated our work in this chapter, which provides an overview of the state-of-the-art in model-based testing, by presenting and discussing existing model-based testing tools, and classifying them based on a sensible and relevant taxonomic schema.

In 2012, Utting *et al.* [4] have proposed a model-based testing taxonomy based on seven dimensions: the modeling subject, the modeling redundancy, the modeling characteristics, the modeling paradigm, the test selection criteria, the test generation technology, and the test execution. We have chosen to modify this taxonomy by proposing a variant in which we have selected four of the previously proposed dimensions, namely the modeling paradigm, the test selection criteria, the test generation method, and the text execution, to which we added two new dimensions: (i) the *test artifact* represented by the type of information encoded in the model for the purpose of testing (i.e., the functional behavior, extra-functional behavior, or the architectural description) and (ii) the *mapping* support between abstract and executable test-cases. Our research overview of the state-of-the-art tool-supported model-based testing frameworks proposed in this paper is thus based on this extended taxonomy. Due to the large number of model-based testing frameworks available nowadays, we focus only on the techniques supported by mature tools that can handle modeling, test-case generation, test-case selection and possibly test-case execution. Based on relevant literature review [1, 5–7] and manual s earch, we have identified 33 model-based testing tools that we consider mature enough to potentially have an impact on both state-of-the-art and -practice. These tools are presented in the chapter and classified based on our taxonomy. In an attempt to address the concerns mentioned above, with respect to answering the relevant questions, we have applied four of the considered tools, each belonging to a different category with respect to the underlying modeling notation, on a simple yet illustrative coffee/tea vending machine example. For each of these four tools, we set the test selection criterion that belongs to the structural coverage class, respectively, and the test-cases generated by each of them are discussed and compared with respect to expressiveness and possible application domain. The fact that we have included the test artifact as one of our taxonomy criteria led to observations regarding the small proportion of frameworks that consider generating test-cases for extra-functional models, or software architectures.

---

[1] Challenges in Adopting and Deploying Research Ideas into Industrial Teams, Keynote by Brian Robinson, COMPSAC 2014. The presentation is available at: http://www.computer.org/portal/web/COMPSAC-2014/Keynotes.

Other similar works are available. Fraser *et al.* [3] recognize the importance of model-based testing in the area of automated test generation, and survey the state-of-the-art in testing with model checkers. We do not restrict the test generation method, and present other techniques like graph search algorithms and theorem proving also. More recently, Shafique *et al.* [6] have written a comprehensive systematic literature review on state-based testing, showing the application of the tools by comparing them with respect to coverage criteria and level of automation. Our work is not a systematic literature review, we rather attempt to overview the existing tool-supported model-based testing that employs a comprehensive class of models designed based on the system's requirements, and not on code. In this context, the outcome of our work is threefold: (i) we propose an extension to an existing model-based testing taxonomy that would potentially allow us to collect more evidence on the type of information contained in the tools, (ii) we discuss 33 model-based testing tools by using our proposed taxonomy, and (iii) we chose four of these tools (ProTest, UPPAAL Cover, MaTeLo, and CompleteTest) and apply each of them on the same running example to show the inner-workings from model creation to test execution.

The chapter is structured as follows. In Section 2 we provide a brief overview of the model-based testing process. In Section 3 we describe our proposed taxonomy, and in Section 4 we introduce the literature review process, as well as the selected list of tools, after applying the mentioned review process. Next, we describe the tools based on their underlying modeling notation, as follows: model-based testing tools for pre/post notations in Section 6, for transition-based notations in Section 7, for stochastic models in Section 8, and for data-flow models in Section 9. In Section 10, we discuss our results and gained insights, before concluding the chapter in Section 11.

2. THE GENERIC MODEL-BASED TESTING APPROACH

The model-based testing process [4] is done in multiple steps, as depicted in Fig. 1.

The intended behavior of a system is most often expressed through requirements, specifications, and other similar documents, which are encoded into a formal model using explicit behavioral notations (Step 1 in Fig. 1). This model represents an abstraction of the system under test, that is, a smaller and simpler version of the actual system, and (most often) includes only the aspects of the system that are intended to be tested. Since

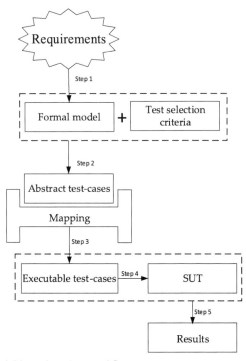

Figure 1 The model-based testing workflow.

there is no model notation that can satisfy all testing purposes, several modeling notations have been used by both academia and industry, for various
purposes. Such examples include state-base notations like the Z language,
transition-based notations like labeled transition system or timed automata,
stochastic notations like Markov chains, etc.

Based on the requirements of the system, the test selection criterion
defines the test-cases to be generated by specifying the features of the system
to be tested prior to the actual test-case generation. Such a test selection criterion most often refers to a certain functionality of the system, to the structure of the model, or to different stochastic characteristics.

The model together with the test selection criteria are used to generate
test-cases (Step 2 in Fig. 1), most often represented as traces or pairs of inputs
and expected outputs of the system. The test selection criterion is used to
automatically generate the desired test-cases from an infinite number of possible tests. In most cases, these tests are called abstract test-cases because they
reflect only the information encoded in the formal model and are independent of the actual implementation, so they cannot be directly executed on

the system under test. Since the system model is an abstraction of the system under test, we need to add to the abstract test-cases all the details of the system implementation that where not mentioned in the abstract model (Step 3 in Fig. 1). This can be done with the help of a transformation tool, or more often by writing an adapter that wraps around the system under test and implements each abstract operation in terms of the low-level system facilities.

The executable test-cases are run on the actual implementation of the system (Step 4 in Fig. 1). At the end of each test execution, a verdict is returned (Step 5 in Fig. 1), which represents the result of comparing the output produced by the system under test with the expected output provided by the test-case (based on the formal model). The verdict can be pass, fail, or inconclusive (in some cases a decision cannot be made). For each failed test, the tester must determine the fault that has caused the failure. The fault can be either in the implementation or in the test itself.

3. PROPOSED TAXONOMY DIMENSIONS

Model-based testing tools are characterized by various features that could be used to intuitively assess the advantages and limitations associated with a potential integration of such tools into a software development process. In 2012, Utting *et al.* [4] have devised a taxonomy that identifies different relevant dimensions of model-based testing. Based on this work, we propose an alternative taxonomic schema, in which we keep four of the existing dimensions, namely the model notations, the test selection criteria, the test generation methods, and the text execution. We extend this restricted taxonomic schema by proposing two new dimensions as shown in Fig. 2: the test *artifact* represented by the model, and the mapping support between abstract and executable test-cases. In the rest of this section, we describe all the dimensions of our taxonomy, presented in Fig. 2.

3.1 The Modeling Notation

The intended behavior of a system is most often expressed through requirements, functional specifications, and other similar documents, which are encoded into a model that uses explicit, unambiguous behavioral notations. The latter make it possible to simulate the execution of the model and use it as an oracle, by predicting the expected output of the system under test. In this chapter, we focus our attention on the model paradigms most often used in practice.

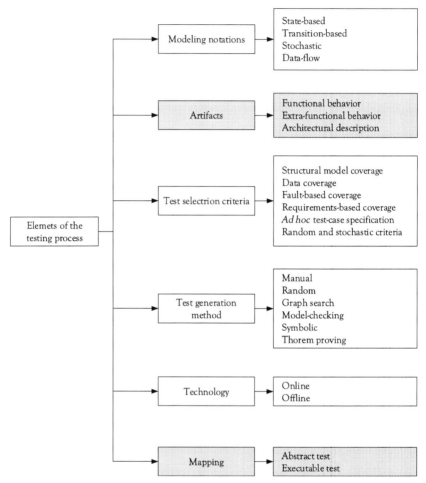

Figure 2 Taxonomy revised.

State-based or pre/post notations. The system is modeled as a collection of variables representing its state at a specific point of the execution, together with a collection of operations defined by a precondition that defines the admissible set of initial states, and a postcondition that specifies the guaranteed set of final states. Examples of such notations include the Z language [8], the B machine [9], UML's Object Constraint Language (OCL) [10], Java Modeling Language (JML) [11], VDM [12], and Spec# [13].

Transition-based notations. In such formalisms, the system is modeled as a set of possible states together with the transitions between them. Typically this is a graphical "node-and-arc" representation, such as the one of finite state machines (FSMs) [14], statecharts [15], labeled transition systems [16], or I/O automata [17], but other textual or tabular notations can be used.

Stochastic notations. The system is described by a probabilistic model of the events and input values. Such notations, like Markov chains [18], tend to be used to model environments rather than the SUT, and can specify the distribution of events on test inputs, but are weaker at predicting the expected output.

Data-flow notations. These notations concentrate on the data rather than the control flow. Examples of such notations are Lustre [19] and the block diagrams as used, for instance, in Matlab Simulink [20] for modeling continuous systems.

3.2 The Test Artifact

The test artifact represents the type of information encoded in the model for the purpose of testing, namely the *functional* behavior, *extra-functional* behavior, or the *architectural* description. These artifacts are in fact the models used for generating test-cases for the system under test.

Functional behavior. A functional behavior is assumed to be a structured description of the software's functionality, by considering solely the system behavior, and not encode architectural information. In the rest of the chapter we will refer to "deriving test-cases from a functional behavior" in case the test model is created from the functional requirements.

Extra-functional behavior. The extra-functional behavior complements the functional behavior of a system, by providing extra-functional information, such as timing annotations in terms of periods, delays, synchronization constraints, end-to-end deadlines etc., reliability annotations etc. In this chapter, we review model-based testing tools that can be used for testing extra-functional properties such as execution time, quality of service, security, usability, and safety.

Architectural description. In this chapter, an architectural description is assumed to define the software's structure in some Architecture Description Language (ADL) [21], from which a model that can be used during model-based testing can be derived. Bertolino *et al.* [22] consider the software architecture description as a way to "implement" the system by architectural components, connectors, together with the system's behavior. In addition, the model should capture architecturally-relevant decisions behind a particular design. In the context of software architectures, model-based testing consists in assessing whether the system satisfies desired architectural properties such as "once a signal is sent to a port, it is always read before a new signal is sent."

In principle, the test artifact might constrain the type of test selection criteria, depending on the modeled behavior. For instance, if one targets requirements-based coverage for a set of requirements that contains real-time requirements (e.g, end-to-end deadlines), such goal cannot be achieved by assuming a purely functional test artifact.

3.3 Test Selection Criteria

Based on the requirements of the system, the test selection criteria define the test-cases to be generated, by providing a "command" to the testing tool, which will determine the algorithm to be used in generating the test-cases. Depending on the type of software system to be developed, different testing methods and strategies come in many different forms. In order to reason about these techniques, test selection criteria are used for evaluating the adequacy reached by a certain test. A test criterion is formulated using the so-called *coverage items*. These items should be exercised during testing in order for the criterion to be satisfied.

Structural Model Coverage Criteria. A test criterion defined on the abstract representation of the software implementation is called a structural model coverage criterion. It exploits the structure of the model, such as the nodes and arcs of a transition-based model, and is specific to each kind of modeling notation. The main families of structural model coverage criteria are: control-flow-oriented coverage criteria, data-flow-oriented coverage criteria, transition-based coverage criteria, UML-based coverage criteria.

Data Coverage Criteria. These criteria deal with choosing the test values from a large input data space. The main families of data coverage criteria are: boundary value testing, statistical data coverage, pairwise coverage, N-wise coverage, or all-combinations coverage [23].

Fault-based Criteria. Mostly applicable to system under test models, fault-based testing is a technique that generates test data, in order to demonstrate the absence of predefined faults. During the last decade *mutation analysis* has been extensively studied. It uses mutation operators to introduce faults represented by small changes, or *mutations*, into the model, hence producing mutant specifications. Black *et al.* have proposed such fault-based criteria for specifications [24].

Requirements-based Coverage Criteria. When the elements of a model can be explicitly associated with informal requirements of the SUT, coverage can also be applied to requirements. All-requirements coverage, or simply requirements coverage, requires that all requirements are covered by a test suite.

Ad hoc Test Case Specification. In addition to the model, the test engineer writes a test-case specification in some formal notation, which is used to determine which tests will be generated.

Random and Stochastic Criteria. Such criteria are especially applicable to environment models, as it is the environment that determines the usage patterns/profiles of the system under test. For instance, stochastic models can be used to specify the expected usage profile of the system under test. When generating the tests, the transitions are fired based on the probability distribution of the outgoing transitions of the model, which results in test-cases with a higher probability being generated first.

3.4 The Test Generation Method

The generation method denotes the technique used to generate the test-cases, which also provides the potential for automation for the model-based testing process.

Manual tests. It is an *ad hoc* process driven by human testers that write test inputs and descriptions of expected test results, manually.

Random generation. This method is the simplest version of test-case automation, where the input space of a system is sampled to generate test-cases.

Graph search algorithms. Dedicated graph search algorithms, such as node or arc coverage algorithms, provide priced traces, or walks through the system as test-cases.

Model-checking. The automatic generation of test-cases can be achieved by verifying or refuting properties for all possible executions of a model, by model-checking techniques.

Symbolic execution. The system is run with a set of input values that allows a symbolic trace to represent many fully instantiated traces.

Theorem proving. This method can be used to check the satisfiability of formulas that directly occur as guards (boolean conditions) of transitions in state-based models.

3.5 The Technology

This dimension provides a direct connection between the generation of test-cases and their execution.

Online. The test generation and test execution are done in an immediate sequence, that is, each generated test-case is immediately executed, and only after that a new test-case will be generated. The outputs of the SUT can have an impact on the test generation algorithms.

Offline. The test-case generation and test execution are done in different and separated steps. This means that, for instance, a whole test-suite (a set of test-cases corresponding to a particular criterion) can be generated before running any of the constituent test-cases.

3.6 The Mapping

The test-case generation process relies on the definition of a formal model, which is used to automate this process. Consequently, the test-cases reflect only the information encoded in the model, and their execution on the SUT is highly dependent on the relation between the model and the implementation.

Abstract Tests. The abstract test-cases can not be directly run on the SUT, since there is no mapping between the model elements and the low-level system elements.

Executable Tests. In this case, the model-based testing tool incorporates transformation rules that connect the model and the implementation of the system under test.

4. A RESEARCH REVIEW OF MODEL-BASED TESTING TOOLS

The goal of this chapter is to give an overview of the state-of-the-art model-based testing frameworks, by presenting existing model-based testing tools, and classifying them based on our proposed taxonomy (presented in Section 3). Due to the large number of models and frameworks proposed by researchers and practitioners, we focus only on model-based testing techniques supported by an associated tool that handles modeling, test-case generation, test-case selection and possibly execution. Fulfilling this goal is, however, far from a trivial task.

First, we intend to include all the relevant model-based testing tools for requirements-based designs. Secondly, we need relevant information about the underlying approaches, to be able to describe the tools with respect to the assumed taxonomy, which allows for a comprehensive comparison. Shafique and Labiche [6] have proposed a systematic literature review [25] on model-based testing tools, by using a review protocol based on the search process, the inclusion/exclusion criteria for selecting tools, and criteria to evaluate the selected tools.

Initially, the authors of the mentioned work have identified 49 model-based testing tools before applying the exclusion criteria. Then, they apply their own exclusion criteria and retain only 11 of them. As a starting point of our current work, we collect the names of the initial tools, which in this first phase of review are: TestMaster, GOTCHA, GraphWalker, TestCast, NModel, TestOptimal, AGEDIS, Conformiq, ParTeG, CertifyItb, AsmL Test Tool, PyModel, SpecExplorer Test Tool, ATD-Automated Test Designer, CTESK,4 errfix, Escalator, Expecco, Focus!MBT, GATel, getmore, Rhapsody-ATG, SDL-TTCN, Test Real-time, JavaTESK4, JUMBL, KeY, MaTelo, MathWorks SystemTest, MISTA, ModelJUnit, MODENA, OSMO, PrUDE, QuickCheck, Reactis, Simulink Tester for T-VEC, Statemate, TDE/UML, Tedeso, TEMA, TestEra, TGSR, TGV, Time Partition Test, TOA, TorX, Uppaal Cover, and Uppaal-TRON. Given the scope of our research review, which is somewhat larger than the one provided in the above mentioned systematic literature review [6], we decide to first consider all of these tools for review. In the next step, we define our selection criteria that we present in the following.

4.1 Selection Criteria and Procedures for Including/ Excluding Model-based Testing Tools

Model-based testing tools have been applied in software engineering for a considerable range of models. To gather more information for our proposed taxonomy, it is imperative to define comprehensive inclusion/exclusion criteria to select only those tools that provide evidence with respect to our taxonomy. The following exclusion criteria is applicable in this research review, concretely, we exclude tools that:

- Contain a model-based testing approach that starts from the code and not from a model of the specification;
- Do not report application of the model-based testing tool on a case-study;
- Do not report the modeling notation, the test generation method, the test selection criteria, the test mapping (e.g., abstract or executable), and the test artifact.

The exclusion has been carried out by one researcher that has excluded 23 of the above list of tools, based on reading the abstract and the full-text of the primary study related to each tool, respectively. For some tools, no primary study has been found and the researcher relies only on other information such as web-sites. Some other tools are excluded because of lack of information. Thus, 26 tools are retained at the end of second selection phase. These 26 tools are then complemented with 7 more tools found by manual search performed by the same researcher. In the end, we reach a final figure of 33 tools, shown in Table 1.

4.2 Our Taxonomy

Further, we present the descriptive characterization of the assessed tools, in relation to our proposed taxonomy dimensions. The 33 model-based testing tools are classified based on the modeling notation, the test generation method, the testing technology, the test selection criteria, the test artifact, and the test mapping. Our taxonomy is shown in Table 1, and contains the relevant information that characterizes each tool in relation to the mentioned taxonomy dimensions. Based on these findings and our proposed taxonomy, in the next sections we describe the different model notations underlying the available model-based testing tools. Before that, we introduce the running example on which we apply four representative tools of the selected pool.

5. RUNNING EXAMPLE: THE COFFEE/TEA VENDING MACHINE

Coffee is very important to researchers. Paul Erdos once said that *"a mathematician is a device for turning coffee into theorems"*, and this can be extrapolated to other areas of research, such as computer science.

In this chapter, we chose to present how a simple Coffee/Tea Vending Machine (a frequently used example of model-based testing) can be modeled using four different modeling notations, and how the associated model-based testing tools can be employed to generate test-cases. Since we are considering software models instead of the intended realizations, this exercise does not guarantee that all busy and impatient researchers will always get coffee (or tea) from their Coffee/Tea Vending Machines, it rather helps us evaluate different modeling notations and some of the model-based testing tools used mainly in academia, but also in industry.

The system specification is simple. The machine is *idle* until the user selects a drink, either coffee or tea. After the drink has been selected, the user has to insert coins within 10 seconds. The machine charges two coins for tea and four coins for coffee. If the user has inserted enough coins for the selected drink, the machine prepares it, serves it to the user, provides the

Table 1 The Collection of Reviewed Tools

Tool	Model	Modeling Notation	Generation Method	Technology	Selection Criteria	Artifact	Mapping
TestMaster [26]	EFSM	Transition-based	Not specified	Offline	Test Case Specification	Functional behavior	Executable tests
GOTCHA [27]	$C^\#$ FSM	Transition-based	Model-checking	Offline	Structural Model Coverage	Functional behavior	Abstract Tests
GraphWalker	FSM	Transition-based	Graph search	Offline and online	Requirements Coverage, Structural Model Coverage	Functional behavior	Executable tests
TestCast	UML	Transition-based	Graph search	Offline	Requirements Coverage, Structural Model Coverage	Functional behavior	Executable tests
NModel [28]	$C^\#$ FSM	Transition-based	Model-checking	Online and offline	Requirements Coverage, Structural Model Coverage, Data Coverage	Functional behavior	Executable tests
PyModel [29]	FSM	Transition-based	Graph search	Online and offline	Not specified	Functional behavior	Executable tests
SpecExplorer [30]	Spec$^\#$ FSM/ASM	Pre–Post	Model-checking	Online and offline	Not specified	Functional behavior	Abstract Tests
TestOptimal [31]	EFSM	Transition-based	Graph search	Online and offline	Structural Model Coverage	Functional behavior, Extra-functional behavior	Executable tests
AGEDIS [32]	UML	Transition-based	Graph search	Offline	Structural Model Coverage	Functional behavior	Executable tests

Continued

Table 1 The Collection of Reviewed Tools—cont'd

Tool	Model	Modeling Notation	Generation Method	Technology	Selection Criteria	Artifact	Mapping
Conformiq [33]	QML	Transition-based	Symbolic and Model-checking	Online and offline	Test Case Specification, Structural Model Coverage	Functional behavior	Executable tests
ParTeG [34, 35]	UML	Transition-based	Not specified	Offline	Structural Model Coverage	Functional behavior	Executable tests
AsmL [36, 37]	AsmL	Pre-Post	Model-checking	Online	Test Case Specification, Structural Model Coverage	Functional behavior	Executable tests
GATel [38]	Lustre	Data-Flow	Constraint solver	Offline	Test Case Specification, Structural Model Coverage	Functional behavior	Executable tests
JUMBL [39]	Markov Chains	Stochastic	Model-checking and Random	Offline	Test Case Specification, Structural Model Coverage	Functional behavior	Executable tests
MaTelo [40]	Markov Chains	Stochastic	Model-checking	Offline	Test Case Specification, Structural Model Coverage	Functional behavior	Executable tests
MISTA [41]	UML	Transition-based	Not specified	Online and offline	Test Case Specification	Functional behavior, Extra-functional behavior	Executable tests
ModelJUnit [1]	EFSM	Transition-based	Graph search and Random	Online and offline	Test Case Specification	Functional behavior	Executable tests

Tool	Notation	Paradigm	Technology	Mode	Test Selection Criteria	Test Objective	Test Type
PrUDE [42]	UML	Transition-based	Theorem proving	Offline	Structural Model Coverage	Functional behavior	Executable tests
Reactis [43]	Simulink StateFlow	Transition-based	Manual and Random	Offline	Structural Model Coverage, Requirements Coverage	Functional behavior	Abstract Tests
Tedeso [44]	UML	Transition-based	Graph search	Offline	Structural Model Coverage	Functional behavior	Executable Tests
TEMA [45]	LTS	Transition-based	Graph search	Online	Test Case Specification	Functional behavior	Executable tests
TGV [46]	FLS	Transition-based	Not specified	Online	Test Case Specification, Structural Model Coverage	Functional behavior	Abstract tests
JTorX [47]	LTS	Transition-based	Not specified	Online	Test Case Specification, Structural Model Coverage	Functional behavior	Executable tests
CoVer [48]	TA	Transition-based	Model-checking	Offline	Structural Model Coverage	Functional behavior	Abstract Tests
Uppaal-TRON [49]	TA	Transition-based	Model-checking	Online	Not specified	Functional behavior	Executable tests
Isabelle/HOL [50]	Z	Pre-Post	Theorem proving	Offline	Test Case Specification	Functional behavior	Abstract Tests
BZ [51]	B, Z	Pre-Post	Constraint solver	Offline	Boundary Value Analysis	Functional behavior	Abstract Tests

Continued

Table 1 The Collection of Reviewed Tools—cont'd

Tool	Model	Modeling Notation	Generation Method	Technology	Selection Criteria	Artifact	Mapping
ProTest [52]	B	Pre–Post	Model–checking	Offline	Not specified	Functional behavior	Abstract Tests
JSXM [53]	Stream X-Machine	Transition-based	Not specified	Online and offline	Not specified	Functional behavior	Executable tests
TestUml [54]	UML	Transition-based	Random	Offline	Random	Functional behavior	Executable tests
LTG [55]	UML	Transition-based	Not specified	Offline	Structural Model Coverage	Functional behavior	Executable tests
Simulink Verification and Validation [56]	Simulink	Data-Flow	Graph search	Offline	Test Case Specification, Structural Model Coverage	Functional behavior	Executable tests
CompleteTest [57]	Function Block Diagram	Data-Flow	Model–checking	Offline	Test Case Specification, Structural Model Coverage	Functional and extra-functional behavior	Executable tests

change (when needed), and returns to *idle*. If the user has not inserted enough coins for the selected drink within 10 seconds from drink selection, the machine returns all the already inserted coins, and returns to *idle*.

We consider that a correct functioning of the Coffee/Tea Vending Machine means that the user will always receive the selected drink (assuming that one has inserted enough coins for it) and the correct change (including none if the case), and the entire process does not take more than 60 seconds. Throughout the chapter we will use this example in order to test the functionality and the timing behavior of the vending machine. By running selected model-based testing tools that rely on different formalisms, we can gain more insight into the actual usage of the respective tool, in order to get an intuition of the applicability of such approaches.

6. MODEL-BASED TESTING TOOLS FOR PRE/POST NOTATIONS

The *state-based* or *pre/post* notation is the first category of formal modeling languages that we examine in this chapter. A formal specification uses mathematical notations to precisely describe the properties of the system, without considering the ways in which such properties are met by the real system. Model-based testing that relies on such formal specifications has received a lot of attention during mid 90's. Generating test-cases from pre/post models subsumes choosing the high-level test objective, and modeling the system based on state variables and pre- and postconditions for each operation allowed by the model [58, 59]. Each operation is specified semantically as a pre/postcondition relation that can then be reduced to the Disjunctive Normal Form (DNF) [60], and the terms can be used to partition the test domain. The method is originally proposed by Dick *et al.* [61], and serves as a reference method for model-based testing based on notations such as Z, or B. During the last few years, various extensions of high-level programming languages, such as C# and Java, have been proposed based on pre/post notations, in order to enable programmers to test their code through model-checking techniques. Such extensions are used in model-based testing tools for Spec# and AsmL.

In the following, we present and discuss some of the most popular pre/post notations such as Z language, B method, Spec#, and AsmL, together with some of the most mature model-based testing tools that use such formal notations.

6.1 The Z Language

The Z language [8] is a formal modeling language that uses simple mathematical notations to describe hardware and software systems. In Z, the model relies on *mathematical data types* that capture the system data, and *predicate logic* that describes the system behavior. Often, a Z specification is made of smaller pieces called *schemas*, which allow different features of the system to be described separately, and then related and combined. This modeling style is a good match for imperative, procedural programming languages that provide a rich collection of data types, physical systems that include storage elements, or object-oriented programming. However, Z is not an executable notation and cannot be directly interpreted or compiled into a running program.

ISABELLE/HOL. Encoding Z specifications into a higher-order logic [62] allows state-of-the-art theorem provers (e.g., Isabelle) to be used on Z models [63]. With such an encoding at hand, all the deductive power of Isabelle is available to reason about Z specifications. In order to obtain test-cases from Z specifications, the prover transforms each predicate of each operation schema into a DNF form, respectively. This is done in three steps: (i) separate disjunctive predicates from non-disjunctive ones at a "syntactic" level, where one does not reason about semantic equalities or equivalences, but about permutations of sub-formulas of a conjunction, (ii) compute the DNF with an algorithm that first transforms implications and equivalences into disjunctions, then builds a negation normal form, and finally distributes conjunctions over disjunctions, and (iii) eliminate unsatisfiable disjuncts and simplify test cases by employing Isabelle's simplifier with the standard simplifier set for higher-order logic.

Even if the techniques mentioned above are not novel, the tool shows the feasibility and usefulness of implementing verification techniques on top of a modern state-of-the-art theorem prover.

6.2 The B-Method

The B-method [9] uses the Abstract Machine notation [64] as the specification and design language, which is a generalized version of Dijkstra's guarded command language [65]. The formal specifications can be constructed and verified in an incremental way, and existing specifications can be reused to form new specifications by employing the semi-hiding principle (a variable of one Abstract Machine can be mentioned in other Abstract Machines, but not modified by the latter). The theory of generalized substitutions, used by the Abstract Machine, includes laws that permit the calculation of the weakest precondition of each machine, on which the system's formal verification relies. A generalized substitution is defined as a predicate function that transforms a postcondition into its weakest precondition, that is, the largest set of initial states from which the machine is guaranteed to establish the postcondition at the end of its execution, provided that the latter terminates.

BZ Testing Tool. Compared to Isabelle/HOL, the BZ Testing Tool provides boundary testing from B and Z specifications, where every operation of the system is tested at every boundary state (minimum and maximum) using all input boundary values of that operation [66]. The process is automated by employing the CLPS-B constraint solver [67] to animate the specification. The tool performs a transformation of the formal specification (e.g., B or Z) into a common subset format called BZ-Prolog. Then, the DNF is computed to determine the set of boundary goals, which are predicates that describe subsets of the state space, respectively. Each of these boundary goals are then instantiated to provide one or more boundary states, by traversing the state space. The tool allows for both positive and negative test-cases. The test-case trace consists of: (i) the preamble that takes the system from its initial state to a boundary state, (ii) the body that invokes an update operation with input boundary values, (iii) the identification that represents a sequence of observation operations to enable the assigning of pass/fail verdicts, and (iv) the postamble that takes the system back to the boundary state or to an initial state, which enables the concatenation of test-cases. For negative test-cases (a legal trace of invoked operations whose precondition is false), the body part is generated with invalid input boundary values, and no identification, or postamble parts are generated, as the system reaches an indeterminate state of the model. In the end, all traces are automatically translated into executable test-scripts.

ProTest. ProTest [52] is an automatic test environment for B specifications based on model-checking techniques. Since it relies on the ProB model-checker [68], the testing tool can take as input specifications that are modeled as single B machines. As in the previously described tools, ProTest first computes the DNF of the machine's precondition. Once the disjunctive form of the precondition is obtained, the contradictory disjuncts are filtered out with a naive theorem prover. The remaining disjuncts partition the input space into subspaces that create instances of the machine. Next, the full state space of the B machine is explored through exhaustive model-checking to construct a finite state machine (FSM) of the specification. This state space search is performed with the ProB tool. Starting from the initial state, the FSM is traversed to generate a set of operation sequences, where each operation instance in the FSM appears in the generated sequences at least once. Each such sequence of B operations constitutes one test-case for the subsequent implementation.

6.3 Spec#

Spec# [13] is an extension of the C# programming language that allows the specification of different constructs, such as pre- and postconditions, non-null types, and higher-level data abstractions. The specifications also become part of program execution, where they are checked dynamically to ensure the consistency between the program and its specification. Thus, Spec# provides means for programmers to write down and verify their assertions/method contracts.

Spec Explorer. Spec Explorer [30] provides online and offline testing for model programs written in Spec#. A model program defines the state variables and update rules of an abstract state machine (ASM) [69]. An ASM is a state machine that in each step computes a set of updates of the machine's variables, and commits all updates simultaneously. The states of the machine are defined by the values of the variables at each step, whereas the transitions between states are invocations of the model program's methods that satisfy the given preconditions. The tool uses the theory of interface automata [70], and the test generation can be viewed as a game between the SUT and the test generator, where the model program is annotated with an action method for the test generator, and an observation method for the SUT. The test-case generation algorithm starts from the initial state of the system, and, in each state, waits for the SUT to perform an observable event, otherwise it executes one of the controllable methods in the model for which the precondition is true. This stops when the system reaches an accepting state. At this point, each test-case is nothing but a sequence of operations of the abstract state machine. By animating the ASM, we obtain a state at the end of the test sequence corresponding to a particular test-case. With the implementation of the ASM in Java at hand, one executes the implementation in relation to the same test-case and obtained state. If the two states match, then a pass verdict specifies that the implementation has passed the test.

6.4 AsmL

The Abstract State Machine Language (AsmL) [37] is a fusion of the Abstract State Machine paradigm and the .NET language runtime system. AsmL can be integrated with any .NET language: AsmL models can perform callouts, and AsmL models can be called and referred to from other .NET languages. AsmL supports meta-modeling that allows a programmatic exploration of the non-determinism in the model. This allows one to realize various state exploration algorithms for AsmL models, including explicit state model-checking, and in particular test generation and test evaluation.

AsmL. The AsmL tool environment [37] generates a FSM by exploring the state space of the AsmL model by explicit-state model-checking techniques. Starting at the initial state, enabled actions are fired, leading to a set of successor states, from where the exploration is continued. An action is enabled if the precondition of the method is true in the current state. From the FSM, test cases (i.e., call sequences) can be generated to provide conformance testing between the model and an implementation, where the implementation can be written in any of the .NET languages. To enable this, the implementation assemblies are rewritten on the intermediate code level by inserting callbacks monitored methods to the runtime verification engine. Each time a monitored method is called, its parameters and output result are propagated to the conformance test manager. On each of the currently possible model states, the according model method will be called. The resulting states of those calls constitute the set of next model states. If this set becomes empty, the conformance test fails.

Next, we select a representative tool of the pre/post notation category, and apply it on our running example.

6.5 The Coffee/Tea Vending Machine in ProTest

Generating test-cases in ProTest consists of five distinct steps. We present the tool and its test-case generation process on the Coffee/Tea Vending Machine introduced in Section 5.[2]

Step 1: Identify the factors. In a B machine, the factors (or the variables) are "items" that can satisfy different conditions during the execution. For the Coffee/Tea Vending Machine, the factors are the *selected drink*, the *provided drink*, the *inserted coins*, and the provided *change*.

Step 2: Identify the Levels for Each Factor. For each factor, we identify the levels of interest, which are the possible different values of the variables that we intend to test. For the set of variables described in **Step 1**, we present the possible values in Fig. 3. For example, the *selected drink* can be *empty*

---

[2] We have followed the ProTest tutorial available on the Web: http://www.sigmazone.com/protest_HowTo.htm.

Factor #	Factor 1	Factor 2	Factor 3	Factor 4
Factor Name	selected	coins	change	provided
Level 1	empty	0	0	empty
Level 2	tea	1	1	tea
Level 3	coffee	2	2	coffee
Level 4		3	3	
Level 5		4	4	
Level 6		5	5	

Figure 3 The levels for the factors of the coffee/tea vending machine.

	If Factor ...	is at level ...	then Factor ...	can't be ...
Constraint 1	selected drink ▼	tea ▼	coins ▼	0 ▼
Constraint 2	selected drink ▼	tea ▼	coins ▼	1 ▼
Constraint 3	selected drink ▼	coffee ▼	coins ▼	0 ▼
Constraint 4	selected drink ▼	coffee ▼	coins ▼	1 ▼
Constraint 5	selected drink ▼	coffee ▼	coins ▼	2 ▼

Figure 4 The constraints of the coffee/tea vending machine.

(no drink has been selected), *tea*, or *coffee*, whereas the user can insert a number of *coins* between 0 and 5.

Step 3: Establish the Constraints. Assuming the given levels of each factor, respectively, we identify a series of constraints representing infeasible relationships between factors. Such constraints are expressed according to the following rule: "*If <FactorA> is at <Level1> then <FactorB> can't be at <Level2>.*" For the Coffee/Tea Vending Machine, we have identified a set of 19 constraints. In Fig. 4, we present some of these constraints.

Step 4: Enter Any Previous Runs. Previous testing attempts can be specified through the tuple: *<selected drink, coins, change, provided drink>*, and they are used to reduce the total number of tests provided by the tool. For the Coffee/Tea Vending Machine, we have not specified any such previous runs.

Step 5: Generate All Two-Way Combinations. At this point, ProTest will generate the test-cases for the model described by steps 1 to 4. For the Coffee/Tea Vending Machine, the tool automatically generates 85 test-cases, out of 101 possible input combinations. In Fig. 5, we present some of these test-cases.

7. MODEL-BASED TESTING TOOLS FOR TRANSITION-BASED NOTATIONS

Instead of characterizing the system based on its admissible states, one might model the system as transitions from one state to another. In such a

	Factor_A	Factor_B	Factor_C	Factor_D
Factor Name	selected drink	coins	change	provided drink
Case 1	empty	0	0	coffee
Case 2	tea	5	1	tea
Case 3	tea	4	3	tea
Case 4	coffee	3	4	coffee
Case 5	tea	3	0	tea
Case 6	empty	4	1	coffee
Case 7	coffee	5	3	coffee
Case 8	tea	5	4	tea

Figure 5 Test-cases for the coffee/tea vending machine.

model, the properties are specified as a set of transitions functions, which map each input state to the corresponding output state. Based on the notations used, the model can be annotated with triggering events, which are conditions sufficient for the transition to take place, or guards that are necessary preconditions for the transition to be fired.

In the next sections, we present some of the techniques used for generating test-cases from transition-based notations, starting with simple finite state machines and progressing towards more complex notations such as UML diagrams.

7.1 Finite State Machines

A finite state machine (FSM) [71] is a mathematical model of computation usually represented as a graph, with a finite number of nodes describing the possible states of the system, and a finite number of arcs representing the transitions that do or do not change the state, respectively. Such a machine is mostly used to model computer programs and sequential logic. There are two types of FSMs: *Mealy machines*, where the output values are determined based on the current state together with the current input, and *Moore machines*, where the output is determined solely based on the current state. Extended finite state machines (EFSMs) [72] allow for internal variables than can store more detailed internal state information. Thus, EFSMs allow for a larger number of internal states. Mapping the large number of internal states to a smaller number of visible states requires an abstraction of the system, which can influence the testing process.

The early publications on testing FSMs discuss and propose solutions to two major types of testing problems: (i) state identification [73], and (ii) state verification [74]. In the state identification problem, one aims to identify the initial state of the machine. This is done through a trace called *distinguish sequence*, where one applies an input sequence to the FSM so that from its input/output behavior one can deduce the desired information about the state of the machine. In the state verification, we verify if the FSM is in a specified state, by a trace called *unique input/output* (UIO) sequence[75, 76]. Nowadays, FSMs are mostly employed in the conformance testing of communication protocols. Given the specification of the systems as an FSM, and an implementation for which one can observe only the I/O behavior, conformance testing aims to check weather the implementation conforms with its specification through a test sequence called *checking sequence*. One of the main disadvantages of such representation is that it rapidly becomes too big for real, industrial systems, so it is mainly used to model small reactive systems, like various communication protocols. Also, the FSM model is not expressive enough to allow internal variables to store more information about the states, and the actions to have guards, which is the case with extended finite state machines.

TestMaster. The TestMaster [26, 77] tool uses extended finite state machines to specify the system model, and the test-case generation is performed based on identifying input sequences that enable the transitions, and guide the system through a path defined by the EFSM's states. Each input sequence so constructed represents a test-case for the system-under-test, and the tool generates test-cases following user-specified path coverage schemes. TestMaster uses a combination of basic graph coverage algorithms like depth-first search, breadth-first search, and minimum spanning tree, to derive the paths of EFSMs.

GOTCHA. GOTCHA [27, 78] is a prototype test generator based on the Murφ model-checker [79]. The Murφ definition language is extended to allow to designate coverage variables and characterize final states when modeling the unit-under-test. The GOTCHA compiler builds a C++ file containing both the test generation algorithm and the embodiment of the finite state machine that is explored via a depth-first search or a breadth-first search, from each of the start states. On completion of the enumeration of the entire reachable state space, a random coverage task is chosen from amongst those that have not yet been covered. A test-case is generated by constructing an execution path to the coverage task (state or transition), then continuing to a final state. A task is deemed not coverable if no path that exercises the task has an extension to any designated final state.

GraphWalker. GraphWalker is a tool that generates test-cases from FSMs, by using search algorithms like A* or random, for various coverage criteria (e.g., state, edge, requirement). There is little scientific documentation about the tool, and for information we refer the reader to the tool's webpage: http://www.graphwalker.org/.

TestOptimal. TestOprimal is a commercial tool for generating executable test-cases for FSMs, based on graph search techniques. Due to the limited scientific documentation about the tool, we refer the reader to the tool's web site for more information: http://testoptimal.com/.

NModel. In NModel [80] the implementation is modeled based on a library of attributes and data types for writing model programs in C#. This implementation is used to generate a graphical FSM using the integrated visualization and analysis tool. Next, the offline test generator performs link coverage of model programs to produce test-cases. To test the test-suite on the implementation, a test harness needs to be manually implemented to couple the test-cases described in the model program with the implementation. Finally, running the conformance tester with the test-suite and the implementation coupled by the test harness checks for consistency between the implementation and the model.

PyModel. PyModel [29] is an open-source model-based testing framework for Python programs. It takes as input one or more models such as model programs, FSMs, or test suites. An analyzer generates a finite state machine from the product of input models, for validation, visualization, and checking of safety properties by concrete state model-checking. The PyModel Graphics program generates a file of graphical visualization of the analyzer's output. Last, the PyModel Tester displays traces, generates and executes test-cases both offline and on-the-fly.

JSXM. JSXM [53] takes as input Stream X-Machines (SXMs), which are EFSMs enriched with a memory structure and functional label transitions, and eventually generates concrete test-cases for the implementation-under-test. In order to obtain such test-cases, the tool starts by animating SXM models for model validation, and uses the SXM formalism to implement an extension of the W-method to generate abstract test-sets that are able to guarantee the functional conformance of an implementation to its specification. Since these are abstract test-cases, which are independent of the programming language of the implementation, a transformation is used to convert them into concrete test-cases in the underlying technology of the implementation.

ModelJUnit. The ModelJUnit library is a set of Jave classes designed to be used as an extension of the JUnit for model-based testing of Java classes. The tool allows for the FSM or EFSM model to be written as in Java, and provides a collection of algorithms for traversing the model and generating the test-cases. The test-cases are generated online, and the EFSM model is used to define both the possible states and transitions in the model, and also the adaptor that connects the model to the SUT, which can be another Java class. The test-cases are run in the same way as the JUnit tests.

7.2 Labeled Transition Systems

Since an FSM defines only the possible sequences of interactions that the model might have with its environment, but there is no notion of direction on interactions (e.g., inputs, outputs), one needs to extend the model of the system and of the environment with inputs and outputs. We consider as *outputs* the interactions initiated by the system and never refused by the environment, and as *inputs* the interactions initiated by the environment and never refused by the system. Unlike FSMs, labeled transition systems (LTSs) allow for an infinite set of states and an infinite set of labels. Most of the work carried out in the area of testing LTSs is due to Jan Tretmans[16]. He proposes a method to test an implementation for compliance with a model that describes the required behavior, with the models being expressed as LTSs, and compliance being defined by the *ioco* implementation relation.

TorX. The TorX tool [81] is based on the 'ioco' test theory, the theory of testing equivalences and preorders for LTSs. This means that an implementation is ioco-correct with respect to a specification (both modeled as LTSs), if any output action produced by the implementation can also occur as an output of the specification. The execution of an exhaustive test-suite, which may contain infinitely many cases, is unrealistic. Therefore, we need to select a finite number of test-cases. The selection of such cases is not easy, and a selection strategy could help in detecting as many erroneous implementations as possible, within a restricted period of time. TorX provides automatic test-case generation, test-case implementation, test-case execution and analysis in an on-the-fly manner. The latter implements the ioco-test derivation algorithm to derive test-cases from formal, transition-based system specifications. The specifications can be expressed in the formal languages Lotos, Promela, or directly as an LTS. During test execution, test-cases are derived on-the-fly. For each test step, TorX computes only the test primitives from the formal specification, which are needed in that step, that is, the stimuli that can be given, and the observations that are expected. Then, it decides between stimulating or observing (either chooses a stimulus and sends it to the implementation, or it acquires an observation from the implementation and checks whether it was expected), and computes the test primitives for the next test step. A test run is collected in a log that contains all the executed test steps, and it can be visualized as a message sequence chart.

TGV. The TGV tool [46] employs an approach based on formal specification of the intended behavior of the system provided as labeled transition models, and on a precise testing theory that allows one to describe test generation algorithms, and establish important properties on generated test-cases from the original specifications. TGV is an efficient on-the-fly tool that generates test-cases by a partial exploration of state graphs, thus avoiding the state explosion problem. The tool gets as input the LTS together with a second input representing the test selection directive, e.g., random test selection, selection guided by coverage criteria, guided by test purposes (originally), or a mixture of these. The test purpose is specified by an automaton that accepts the behaviors of the specification. TGV generates abstract test-cases that describe the behaviors in terms of input/output interactions between the tester and the implementation, and provides verdicts associated with these behaviors.

TEMA. The TEMA tool-chain [45] contains tools for different phases of the model-based testing process: test modeling, test design, test generation, and test debugging. TEMA models support two types of test data: localization tables and data tables. Localization tables are used to separate localized strings from the refinement machines, where the string is referred to by a symbolic name. Data tables can be used to store complex structured data, such as inputs given to the SUT, and they are accessed using Python code embedded in the transitions. The test generation presents a number of algorithms that use the models and the test objectives to produce the actual test-cases (also called tests). It performs online test-case generation, and after a test-case has been generated from the model, that respective test-case is executed on the SUT, and a Boolean value describing the result is returned to the test generator. This enables long-period random tests that have no other specific goals but to find system faults.

7.3 Timed Automata

Timed automata (TA) formalism is a finite automata model extended with clock variables and simple constraints over clocks and states. The timed automata model has been successfully used for verification of real-time systems, and forms the basis of several model-checking tools, e.g., UPPAAL. Some of the tools that use TA to generate test-cases are described below.

UPPAAL CoVer. CoVer [48] is a test-case generation tool that takes as input the timed automata model of a system, and generates abstract test-cases based on a coverage criterion expressed in an observer language. CoVer extends the UPPAAL model-checker with coverage-based test-case generation capabilities, by implementing an observer language expressive enough to capture coverage criteria like structural coverage (i.e., edge coverage) and semantic coverage (i.e., definition-use pairs). The tool uses a query language to specify from which timed automata should the tests be generated. The system is modeled as a network of TA, consisting of a controller that specifies the behavior of the system to be tested, and an environment that specifies the components surrounding the controller. The tool imposes some restrictions on the model, that is, the controller needs to be modeled by deterministic, input-enabled, and output-urgent timed automata. CoVer extends the query language of UPPAAL with the prefix "cover," which instructs the tool to generate a test-suite that fulfills the coverage criterion specified by an observer, the latter being a monitoring automaton formally describing the coverage criterion. To generate and select test-cases, CoVer performs state-space exploration, by on-the-fly reachability analysis of the timed automata state-space combined with the coverage criterion.

UPPAAL TRON. UPPAAL TRON [49] is an online testing tool that performs model-based black-box conformance testing of embedded systems. TRON replaces the environment of the system and performs two logical functions, stimulation and monitoring. Based on the timed sequence of input and output actions that have been performed, it stimulates the system model with the input that is deemed relevant, while it monitors the outputs and checks the conformance of these against the expected behavior. To perform such functions, TRON computes the set of states that the model can possibly occupy after the timed trace observed so far, based on the idea of symbolically computing the current possible set of states.

7.4 UML statecharts

UML statecharts, also known as UML state machines, are finite state machines extended with hierarchy and concurrency [82]. By using this model one can use state machines to model complex real-time systems. A statechart model shows the possible states and the transitions that cause a state change.

Conformiq. The commercial tool Conformiq [83] contains two distinctive parts: (i) one for test generation and the other one (ii) for modeling the specification. Conformiq Modeler is used to design a functional model in QML (a user interface markup language) that is an UML language and an action language derived from Java. Conformiq Designer generates test-cases using structural model coverage criteria. The generated abstract test-cases can be executed on the model, or can be transformed into executable test-cases for many different languages, such as C, Java, etc.

TestCast. The TestCast tool is a commercial tool that provides testing for UML statecharts that encapsulate the system behavior, and it assumes structural test coverage criteria. Abstract test-cases are automatically designed and generated based on graph search techniques, which are converted to executable test-scripts. There is little scientific documentation about the tool, so we refer the reader to the tool's website, for more information: http://www.elvior.com/test-generation/.

AGEDIS. This tool [32] is a research prototype that takes as input an UML model representing the behavioral model of the system, and the test generation directives, describing the test strategy. The latter are provided by the user as test purposes, using UML state diagrams for global model coverage at varying levels of detail. The execution engine presents each stimulus described in the abstract test-suite to the SUT, and observes the responses, waits for callbacks, and traps any thrown exceptions. The responses are compared with those predicted by the model, and a verdict is reached. Next, the test execution directives describe the testing interface to the SUT, and give the mappings from the model's abstractions to the concrete SUT interfaces, for control and observation.

ParTeG. ParTeG [35] is an Eclipse plug-in that generates test cases automatically, from UML state machines and class diagrams that are annotated with Object Constraint Language (OCL) expressions. The tool has the ability to satisfy combined coverage criteria, that is, transition-based coverage criteria (e.g., All-Transitions) can be combined with boundary-based coverage criteria (e.g., Multi-Dimensional). Assuming the combination of coverage criteria, the state machine paths are converted into executable test-cases, and the tool supports test goal monitoring so that already covered test goals are excluded from further test-case generations.

PrUDE. The tool [42] uses the Unified Modeling Language (UML) as graphical notation and the Prototype Verification System's Specification Language (PVS-SL) as formal notation. To facilitate industrial adoption, the tool provides: (i) a graphical interface in UML that completely hides the formal notation of PVS-SL, and (ii) automation using existing tools. The interface of PrUDE with UML is based on XMI, which provides an explicit interchange format for UML-based tools. The PrUDE tool provides support for consistency-checking, model-checking, proof-checking, and testing based on the PVS toolkit.

Tedeso. Tedeso [44] is a research model-based testing tool that supports the automatic generation of test-cases, according to different data and control coverage algorithms, and uses the category partition method [84] to generate abstract and executable test-cases. The generation process is based on annotated activity and sequence UML diagrams, with control and proprietary data constraints attached to nodes and transitions in those diagrams. These diagrams are then parsed to generate abstract test-cases that can be converted into executable test-cases and the associated test reports.

TestUml. The TestUml reserach prototype [54] proposes a testing framework for legacy Web applications, through semi-automatic test-case generation based on random walks on the UML model of the system. The tool uses a set of criteria (i.e., software metrics such as structural coverage criteria) as test stop criteria. Traditionally, such criteria are used apriori to guide the test-case generation process, but TestUml uses them at runtime, to also help the user in driving testing operations. TestUml uses WebUml-generated UML models and defines a set of test-cases. Then, it executes them and generates test results and coverage level reports. With TestUml, the user may verify testing coverage status step-by-step during test-case iterations and may decide (on-the-fly) when to stop testing. Alternatively, the user may define the testing coverage level apriori, so that TestUml executes test-cases until this level is reached.

LTG. The LEIRIOS Test Generator (LTG) [55] is a research prototype based on the symbolic animation of formal specifications (i.e, B machines, UML/OCL models, Z specifications) and various test generation strategies like cause-effect testing and boundary testing. The symbolic animation that the tool performs makes it possible to traverse the reachability graph of the formal model, and generate test-cases as sequences of operations. The generated abstract test-cases are then transformed into executable test-scripts.

Mista. Given a model-implementation description, MISTA [41] (a research tool) automatically generates executable test cases in the target language, and the test cases can then be executed against the system under test. The model-implementation description consists of a test model in function nets or UML, a model-implementation mapping that maps individual elements in a test model into target code, and user-provided helper code. Tests can be generated automatically to meet various coverage criteria of test models, such as reachability coverage (round-trip paths), sneak path, state coverage, transition coverage, depth coverage, and random generation.

Partial ordering and pairwise techniques can be applied to reduce the set of tests. Executable test scripts can be generated automatically in various languages and test frameworks (Java, C#), and the tool supports on-the-fly testing and online execution of existing tests.

7.5 The Coffee/Tea Vending Machine in UPPAAL CoVer

Generating abstract test-cases with CoVer consists of three steps. In this section, we present the tool and its test-case generation process for the Coffee/Tea Vending Machine introduced in Section 5.[3]

Step 1: Creating the formal model. We have modeled the Coffee/Tea Vending Machine in timed automata, with the machine itself being depicted in Fig. 6, and the use of the machine in Fig. 7. For more detail on TA modes, we refer the reader to the relevant literature [85, 86]. Since the TA paradigm allows measuring of elapsed time, we are able to capture information regarding the extra-functional behavior of the Coffee/Tea Vending Machine, in our model, yet the tool generates test-cases only for the functional behavior of the system.

Step 2: Provide the coverage criterion. CoVer supports two types of coverage criteria: *definition-use* coverage criteria, and *all edges* coverage criteria. In this example, we have chosen to generate test-cases based on the definition-use of the variable "coin," which is a type of structural criteria. To model this, we have used the observer and the system property specification guidelines presented on the tool's website.

Step 3: Generate the test-cases. The CoVer tool is called from the command line, and generates automatically a set of test-cases for the given coverage criteria. For this particular example, the tool has generated four test-cases, and in Fig. 8, we present the first test-cases in the set.

8. MODEL-BASED TESTING TOOLS FOR STOCHASTIC MODELS

For many software programs, probabilistic models are a useful asset in modeling statistical behavior, such that coverage testing is possible by automating test-case selection, execution and evaluation. In the following, we overview and discuss some the underlying models and tools found in our review of model-based testing of stochastic behavior, which are used for testing software designs.

---

[3] We have followed the UPPAAL CoVer tutorial from http://www.hessel.nu/cover/putting.php.

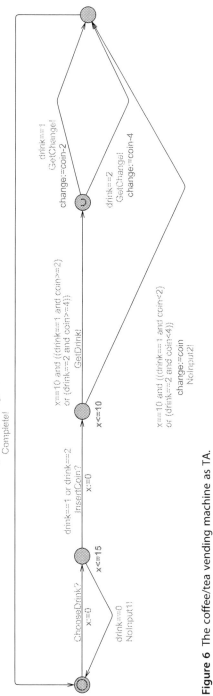

Figure 6 The coffee/tea vending machine as TA.

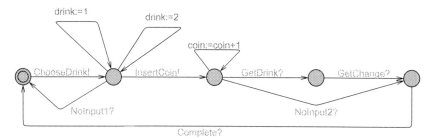

Figure 7 The user of the coffee/tea vending machine as TA.

```
===== Trace #1====================================
du<varid offset=1, edgeid User._id2_to__id2, edgeid User._id2_to__id2>
du<varid offset=1, edgeid User._id2_to__id2, edgeid Machine._id7_to__id5>
State:( User._id4 Machine._id9 ) x=0 drink=0 coin=0 change=0
Transitions:
User._id4->User._id3 { 1, ChooseDrink!, 1 }
Machine._id9->Machine._id8 { 1, ChooseDrink?, x := 0 }
State: ( User._id3 Machine._id8 ) x=0 drink=0 coin=0 change=0
Transitions: User._id3->User._id3 { 1, tau, drink := 2 }
State:( User._id3 Machine._id8 ) x=0 drink=2 coin=0 change=0
Transitions:
User._id3->User._id2 { 1, InsertCoin!, 1 }
Machine._id8->Machine._id7 { drink == 1 || drink == 2, InsertCoin?, x := 0 }
State: ( User._id2 Machine._id7 ) x=0 drink=2 coin=0 change=0
Transitions: User._id2->User._id2 { coin <= 10, tau, coin := coin + 1 }
State: ( User._id2 Machine._id7 ) x=0 drink=2 coin=1 change=0
Transitions: User._id2->User._id2 { coin <= 10, tau, coin := coin + 1 }
State: ( User._id2 Machine._id7 ) x=0 drink=2 coin=2 change=0
Transitions: User._id2->User._id2 { coin <= 10, tau, coin := coin + 1 }
State: ( User._id2 Machine._id7 ) x=0 drink=2 coin=3 change=0
Delay: 10
State: ( User._id2 Machine._id7 ) x=10 drink=2 coin=3 change=0 Transitions:
Machine._id7->Machine._id5 { x == 10 && (drink == 1 && coin < 2 || drink == 2 &&
coin < 4), NoInput2!, change := coin }
User._id2->User._id0 { 1, NoInput2?, 1 }
State:( User._id0 Machine._id5 ) x=10 drink=2 coin=3 change=3
```
Figure 8 Abstract test-case generated by CoVer.

8.1 Markov Chains

A Markov chain [87] is simply a sequence of random values in which the next value is in some way dependent on the current value, rather than being completely random. To generate test-cases from models, one needs to represent the system behavior and its constraints in a non-ambiguous way. However, the respective system behavior changes depending on how the system is used, that is, assuming various computational loads, an experienced or novice user, different usage frequencies etc. Modeling notations like Markov chains are appropriate abstractions of such *usage profiles* that characterize the operational use of a software system.

Markov chains have a simple structure and consequently they provide an intuitive view of the system execution. Markovian models allow test input sequences to be generated from multiple probability distributions, making the notation more general than other existing ones. In addition, the stopping criteria of the test-case generation algorithms based on Markov chain representations could lead to the system's reliability assessment, via the included failure information. One of the obvious drawbacks of the model is its somewhat poor scalability. The transition probabilities in the model are stored in a matrix that becomes hard to comprehend as the states and their transitions accumulate.

In the following, we describe two of the MBT tools that rely on Markov chains, after which we apply one of them on our running example.

MaTeLo Testing Tool. This is a commercial tool that has been developed in an European project named Markov Test Logic (MaTeLo) [88] and it is mainly targeted at deriving test-cases from the intended usage of the software under test, modeled as a Markov chain. The focus of MaTeLo is not on requirements coverage (although this could be considered as a secondary goal) but on covering the ways in which the software is intended to be used, in order to detect the most critical faults that could appear from the respective use. The input to MaTeLo that describes the usage profile can be given as a Message Sequence Chart (MSC), a UML sequence diagram, or a state-chart.

J Usage Model Builder Library (JUMBL). This research prototype [39] provides support for the automated test-case generation from usage models described in TML, the modeling language used in the tool to describe probabilities as constraints, along with simple objective functions that facilitate defining the probability distribution for a usage model, similar to those in Markov models. In comparison to MaTeLo, JUMBL does not provide any usage model editor, instead it allows users to develop usage models as spreadsheets, in text editors, or graphical editors. Another difference from MaTeLo is that it uses three different algorithms to automatically generate test-cases: (i) Postman-based test-generation, (ii) Random-based test-generation, and (iii) Probability-based test-generation, as well as a way of manually generating test-cases in an interactive editor.

8.2 The Coffee/Tea Vending Machine in MaTeLo

We have modeled the Coffee/Tea Vending Machine as a Markov chain depicted in Fig. 9. Since the model paradigm allows transition probabilities,

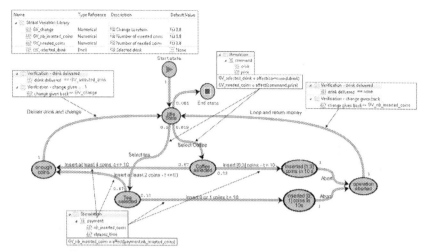

Figure 9 Coffee/tea vending machine modeled in MaTeLo.

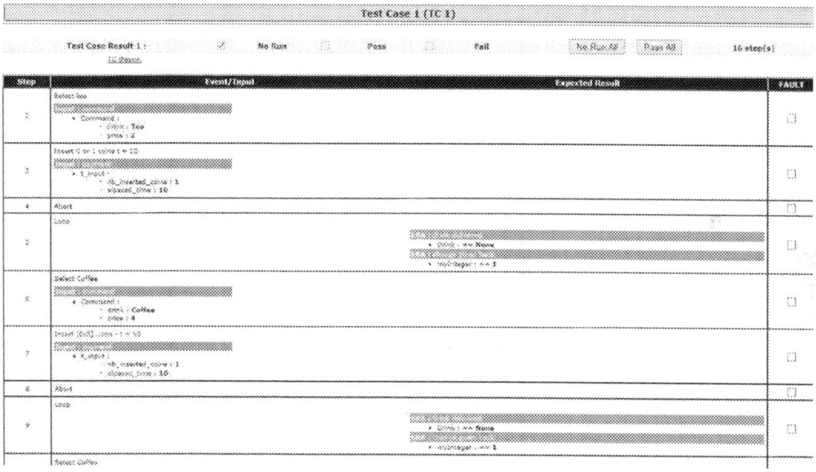

Figure 10 Test cases generated in MaTeLo for transition coverage.

we can impose extra conditions on the test data of the Vending Machine. Here, we employ MaTeLo to generate abstract test-cases. Assuming a transition coverage criterion, the test-cases are saved as a sequence of inputs/events and expected outputs, as shown in Fig. 10. For example, if the user selects tea (see Step 2 in Fig. 10) and inserts 1 coin (see Step 3 in Fig. 10), then the Coffee/Tea Vending Machine will return no drink and 1 coin as change (see Step 5 in Fig. 10).

9. MODEL-BASED TESTING TOOLS FOR DATA-FLOW MODELS

The usage of data-flow models in model-based design has been established as an essential paradigm in software development in embedded systems. In this scenario, there is a need for powerful tools for model-based testing in which automation is the key to more efficient development.

9.1 Simulink, Lustre and Function Block Diagram

Lustre [19], Simulink [89] and Function Block Diagram (FBD) [90] are examples of data-flow languages that describe the relation between software inputs and outputs, instead of describing the control flow of the software. Simulink started as a simulation environment and its semantics is informally described. Lustre, on the other hand, is a synchronous language for critical applications and has several features, such as formal semantics and modularity. Simulink and Lustre are models manipulating signals and computational blocks. For instance, Simulink has a graphical language where signals are wires connecting the various blocks (e.g., adders, transfer functions etc.).

Simulink has become a de-facto standard in many industrial domains, such as the automotive domain. International safety standards such as DO-178B or IEC 61508 strongly recommend the application of testing tools for Simulink models. In particular, they require the design engineers to provide test-cases that exercise the system according to structural coverage criteria. Therefore, there is a strong need to automate this process by using model-based testing tools.

Simulink Verification and Validation. This commercial tool[4] is created for automated tracing of requirements, compliance to modeling standards checking, and model coverage. The tool integrates a harness model used for executing the generated test-cases on the actual code, providing at the same time checks for the DO-178B and IEC 61508 industry standards.

An engineer using Simulink Verification and Validation can generate test-cases, test-harness models, and perform component testing via simulation. The resulting test-case can be used to check that the model satisfies requirements or can be applied on the implementation.

---

[4] For more details on Simulink Verification and Validation Tools we refer the reader to the following link: http://se.mathworks.com/products/simverification/.

GATel. This tool [38] has been developed by the French Nuclear Research Agency (CEA), with the main goal of automatically generating test-cases from specifications written in the Lustre language. The property to be tested, that is, the test objective, can be either an invariant property (expressed via assert directives), or a reachability property, both specified in Lustre. The properties that must be satisfied in at least one cycle are stated by reach directives. The test generation engine uses a constraint solver and outputs input sequences. The software is executed with these inputs in order to obtain the corresponding outputs. The tool automates the test selection and computes expected outputs at each cycle. The tool can be used for both unit and integration testing, at both model and implementation level.

Reactis. Reactis [43] is a commercial testing and validation tool implemented almost entirely in Standard ML (SML) and tailored for the paradigm in which an executable model of a program's behavior is developed prior to the actual implementation. Such executable models include Simulink and Stateflow (for MathWorks). Reactis can automatically generate test-cases to debug the model itself, but also to check conformance between the Simulink model and the C implementation. The tool allows users to specify a structural coverage criterion in order to indicate how exhaustive the testing should be. Reactis can also automatically check for violations of user-defined assertions regarding the functionality of the system, through manual instrumentations of the model. The assertions should remain true while the artifact executes, so the tool attempts to find violations of such assertions. When a violation is found, the tool provides a diagnostic feedback in the form of an execution sequence leading to the violation.

CompleteTest. CompleteTest[5] is a research testing tool that is automatically generating tests for FBD models. These models are used by an application generator and automatically transformed into executable code. CompleteTest can transform an FBD model into a formal representation with both functionality and timing information. This is done in CompleteTest by an automatic model-to-model transformation from FBDs to timed automata. CompleteTest is using the Uppaal model-checker as the underlying generator engine. The tool supports test-cases to be generated based on a test specification or requirement. In addition, CompleteTest can generate test-cases that satisfy different logic coverage criteria (e.g., decision coverage, condition Coverage, MCDC).

---

[5] For more details we refer the reader to the following link: http://www.completetest.org/.

9.2 The Coffee/Tea Vending Machine in CompleteTest

We have modeled the Coffee/Tea Vending Machine as an FBD model using Beremiz, an open-source editor for modeling FBDs in PLCOpen[6] standard format. As shown in Fig. 11, the model consists of different blocks and a timer that is operated by an internally generated clock. Based on the value of the input signals (e.g., ChooseDrink), the machine is calculating when the coffee is served. The model executes in a cyclic loop and the blocks are running without interruption. Using COMPLETETEST we have generated test-cases that fulfill decision coverage criteria, as shown in Fig. 12.

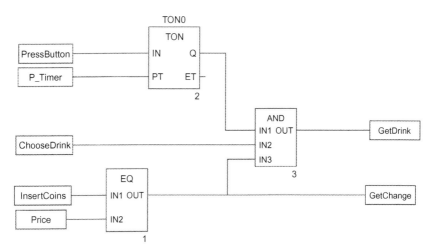

Figure 11 Coffee/tea vending machine modeled in function block diagram.

Step	Time	ChooseDrink	PressButton	InsertCoins	GetDrink	GetChange
1	1 s	10	false	4	false	0
2	2 s	15	true	38	false	0
3	5 s	15	true	38	false	0
4	6 s	14	false	40	false	1
5	7 s	8	true	40	false	0
6	9 s	8	true	40	false	1
7	10 s	8	true	40	false	0

Decision Coverage: 100,0 % User name: Mikael Johansson   Validate Test

Figure 12 Test cases generated in CompleteTest for decision coverage.

[6] The standard can be found at the following link: http://www.plcopen.org/.

The generated test-case consists of a sequence of input vectors, time information, and outputs. In Fig. 12, when the specification agrees with the actual output, the tool displays the outputs in light gray (or green color). Otherwise the outputs are displayed in dark gray (or red color) revealing a bug in the program or a problem in the specification.

10. RESULTS AND DISCUSSION

The results of this chapter are mainly captured in Fig. 13A, F, and B, as follows:

- As shown in Fig. 13A a large majority of model-based testing tools rely on transition-based notations (23) and pre/post notations (5). Just a few tools can handle stochastic (2) and data-flow notations (3). This is in line with two main facts: (i) transition-based notations are a simple and effective way of capturing system behavior, and (ii) testing for stochastic behavior assumes that testers create stochastic models of software behavior rather than individual test-cases, which is not common practice in industry.
- Regarding test execution, 18 out of 33 model-based testing tools that we have reviewed support only offline test execution, while 4 are supporting online test execution. In addition, as shown in Fig. 13F, 8 tools can use a test harness both online and offline. The result is favoring offline test-case generation, which might be due to the fact that online testing is preferred when testing non-deterministic systems, but many implementations are merely deterministic; the combination of online and offline testing assumes on-the-fly and monitoring techniques besides offline algorithms, which fewer tools are able to provide.
- All 33 of the model-based testing tools that we have studied support functional artifacts, while 3 are dealing also with extra-functional artifacts as well (see Fig. 13B). From our review none of the considered model-based testing tools are dealing directly with architectural artifacts. We have to mention that during the search process we have discovered a study [91] on architectural testing that proposes a proof-of-concept tool named ABATT. As the tool is just briefly described and no information is provided on the design of the prototype tool, we have decided to disregard it from the collected tools. However, we consider it an encouraging result towards a mainstream adoption of model-based testing tools for architectural artifacts.
- Regarding the mapping of tests, 25 of the model-based testing tools can generate executable tests while 8 tools are just generating abstract tests.

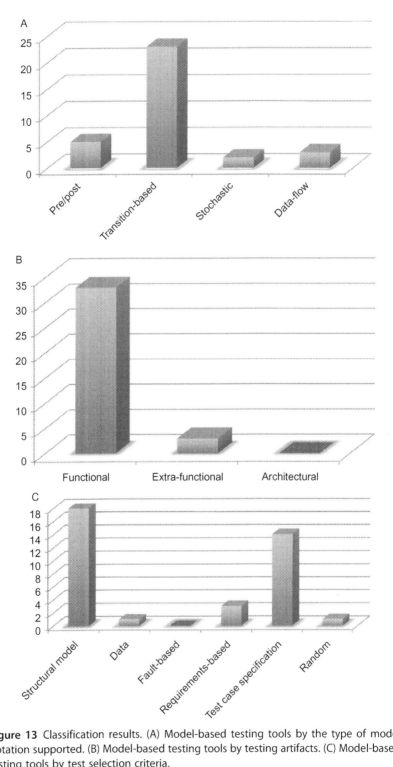

Figure 13 Classification results. (A) Model-based testing tools by the type of model notation supported. (B) Model-based testing tools by testing artifacts. (C) Model-based testing tools by test selection criteria.

(Continued)

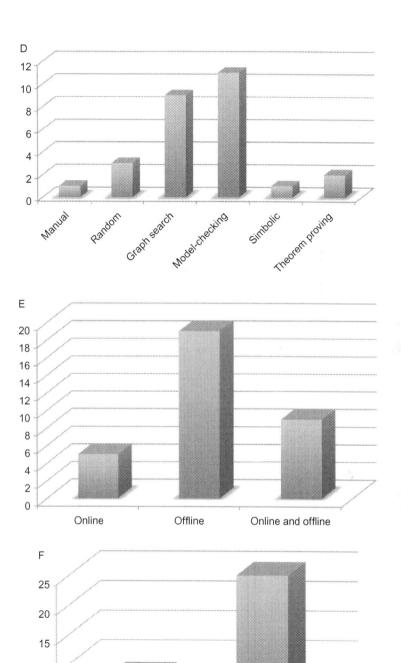

Figure 13—Cont'd (D) Model-based testing tools by test generation method. (E) Model-based testing tools by technology. (F) Model-based testing tools by test mapping.

This result reinforces the ultimate goal of model-based testing frameworks: automating the generation of test-cases that would eventually be run against the system-under-test.

Tool-related insights We have chosen to apply on a toy example four representative model-based testing tools, that is, **ProTest**, **UPPAAL CoVer**, **MaTeLo**, and **CompleteTest**, each assuming a different underlying notation. This endeavor has provided us with useful insights on the type of information contained in the output of each tool, and their possible applicability to a larger extent. Here, we will summarize our findings.

ProTest is a research prototype that uses B machines as the specification model, and model-checking as the test generation method. The tool's user interface is intuitive and easy to grasp. The tester's input to the tool consists basically in introducing the variables' input values, and the rules that constrain the behavior of the system. The tool computes automatically all the possible combinations of variable values that result by executing the model, which represent the test-cases. The simple and intuitive nature of the tool makes it a good candidate for practical use, on untimed system models; the information contained in a generated test-case is basic, in the sense that one cannot observe the system operationally, by following its transitions and their impact on variable values, but rather the final result only. One possible advantage is the fact that the tool could be extended with support for generating test-cases by theorem proving, since it relies on B machines that are backed by deductive analysis theories also. Such an extension would serve the cases in which the state-space explosion problem is encountered.

UPPAAL CoVer is a research prototype that uses networks of timed automata as the input model of the system that consists of a controller and the environment, and model-checking for generating test-cases. In contrast to ProTest, Cover can be applied to timed systems; however, the tool cannot handle generating test-cases for real-time requirements, for instance, response times or end-to-end deadlines. On the other hand, the observer language could be extended in this direction. When applied on the vending machine example, the user is presented with the trace of execution, as the actual test-case. Such trace describes the system operationally, with details on transitions and possible time delays associated with particular states. The information contained in the abstract test-cases is rich, yet the output is not directly applicable to test implementations.

MaTeLo is a commercial tool (developed by ALL4TEC, France) that uses Markov chains as the underlying model, and model-checking method for generating test-cases. The tool is compliant with numerous industrial test frameworks, and unlike the other tools, it allows for specifying usage scenarios by different probability distributions. The model describes the system functionally, however timing information is also encoded such that the elapsed time between states is presented in the computed test-case. The tool provides rich information on the model and the resulting test-case also. One can visualize the library of global variables, whose values change while the model executes. Consequently, the tool can be applied on timed systems to asses the system's reliability via the probabilistic testing. MaTeLo has already been applied on industrial use-cases in the European projects MBAT (transportation domain) and iFEST (process control domain), with encouraging results.

CompleteTest is a research prototype that uses function block diagrams (FBDs) as the underlying modeling notation, and model-checking for generating executable test-cases. The application of CompleteTest on our running example revealed the usability of the tool, and its practical touch. Although timed automata is the formal model that encodes each FBD's behavior, this is hidden from the user, who does not have to master the associated formal underpinnings. For any given set of inputs, the tester is supposed to supply the expected outputs, respectively, and the tool uses model-checking to evaluate whether the real output is equal to the expected output, in each case. The coverage criteria does not include real-time requirements, yet the tool caters for a large set of coverage criteria, as presented previously. The tool has been successfully applied in industry, on real-sized systems from the transportation domain, and the engineers have reported an efficiency increase in testing of 80% [92].

11. CONCLUSIONS

In this chapter, we have presented an overview of the most prominent state-of-the-art tools for model-based testing of requirements-based designs. The model-based testing tools that we have reviewed rely on different classes of underlying notations, which give one hints on their applicability and expressiveness. The application of the chosen representative tools on the toy example has helped us to gain insight in their inner functionality, as well as in some of their advantages and limitations. In this chapter, we have relied on the taxonomy proposed by Utting *et al.* [4], which we have extended with two new dimensions: the test artifact, and mapping of tests. The test artifact represents the type of information encoded in the model for the purpose of testing (i.e., functional behavior, extra-functional behavior, or the architectural description), while the mapping specifies if the tools provide mapping rules that connect the model and the implementation, in order to allow the transformation of the generated test-cases into executable ones.

Based on our proposed taxonomy, we have classified and reviewed 33 model-based testing tools that can handle modeling, test-case generation, and possibly test-case execution, and that we consider mature enough to potentially impact both state-of-the-art and state-of practice. The review process itself has allowed us to observe different trends and gaps in current model-based testing frameworks, which we have reported in the results and discussion section. For instance, we have observed that only a small proportion of the presented frameworks consider generating test-cases for extra-functional models, or software architectures. Last but not least, we have selected four of these tools (ProTest, UPPAAL Cover, MaTeLo, and CompleteTest) and apply them on a running example to show the inner-workings from model creation to test execution. The endeavor has provided us with valuable insights with respect to the state-of-the-art of model-based testing tools that focus on requirements-based designs, as well as with a deeper understanding of the gaps that need to be addressed in the future.

ACKNOWLEDGMENTS
The authors would like to thank Eduard Enoiu for his valuable comments on the CompleteTest tool. This research has received funding from the ARTEMIS JU, grant agreement number 269335, and from VINNOVA, the Swedish Governmental Agency for Innovation Systems, within the MBAT project.

REFERENCES
[1] M. Utting, B. Legeard, Practical Model-Based Testing: A Tools Approach, Morgan Kaufmann, 2010.
[2] J. Boberg, Early fault detection with model-based testing, in: Proceedings of the 7th ACM SIGPLAN Workshop on ERLANG, 2008, pp. 9–20.
[3] G. Fraser, F. Wotawa, P.E. Ammann, Testing with model checkers: a survey, Softw. Test. Verif. Rel. 19 (3) (2009) 215–261.
[4] M. Utting, A. Pretschner, B. Legeard, A taxonomy of model-based testing approaches, Softw. Test. Verif. Rel. 22 (5) (2012) 297–312.
[5] M. Utting, A. Pretschner, B. Legeard, A taxonomy of model-based testing, 2006).
[6] M. Shafique, Y. Labiche, A systematic review of state-based test tools, Int. J. Softw. Tools Technol. Transfer (2013) 1–18.
[7] A.C. Dias Neto, R. Subramanyan, M. Vieira, G.H. Travassos, A survey on model-based testing approaches: a systematic review, in: Proceedings of the 1st ACM International Workshop on Empirical Assessment of Software Engineering Languages and Technologies: Held in Conjunction with the 22nd IEEE/ACM International Conference on Automated Software Engineering (ASE 2007), 2007, pp. 31–36.
[8] J.M. Spivey, J. Abrial, The Z Notation, Prentice-Hall, 1992.

[9] J.-R. Abrial, M.K. Lee, D. Neilson, P. Scharbach, I.H. Sørensen, The B-method, in: VDM'91 Formal Software Development Methods, 1991, pp. 398–405.

[10] J.B. Warmer, A.G. Kleppe, The Object Constraint Language: Precise Modeling With UML (Addison-Wesley Object Technology Series), Addison-Wesley Longman Publishing Co., Inc., 1998

[11] G.T. Leavens, A.L. Baker, C. Ruby, JML: a notation for detailed design, in: Behavioral Specifications of Businesses and SystemsSpringer, 1999, pp. 175–188.

[12] J.S. Fitzgerald, P.G. Larsen, M. Verhoef, Vienna development method, in: Wiley Encyclopedia of Computer Science and EngineeringWiley Online Library, 2008.

[13] M. Barnett, K.R.M. Leino, W. Schulte, The Spec# programming system: an overview, in: Construction and Analysis of Safe, Secure, and Interoperable Smart DevicesSpringer, 2005, pp. 49–69.

[14] C. Bolchini, D. Sciuto, Finite State Machine, 1995.

[15] D. Harel, Statecharts: a visual formalism for complex systems, Sci. comput. program. 8 (3) (1987) 231–274.

[16] J. Tretmans, Model based testing with labelled transition systems, in: Formal Methods and TestingSpringer, 2008, pp. 1–38.

[17] D.K. Kaynar, N. Lynch, R. Segala, F. Vaandrager, The theory of timed I/O automata, in: Synthesis Lectures on Distributed Computing TheoryMorgan & Claypool Publishers, 2010, pp. 1–137.

[18] J.G. Kemeny, J.L. Snell, Finite Markov Chains, vol. 356, van Nostrand, 1960.

[19] D. Pilaud, N. Halbwachs, J. Plaice, LUSTRE: a declarative language for programming synchronous systems, in: Proceedings of the 14th Annual ACM Symposium on Principles of Programming Languages (14th POPL 1987), ACM, 1987, pp. 178–188.

[20] J.B. Dabney, T.L. Harman, Mastering Simulink 4, Prentice Hall PTR, 2001.

[21] N. Medvidovic, R.N. Taylor, A classification and comparison framework for software architecture description languages, IEEE Trans. Softw. Eng. 26 (1) (2000) 70–93.

[22] A. Bertolino, P. Inverardi, H. Muccini, Software architecture-based analysis and testing: a look into achievements and future challenges, Computing 95 (8) (2013) 633–648.

[23] S. Rapps, E.J. Weyuker, Selecting software test data using data flow information, IEEE Trans. Softw. Eng. 11 (4) (1985) 367–375.

[24] P.E. Black, V. Okun, Y. Yesha, Mutation operators for specifications, in: Proceedings of the Fifteenth IEEE International Conference on Automated Software Engineering (ASE 2000), 2000, pp. 81–88.

[25] B.A. Kitchenham, S.L. Pfleeger, L.M. Pickard, P.W. Jones, D.C. Hoaglin, K. El Emam, J. Rosenberg, Preliminary guidelines for empirical research in software engineering, IEEE Trans. Softw. Eng. 28 (8) (2002) 721–734.

[26] J. Zander, I. Schieferdecker, P.J. Mosterman, Model-Based Testing for Embedded Systems, CRC Press, 2011.

[27] E. Farchi, A. Hartman, S.S. Pinter, Using a model-based test generator to test for standard conformance, IBM Syst. J. 41 (1) (2002) 89–110.

[28] J. Ernits, R. Roo, J. Jacky, M. Veanes, Model-based testing of web applications using NModel, in: Testing of Software and Communication SystemsSpringer, 2009, pp. 211–216.

[29] J. Jacky, PyModel: model-based testing in python, in: Proceedings of the Python for Scientific Computing Conference, 2011.

[30] M. Veanes, C. Campbell, W. Grieskamp, W. Schulte, N. Tillmann, L. Nachmanson, Model-based testing of object-oriented reactive systems with spec explorer, in: Formal methods and testingSpringer, 2008, pp. 39–76.

[31] H. Achkar, Model based testing of web applications, in: Proceedings of 9th Annual STANZ, Australia, 2010.

[32] A. Hartman, K. Nagin, The AGEDIS tools for model based testing, SIGSOFT Softw. Eng. Notes 29 (4) (2004) 129–132.

[33] A. Huima, Implementing conformiq qtronic, in: Testing of Software and Communicating SystemsSpringer, 2007, pp. 1–12.

[34] S. Weißleder, B.-H. Schlingloff, Deriving input partitions from UML models for automatic test generation, in: Models in Software EngineeringSpringer, 2008, pp. 151–163.

[35] D. Sokenou, S. Weißleder, ParTeG-integrating model-based testing and model transformations, in: Software Engineering, 2010, pp. 23–24.

[36] K. Stobie, Model based testing in practice at Microsoft, Electron. Notes Theor. Comput. Sci. 111 (2005) 5–12.

[37] M. Barnett, W. Grieskamp, L. Nachmanson, W. Schulte, N. Tillmann, M. Veanes, Towards a tool environment for model-based testing with AsmL, in: Formal Approaches to Software TestingSpringer, 2004, pp. 252–266.

[38] B. Marre, A. Arnould, Test sequences generation from LUSTRE descriptions: GATEL, in: Proceedings of the Fifteenth IEEE International Conference on Automated Software Engineering (ASE 2000), 2000, pp. 229–237.

[39] S.J. Prowell, JUMBL: a tool for model-based statistical testing, in: Proceedings of the 36th Annual Hawaii International Conference on System Sciences, 2003, p. 9.

[40] H. Le Guen, T. Thelin, Practical experiences with statistical usage testing, in: Eleventh Annual International Workshop on Software Technology and Engineering Practice, 2003, pp. 87–93.

[41] D. Xu, L. Thomas, M. Kent, T. Mouelhi, Y. Le Traon, A model-based approach to automated testing of access control policies, in: Proceedings of the 17th ACM Symposium on Access Control Models and Technologies, 2012, pp. 209–218.

[42] I. Traoré, An integrated V&V environment for critical systems development, in: 21st IEEE International Requirements Engineering Conference (RE 2013), 2001, p. 287.

[43] S. Sims, D.C. DuVarney, Experience report: the reactis validation tool, ACM SIGPLAN Not. 42 (9) (2007) 137–140.

[44] C. Budnik, et al., An integrated model-driven approach for mechatronic systems testing, in: IEEE Fifth International Conference on Software Testing, Verification and Validation (ICST 2012), 2012, pp. 447–456.

[45] T. Takala, M. Katara, J. Harty, Experiences of system-level model-based GUI testing of an Android application, in: IEEE Fourth International Conference on Software Testing, Verification and Validation (ICST 2011), 2011, pp. 377–386.

[46] C. Jard, T. Jéron, TGV: theory, principles and algorithms, Int. J. Softw. Tools Technol. Transfer 7 (4) (2005) 297–315.

[47] A. Belinfante, JTorX: a tool for on-line model-driven test derivation and execution, in: Tools and Algorithms for the Construction and Analysis of Systems, Springer, 2010, pp. 266–270.

[48] A. Hessel, P. Pettersson, CoVer-a real-time test case generation tool, in: 19th IFIP International Conference on Testing of Communicating Systems and 7th International Workshop on Formal Approaches to Testing of Software, 2007.

[49] K.G. Larsen, M. Mikucionis, B. Nielsen, A. Skou, Testing real-time embedded software using UPPAAL-TRON: an industrial case study, in: Proceedings of the 5th ACM International Conference on Embedded Software, 2005, pp. 299–306.

[50] S. Berghofer, T. Nipkow, Random testing in Isabelle/HOL, in: SEFM, vol. 4, 2004, pp. 230–239.

[51] F. Bouquet, C. Grandpierre, B. Legeard, F. Peureux, A test generation solution to automate software testing, in: Proceedings of the 3rd International Workshop on Automation of Software Test, 2008, pp. 45–48.

[52] M. Satpathy, M. Leuschel, M. Butler, ProTest: an automatic test environment for B specifications, Electron. Notes Theor. Comput. Sci. 111 (2005) 113–136.

[53] D. Dranidis, K. Bratanis, F. Ipate, JSXM: a tool for automated test generation, in: Software Engineering and Formal Methods, Springer, 2012, pp. 352–366.

[54] C. Bellettini, A. Marchetto, A. Trentini, TestUml: user-metrics driven web applications testing, in: Proceedings of the 2005 ACM Symposium on Applied Computing, 2005, pp. 1694–1698.

[55] E. Bernard, F. Bouquet, A. Charbonnier, B. Legeard, F. Peureux, M. Utting, E. Torreborre, Model-based testing from UML models, in: GI Jahrestagung, 2006, pp. 223–230(2).

[56] Inc Mathworks, SimulinkVerification and Validation™ User's Guide, 2004. http://www.mathworks.com.

[57] E.P. Enoiu, A. Čaušević, T.J. Ostrand, E.J. Weyuker, D. Sundmark, P. Pettersson, Automated test generation using model checking: an industrial evaluation, Int. J. Softw. Tools Technol. Transfer (2014) 1–19.

[58] H.-M. Hörcher, Improving software tests using Z specifications, in: ZUM'95: The Z Formal Specification Notation, Springer, 1995, pp. 152–166.

[59] H.-M. Hoercher, J. Peleska, Using formal specifications to support software testing, Softw. Qual. J. 4 (4) (1995) 309–327.

[60] R.J. Nelson, Simplest normal truth functions, J. Symbol. Log. 20 (02) (1955) 105–108.

[61] J. Dick, A. Faivre, Automating the generation and sequencing of test cases from model-based specifications, in: FME'93: Industrial-Strength Formal Methods, 1993, pp. 268–284.

[62] T. Santen, B. Wolff, A structure preserving encoding of Z in Isabelle/HOL, in: TPHOLs '96 Proceedings of the 9th International Conference on Theorem Proving in Higher Order Logics, Springer, 1996, pp. 283–298.

[63] S. Helke, T. Neustupny, T. Santen, Automating test case generation from Z specifications with Isabelle, in: ZUM'97: The Z Formal Specification Notation, Springer, 1997, pp. 52–71.

[64] K. Lano, H. Haughton, Formal development in B abstract machine notation, Inform. Softw. Technol. 37 (5) (1995) 303–316.

[65] E.W. Dijkstra, E.W. Dijkstra, E.W. Dijkstra, E.W. Dijkstra, A Discipline of Programming, vol. 4, Prentice-Hall, 1976.

[66] B. Legeard, F. Peureux, M. Utting, Automated boundary testing from Z and B, in: FME 2002: Formal Methods–Getting IT Right, Springer, 2002, pp. 221–236.

[67] F. Bouquet, B. Legeard, F. Peureux, CLPS-B–a constraint solver for B, in: Tools and Algorithms for the Construction and Analysis of Systems, Springer, 2002, pp. 188–204.

[68] M. Leuschel, M. Butler, ProB: a model checker for B, in: FME 2003: Formal Methods, Springer, 2003, pp. 855–874.

[69] Y. Gurevich, Evolving algebras 1993: lipari guide, in: Specification and Validation Methods, 1995, pp. 9–36.

[70] L. De Alfaro, T.A. Henzinger, Interface automata, ACM SIGSOFT Softw. Eng. Notes 26 (5) (2001) 109–120.

[71] Y. Hardy, W.-H. Steeb, Finite state machines, in: Classical and Quantum Computing, Springer, 2001, pp. 229–250.

[72] V. Alagar, K. Periyasamy, Extended finite state machine, in: Specification of Software Systems, Springer, 2011, pp. 105–128.

[73] R. Alur, C. Courcoubetis, M. Yannakakis, Distinguishing tests for nondeterministic and probabilistic machines, in: Proceedings of the Twenty-Seventh Annual ACM Symposium on Theory of Computing, 1995, pp. 363–372.

[74] A.V. Aho, A.T. Dahbura, D. Lee, M.U. Uyar, An optimization technique for protocol conformance test generation based on UIO sequences and rural Chinese postman tours, IEEE Trans. Commun. 39 (11) (1991) 1604–1615.

[75] D. Lee, M. Yannakakis, Testing finite-state machines: state identification and verification, IEEE Trans. Comput. 43 (3) (1994) 306–320.

[76] D. Lee, M. Yannakakis, Principles and methods of testing finite state machines–a survey, Proc. IEEE 84 (8) (1996) 1090–1123.

[77] A. Sinha, C.E. Williams, P. Santhanam, A measurement framework for evaluating model-based test generation tools, IBM Syst. J. 45 (3) (2006) 501–514.

[78] M. Benjamin, D. Geist, A. Hartman, Y. Wolfsthal, G. Mas, R. Smeets, A study in coverage-driven test generation, in: Proceedings of the 36th Design Automation Conference, 1999, pp. 970–975.

[79] D.L. Dill, The Mur ϕ verification system, in: Computer Aided Verification1996, pp. 390–393.

[80] V. Chinnapongse, I. Lee, O. Sokolsky, S. Wang, P.L. Jones, Model-based testing of GUI-driven applications, in: Software Technologies for Embedded and Ubiquitous SystemsSpringer, 2009, pp. 203–214.

[81] J. Tretmans, E. Brinksma, Torx: Automated model-based testing, 2003.

[82] J. Rumbaugh, I. Jacobson, G. Booch, The Unified Modeling Language Reference Manual, Pearson Higher Education, 2004.

[83] M. Sarma, P. Murthy, S. Jell, A. Ulrich, Model-based testing in industry: a case study with two MBT tools, in: Proceedings of the 5th Workshop on Automation of Software Test, 2010, pp. 87–90.

[84] T.J. Ostrand, M.J. Balcer, The category-partition method for specifying and generating fuctional tests, Commun. ACM 31 (6) (1988) 676–686.

[85] K.G. Larsen, P. Pettersson, W. Yi, Uppaal in a nutshell, Int. J. Softw. Tools Technol. Transfer 1 (1) (1997) 134–152.

[86] G. Behrmann, A. David, K.G. Larsen, A tutorial on uppaal, in: Formal Methods for the Design of Real-Time Systems, Springer, 2004, pp. 200–236.

[87] J.R. Norris, Markov Chains, Cambridge University Press, 1998, (2008).

[88] A. Guiotto, B. Acquaroli, A. Martelli, MaTeLo: automated testing suite for software validation, in: DASIA 2003, vol. 532, 2003, p. 30.

[89] Inc MathWorks, MATLAB: The Language of Technical Computing, Desktop Tools and Development Environment, Version 7, vol. 9, MathWorks, 2005.

[90] R.W. Lewis, Programming Industrial Control Systems Using IEC 1131-3, (50), IET, 1998.

[91] Z. Jin, J. Offutt, Deriving tests from software architectures, in: Proceedings of the 12th International Symposium on Software Reliability Engineering (ISSRE 2001), 2001, pp. 308–313.

[92] E.P. Enoiu, A. Causevic, T. Ostrand, E. Weyuker, D. Sundmark, P. Pettersson, Automated test generation using model-checking: an industrial evaluation, Int. J. Softw. Tools Technol. Transfer 1 (1) (2014) 1–18. http://www.es.mdh.se/publications/3738-.

ABOUT THE AUTHORS

Raluca Marinescu is a PhD student at Mälardalen University, School of Innovation, Design and Engineering, Embedded Systems Division, Västerås, Sweden, working in the Formal Modeling and Analysis of Embedded Systems group. She has received a M.Sc. in Electronics from Politehnica University of Bucharest in June 2009 and a M.Sc. in Computer Science from Mälardalen University in June 2011. Her main research interests are model-based analysis and testing of embedded systems.

Cristina Seceleanu is Associate Professor at Mälardalen University, School of Innovation, Design and Engineering, Embedded Systems Division, Västerås, Sweden, and leader of the Formal Modeling and Analysis of Embedded Systems research group. She holds a M.Sc. in Electronics (Polytechnic University of Bucharest, Romania, 1993) and a Ph.D. in Computer Science (Turku Centre for Computer Science, Finland, 2005). Her research focuses on developing formal models and verification techniques for predictable real-time and adaptive systems. She currently is and has been involved as organizer, co-organizer, and chair for relevant conferences and workshops in computer engineering, and is a member of the Editorial Board of the International Journal of Electrical and Computer Engineering Systems and the International Journal of Embedded and Real-Time Communication Systems.

Héléne Le Guen received her PhD in Model-based Testing from the University of Rennes (FRANCE) in 2005. Since 1999, she is a development and research engineer in ALL4TEC and has participated to the development of MaTeLo tool. Her main interests include model-based testing, probabilities and linking industrial needs with research solutions.

Paul Pettersson is Deputy Vice-Chancellor and Professor of Real-Time Systems, specialized in modeling and verification, at Mälardalen University in Sweden. He received a Ph.D. in Computer Systems in 1999 and was appointed as Associated Professor (Docent) in Computer Science in 2006 at Uppsala University in Sweden. He joined Mälardalen University in 2006 and has been the Deputy Vice-Chancellor since 2012. Prof. Pettersson received the CAV award, together with Prof. Kim G. Larsen and Prof. Wang Yi, in 2013 "for developing UPPAAL which is the foremost tool suite for the automated analysis and verification of real-time systems." His current research interests include component-based modeling and model-based verification and testing of embedded and real-time systems. He is cofounder of several tools including UPPAAL (for model-checking of timed automata models), TIMES (for real-time schedulability analysis), and CompleteTest (for model-based testing of IEC 61131 models). He is also co-founder of the spin-off company UP4ALL International AB.

CHAPTER FOUR

Preference Incorporation in Evolutionary Multiobjective Optimization: A Survey of the State-of-the-Art

Slim Bechikh*, Marouane Kessentini*, Lamjed Ben Said[†], Khaled Ghédira[†]

*SBSE Lab, Computer and Information Science Department, University of Michigan, Dearborn, Michigan, USA
[†]SOIE (Stratégies d'Optimisation et Informatique intelligentE) Lab, Computer Science Department, University of Tunis (ISG–Tunis), Tunis, Tunisia

Contents

Abstract

After using Evolutionary Algorithms (EAs) for solving multiobjective optimization problems for more than two decades, the incorporation of the decision maker's (DM's) preferences within the evolutionary process has finally become an active research area. In fact, EAs have demonstrated their effectiveness and efficiency in providing a well-converged and well-distributed approximation of the Pareto front. However, in reality, the DM is not interested in discovering the whole Pareto front rather than

Advances in Computers, Volume 98
ISSN 0065-2458
http://dx.doi.org/10.1016/bs.adcom.2015.03.001

141

approximating the portion of the front that best matches his/her preferences, i.e., the Region Of Interest. For this reason, many new preference-based Multiobjective Optimization EAs (MOEAs), which are mostly variations of existing methods, have been recently published in the specialized literature. The purpose of this chapter is to summarize and organize the information on these current approaches in an attempt to motivate researchers to further focus on hybridizing between decision making and evolutionary multiobjective optimization research fields; consequently facilitating the DM's task when selecting the final alternative to realize. Hence, a summary of the main preference-based MOEAs is provided together with a brief criticism that includes their pros and cons. Furthermore, we propose a classification of such type of algorithms based on the DM's preference information structure. Finally, the future trends in this research area and some possible paths for future research are outlined.

ABBREVIATIONS

AS absolutely satisfying objective value
ASF achievement scalarizing function
BC-EMOA Brain-Computer Evolutionary Multiobjective Optimization Algorithm
DF desirability function
DF-SMS-EMOA Desirability Function-based S Metric Selection-based Evolutionary Multiobjective Optimization Algorithm
DM decision maker
DPs diversity problems
DTLZ Deb–Thiele–Laumans–Zitzler
DWA dynamic weighted aggregation
EA Evolutionary Algorithm
EMO evolutionary multiobjective optimization
G-MOEA Guided-Multiobjective Optimization Evolutionary Algorithm
g-NSGA-II goal-based Nondominated Sorting Genetic Algorithm-II
IBEA Indicator-Based Evolutionary Algorithm
iTDEA interactive Territory Defining Evolutionary Algorithm
LBS light beam search
MCDM multicriteria decision making
MI marginally infeasible objective value
MMPSO MaxiMin particle swarm optimization
MOEA Multiobjective Optimization Evolutionary Algorithm
MOP multiobjective optimization problem
MROI multiple regions of interest
NEMO necessary preference-enhanced evolutionary multiobjective optimizer
NN-DM neural network-based decision maker
NOSGA Nonoutranking Sorting Genetic Algorithm
NSGA-II Nondominated Sorting Genetic Algorithm-II
NSPSO nondominated sorting particle swarm optimization
PBEA Preference-Based Evolutionary Algorithm
PDP Pareto dominance preservation
PI-EMOA Progressively interactive evolutionary multiobjective optimization algorithm
PSO particle swarm optimization

R-NSGA-II reference point-based NSGA-II
r-NSGA-II reference-solution-based Nondominated Sorting Genetic Algorithm-II
ROI region of interest
ROR robust ordinal regression
RPSO-SS reference point-based particle swam optimization using a steady-state approach
RWA random weighted aggregation
SC spread control
SCAD SCAlability Demonstration with respect to the number of objectives
SIBEA Simple Indicator-Based Evolutionary Algorithm
SOP single-objective optimization problem
SQP sequential quadratic programming
SVM support vector machine
TDEA Territory Defining Evolutionary Algorithm
VFOP value function optimization problem

1. INTRODUCTION

Most real world optimization problems encountered in practice involve multiple criteria to be considered simultaneously [1,2]. These criteria, also called objectives, are often conflicting. The decision on a cell phone purchase, for instance, among other things, can be influenced by several criteria such as the price, the battery life, the weight, the performance, and so forth. Usually, there is no single solution that is optimal with respect to all these objectives at the same time, but rather many different designs exist which are incomparable *per se*. Consequently, contrary to single-objective optimization problems (SOPs) where we look for the solution presenting the best performance, the resolution of a multiobjective optimization problem (MOP) yields a set of compromise solutions presenting the optimal trade-offs between the different objectives. When plotted in the objective space, the set of compromise solutions is called the Pareto front. The main goal in multiobjective optimization is to find a well-converged and well-distributed approximation of the Pareto front from which the decision maker (DM) will subsequently select his/her preferred alternative. A MOP consists in minimizing or maximizing an objective function vector under some constraints. The general form of a MOP is defined in (1) [1,2]:

$$\begin{cases} \text{Min } f(x) = [f_1(x), f_2(x), \ldots, f_M(x)]^T \\ g_j(x) \geq 0 \quad j = 1, \ldots, P; \\ h_k(x) = 0 \quad k = 1, \ldots, Q; \\ x_i^{\text{L}} \leq x_i \leq x_i^{\text{U}} \quad i = 1, \ldots, n. \end{cases} \tag{1}$$

where f_i is the ith objective function, M is the number of objective functions, P is the number of inequality constraints, Q is the number of equality constraints, x_i^L and x_i^U correspond to the lower and upper bounds of the variable x_i. A solution x_i satisfying the $(P+Q)$ constraints is said feasible and the set of all feasible solutions defines the feasible search space denoted by Ω. In this formulation, we consider a minimization MOP since maximization can be easily turned to minimization based on the duality principle by multiplying each objective function by -1.

The resolution of a MOP yields a set of trade-off solutions, called Pareto optimal solutions or nondominated solutions, and the image of this set in the objective space is called the Pareto front. Hence, the resolution of a MOP consists in approximating the whole Pareto front. In the following, we give some background definitions related to multiobjective optimization:

Definition 1.1

Pareto optimality

A solution $x^* \in \Omega$ is Pareto optimal if $\forall x \in \Omega$ and $I = \{1, ..., M\}$ either $\forall m \in I$ we have $f_m(x) = f_m(x^*)$ or there is at least one $m \in I$ such that $f_m(x) > f_m(x^*)$.

The definition of Pareto optimality states that x^* is Pareto optimal if no feasible vector x exists which would improve some objective without causing a simultaneous worsening in at least another one. Other important definitions associated with Pareto optimality are essentially the following:

Definition 1.2

Pareto dominance

A solution $u = (u_1, u_2, ..., u_n)$ is said to dominate another solution $v = (v_1, v_2, ..., v_n)$ (denoted by $f(u) \preceq f(v)$) if and only if $f(u)$ is partially less than $f(v)$. In other words, $\forall m \in \{1, ..., M\}$ we have $f_m(u) \leq f_m(v)$ and $\exists m \in \{1, ..., M\}$ where $f_m(u) < f_m(v)$.

Definition 1.3

Pareto optimal set

For a given MOP $f(x)$, the Pareto optimal set is $P^* = \{x \in \Omega | \neg \exists x' \in \Omega, f(x') \preceq f(x)\}$.

Definition 1.4

Pareto optimal front

For a given MOP $f(x)$ and its Pareto optimal set P^*, the Pareto front is $PF^* = \{f(x), x \in P^*\}$.

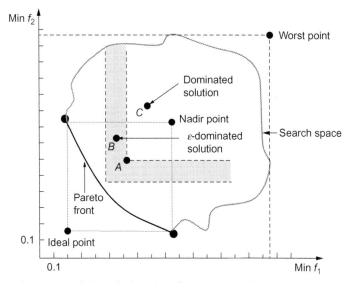

Figure 1 Illustration of the ideal and nadir point in addition to the ε-dominance concept.

Definition 1.5

Ideal point

The ideal point $z^I = (z_1^I, ..., z_M^I)$ is the vector composed of the best objective values over the search space Ω (cf. Fig. 1). Analytically, the ideal objective vector is expressed by:

$$z_m{}^I = \text{Min}_{x \in \Omega} f_m(x), \quad m \in \{1, ..., M\} \tag{2}$$

Definition 1.6

Nadir point

The nadir point $z^N = (z_1^N, ..., z_M^N)$ is the vector composed of the worst objective values over the Pareto set (cf. Fig. 1). Analytically, the nadir objective vector is expressed by:

$$z_m{}^N = \text{Max}_{x \in P*} f_m(x), \quad m \in \{1, ..., M\} \tag{3}$$

Definition 1.7

ε-dominance

A solution u is said to epsilon-dominate a solution $v (u \preceq_{\varepsilon +} v)$ if and only if $\forall m \in \{1, ..., M\}: u_m \leq \varepsilon + v_m$ for a given $\varepsilon > 0$, where u_m / v_m is the mth objective value of solution u / v (cf. Fig. 1).

Figure 1 illustrates the different terms given by definitions (1.1)–(1.7) in a bi-dimensional objective space where we have two-objective functions to minimize (f_1 and f_2). This figure illustrates how the ideal point and the nadir one are obtained based on the extreme solutions of the Pareto front shown with a thick black curved line, which is not the case for the worst point that is build based on the worst objective values over the whole search space. This figure also illustrates how solution C is Pareto dominated by solution A. Besides, although solutions A and B are nondominated with each other, A ε-dominates B since the latter belongs to the region ε-dominated by A that is highlighted with a gray background.

MOPs have received considerable attention in operations research [3]. Traditional methods to solve MOPs transform the MOP to a SOP via an aggregation method. Several aggregative methods were proposed in the specialized literature. We cite, for example, the weighted-sum method, the ε-constraint method, the weighted-metric approach, the goal programming method, the reference direction method, the light beam search (LBS) approach, and so forth (cf. Ref. [4] for an exhaustive review). The main problem with these methods is that they require several parameters to tune subjectively by the DM which is not an easy task. Due to their population-based nature, over the two last decades, Multiobjective Optimization Evolutionary Algorithms (MOEAs) have been demonstrated to be effective black-box tools to handle MOPs. Several survey papers were published in this direction such as in Refs. [5,6]. By January 2011, more than 56,001 publications have been published on the evolutionary multiobjective optimization (EMO) research field. Among these papers, 66.8% have been published in the last 8 years, 38.4% are journal papers and 42.2% are conference papers [6]. Most of these works aim at approximating the Pareto optimal front by following three goals: (1) closeness to the true Pareto front, (2) an even distribution among solutions, and (3) a high spread of solutions. However, in real world applications, the DM is not interested in the whole Pareto front since often the final decision is a unique solution. The final goal of MOEAs is to assist the DM to select the final alternative which satisfies at most his/her preferences. Since MOEAs supply the DM with a huge number of solutions, it seems to be a difficult task to choose the final preferred alternative. In order to facilitate the decision-making task, the DM would like to incorporate his/her preferences into the search process. These preferences are used to guide the search toward the preferred part of the Pareto front, i.e., the region of interest (ROI) which is defined as follows [7,8]:

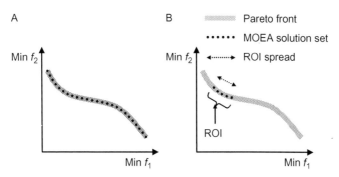

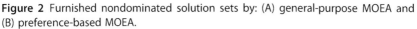

Figure 2 Furnished nondominated solution sets by: (A) general-purpose MOEA and (B) preference-based MOEA.

Definition 1.8
ROI

The ROI is the set of nondominated solutions that are preferred by the DM. These solutions are co-located within the area of the Pareto front on which the DM would like to focus. The ROI spread corresponds to the extent of this region in the M-dimensional objective space (cf. Fig. 2).

Figure 2 shows the difference between the general-purpose MOEA goal and the preference-based MOEA one. We see, from Fig. 2A, how a general-purpose MOEA aims at furnishing a well-converged and well-distributed approximation of the whole Pareto front. However, as shown by Fig. 2B, a preference-based MOEA provides only the ROI according to the DM's preferences and hence facilitating the decision-making task. In preference-based algorithms, the DM can provide his/her preferences before (*a priori*), after (*a posteriori*), or during (interactively) the MOEA run. Each solution belonging to a ROI is a preferred solution by the DM. The DM's preference information can be expressed in several ways. Most of these ways are issued from the classical multicriteria decision making (MCDM) literature [4,9]. In the following, we cite the commonly used preference information structures in the EMO community:

- *Weights*: Each objective is assigned a weighting coefficient expressing its importance. The larger the weight is, the more important the objective is.
- *Solution ranking*: The DM is provided with a sample of solutions (a subset of the current MOEA's population) and is invited to perform pairwise comparisons between pairs of solutions in order to rank the sample's solutions where incomparability and indifference may exist between the solutions to rank.

- *Objective ranking*: Pairwise comparisons between pairs of objectives are performed in order to rank the MOP's objectives where incomparability and indifference may exist between some objectives.
- *Reference point* (also called a *goal* or an *aspiration level vector*): The DM supplies for each objective, the level that he/she would like to achieve.
- *Reservation point* (also called a *reservation level vector*): The DM supplies for each objective, the level that should be achieved according to his/her preferences. The reservation level corresponds to the worst value for which the DM is still satisfied.
- *Trade-off between objectives*: The DM specifies that the gain of one unit in one objective is worth the degradation in some others and vice versa.
- *Outranking parameters*: The DM specifies the necessary parameters to design a fuzzy predicate modeling the truth degree of the predicate "solution x is at least as good as solution y."
- *Desirability thresholds*: The DM supplies: (1) an absolutely satisfying objective value (AS) and (2) a marginally infeasible objective value (MI). These thresholds represent the parameters that define the desirability functions (DFs).

Three survey papers about articulating DM's preferences within MOEAs were published: (1) a first paper by Coello Coello [10], (2) a second one by Rachmawati and Srinivasan [11], and (3) a more recent one by Branke [12]. However, from 2006, there has been a growing interest about the hybridization between decision making and EMO. For this reason, we provide in this work an updated survey of the most prominent works in this research direction. The rest of this chapter is structured as follows. The next section describes in details the main preference-based MOEAs. These search methods are classified based on the DM's preference information structure. A brief criticism is given after the description of each method mentioning its advantages and its possible drawbacks and limitations. The third section is dedicated to provide a synthetic discussion about such types of algorithms. Furthermore, we furnish a comparison between the discussed search methods. Finally, in the last section, we conclude the chapter with some potential direction for future research.

2. PREFERENCE-BASED MOEAs: CLASSIFICATION AND REVIEW

This section provides a classification of preference-based MOEAs based on the structure of the DM's preference information. We focus on the way the preferences are supplied and the mechanism adopted to incorporate these preferences so that the population is guided toward the ROI(s).

2.1 Weight-Based Approaches

2.1.1 Deb [13] Work: The Biased Sharing-Based Approach

In this work, the author incorporated the relative importance of each objective in the form of weight. In fact, he modified the Euclidean distance computation in the sharing mechanism of NSGA (Nondominated Sorting Genetic Algorithm). This mechanism ensures population diversity by penalizing the fitness values of solutions residing within the niche of a particular solution [14]. Originally, the distance between two decision variable vectors x and y is computed as follows:

$$d(x, y) = \sqrt{\sum_{m=1}^{M} \left(\frac{f_m(x) - f_m(y)}{f_m^{\max} - f_m^{\min}} \right)^2} \tag{4}$$

The quantity (4) is modified by incorporating weights into it. The obtained distance metric is called the *weighted Euclidean distance* and is expressed by:

$$d(x, y) = \sqrt{\sum_{m=1}^{M} w'_m \left(\frac{f_m(x) - f_m(y)}{f_m^{\max} - f_m^{\min}} \right)^2} \tag{5}$$

where w'_m is the normalized weighting coefficient and is expressed by:

$$w'_m = \frac{(1 - w_m)}{\max_{m=1}^{M} (1 - w_m)} \tag{6}$$

where w_m is the user-specified weight assigned to the mth objective expressing its importance degree. We note that $w_m \in [0, 1]$ and $\sum_{m=1}^{M} w_m = 1$. The sharing mechanism can then be used in order to bias the Pareto optimal solution distribution toward the preferred part of the front. However, this approach was assessed only on two biobjective problems having convex Pareto fronts with very restricted weight sets that are $(0.9, 0.1)$ and $(0.1, 0.9)$. Hence, further experiments with higher dimension problems and diversified weight sets are required for validation.

2.1.2 Branke and Deb [15] Work: The Biased Crowding-Based Approach

The authors modified the crowding distance calculation in Nondominated Sorting Genetic Algorithm-II (NSGA-II) in order to focus the search on the preferred part of the front. For an objective vector u from a particular front, a biased crowding distance $D(u)$ is defined as follows. Let η be a DM-specified direction vector indicating the most probable or central linearly weighted utility function and let θ be a parameter controlling the bias intensity, then:

$$D(u) = d(u)\left(\frac{d'(u)}{d(u)}\right)^{\theta} \tag{7}$$

where $d(u)$ and $d'(u)$ are, respectively, the original crowding distance and the crowding distance computed based on the locations of the individuals projected onto the (hyper-)plane with η as a direction vector. Figure 3 illustrates this concept. In fact, for a solution from the front more or less parallel to the projected plane (such as solution a), the original crowding distance $d(a)$ and the projected crowding distance $d'(a)$ are more or less the same, thereby making the ratio $d'(a)/d(a)$ close to one. Consequently, according to Eq. (7), solution a will have a biased crowding distance $D(a)$ almost the same as that in the original objective space, i.e., $d(a)$. Contrariwise, for a solution having a large difference in slope on the Pareto optimal front where the tangent has an orientation significantly different from the chosen plane (such as solution b), the projected crowding distance $d'(b)$ is much smaller than the original crowding distance $d(b)$, thereby making the ratio $d'(b)/d(b)$ so smaller than one. For such a solution, the biased crowding distance will be a small quantity which means that solution b is assumed to be artificially

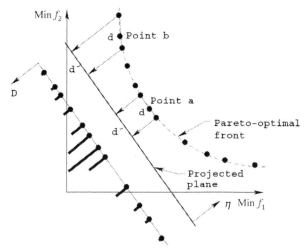

Figure 3 Illustration of the biased crowding-based-approach for the biobjective case. *From Ref. [15].*

crowded. Figure 3 shows also the biased crowding distance values for all nondominated points and how would they typically be distributed for a certain front and a chosen plane. Solutions with large crowding distance are preferred, which allows solutions situated near the tangent point to survive. The parameter θ controls the extent of the obtained solutions. The larger θ is, the smaller the extent is. The main advantages of this approach are: (1) its scalability with the number of objectives and (2) its insensibility to the nonconvexity of the Pareto optimal front. However, the approach was shown to be inferior to the Guided-Multiobjective Optimization Evolutionary Algorithm (G-MOEA) [16] in terms of convergence.

2.1.3 *Zitzler* et al. *[17] Work: The Weighted Hypervolume-Based Approach*

The hypervolume indicator is a performance measure that computes the surface of the objective space dominated by a solution set and bounded by a reference point [18]. The main feature of this performance measure is its Pareto compliance, i.e., it does not contradict the order induced by the Pareto dominance relation [19]. Zitzler and Künzli [20] proposed a MOEA where selection is based on solution marginal contribution to the hypervolume quality indicator, named Indicator-Based Evolutionary Algorithm (IBEA), which has demonstrated its ability to provide a good approximation of the Pareto front for different kinds of MOPs. In Ref. Zitzler *et al.* [17], the authors proposed a weighted version of the hypervolume metric in order to guide the search based on the DM's preferences expressed by: (1) weighting coefficients or (2) a reference point. Three different weighting schemes were proposed for the biobjective case: (1) a weight distribution which favors extreme solutions, (2) a weight distribution which favors one objective over the other (but still keeping the best solution with respect to the less important objective), and (3) a weight distribution based on a reference point, which generates a ridge-like function through a reference point parallel to the diagonal. The reader is invited to confer to the original paper to see the design details of these weighting schemes. In the following, we give the definitions of the hypervolume measure followed by the weighted version of this indicator. The classical definitions of the hypervolume indicator are based on volumes of polytopes [19] or hypercubes [21] and assume that Pareto dominance is the underlying preference relation. Here, we give a generalized definition based on attainment functions that allows considering arbitrary dominance relations. The attainment function [22] gives, for each objective vector the probability that it is dominated by the outcome of a particular multiobjective optimizer. As only single sets are considered here, we can take a slightly simplified definition of the attainment function as follows:

Definition 2.1

Attainment function

Assuming A to be an objective vector set and z to be an objective vector, the attainment function $\alpha_A(z) : [0,1]^M \to \{0,1\}$ for A is defined as:

$$\alpha_A(z) = \begin{cases} 1 & \text{if } A \succeq \{z\} \\ 0 & \text{else} \end{cases} \tag{8}$$

This definition is illustrated in Fig. 4. The concept of attainment function can be used to give a formal definition of the hypervolume indicator. In fact, this latter is defined as the volume of the objective space enclosed by the attainment function and the axes.

Definition 2.2

Hypervolume indicator

The hypervolume I_H^* with reference point $(0,\cdots,0)$ can be formulated via the attainment function as:

$$I_H^*(A) = \int_{(0,\,...,\,0)}^{(1,\,...,\,1)} \alpha_A(z)\mathrm{d}z \tag{9}$$

The attainment function, the integration over which gives the hypervolume for a given set A, is a binary function such that all weakly dominated objective vectors are assigned 1, while the remaining objective vectors are assigned 0. That means all weakly dominated objective vectors have the

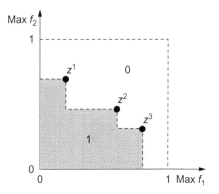

Figure 4 Illustration of the attainment function α_A for $A = \{z^1, z^2, z^3\}$ for the biobjective maximization case.

same weight and contribute equally to the overall indicator value. The main idea behind the weighted hypervolume approach is to give different weights to different regions in the objective space. This can be achieved by defining a weight distribution over the objective space such that the value that a particular weakly dominated objective vector contributes to the overall indicator value can be any strictly positive real value. To this end, the authors introduced a weight distribution function $w : Z \rightarrow \mathfrak{R}^+$. The hypervolume is calculated as the integral over the product of the weight distribution function and the attainment function:

$$I_H^w(A) = \int_{(0, \, ..., \, 0)}^{(1, \, ..., \, 1)} w(z).\alpha_A(z)\mathrm{d}z \qquad (10)$$

The weighted hypervolume is integrated in the Simple IBEA (SIBEA) [17] and the resulting algorithm has shown its ability to drive the search as expected by the authors. However, as noted by the authors, this approach is restricted to the biobjective case. Moreover, there is no control over the ROI spread. It is worth noting that, in a more recent study [23], this work was extended for the M-objective case by defining general indicator classes for an arbitrary number of objectives. Furthermore, this extension enables the DM to control the ROI breadth. The main disadvantage of this more recent approach is that, for the case where the DM would like to find a ROI near his/her expressed reference point, the obtained solution distribution highly depends of the position of this preference point.

2.2 Solution Ranking-Based Approaches

2.2.1 Greenwood et al. [24] Work

In this study, the authors proposed an imprecisely specified multi-attribute utility theory-based weighted-sum approach where the ranking of objectives is implicitly derived from the ranking of some candidate solutions. The imprecisely specified weight coefficients are characterized by a set of constraints describing preferences as revealed in pairwise comparison of the candidate solutions. The used utility function is called imprecise because weights do not have specific values but they are constrained by the DM's preferences. A minimization of the difference in the weighted sums of a pair of solutions, subject to the predetermined constraints, is performed in the fitness computation. This linear optimization is performed for every solution pair in the archive and in the population to obtain the solution fitness values.

Assuming u and v to be two normalized objective vectors (i.e., mapped to the interval $[0,1]$) where the DM prefers u to v, we obtain:

$$u \preceq_{\text{preferred}} v \Rightarrow \sum_{m=1}^{M} w_m(u_m - v_m) \leq 0 \qquad (11)$$

The expression (11) defines a constraint for the objective weights. When several solution pairs are ranked by the DM, a series of such constraints are defined. These constraints confine the objective weighting coefficients to a subspace $W \in \mathfrak{R}_+^M$ where $\mathfrak{R}_+^M$ is the M-dimensional space of positive real numbers. Using the normalized objective values and the constraint subspace W, other configurations created from running a MOEA may be evaluated. More specifically, by definition:

$$\sum_{m=1}^{M} w_m(u_m - v_m) \leq 0 \Rightarrow u \preceq_{\text{preferred}} v \qquad (12)$$

It follows that two alternatives u and u' can be compared by solving the following linear programming problem:

$$\begin{cases} \text{Min} \sum_{m=1}^{M} w_m(u'_m - u_m) \leq 0 \\ w_m \in W \end{cases} \qquad (13)$$

Let $z = \min\limits_{w_m} \sum_{m=1}^{M} w_m(u'_m - u_m)$ and $\bar{z} = \min\limits_{w_m} \sum_{m=1}^{M} w_m(u_m - u'_m)$ then:

- If $z < 0$ then u' is preferred to u;
- If $z \geq 0$ and $\bar{z} < 0$ then u is preferred to u';
- If $z \geq 0$ and $\bar{z} \geq 0$ then u and u' are indifferent.

In summary, the DM is invited to make pairwise comparisons in order to define the constraint subspace W. W is subsequently used in the series of linear programming problems that should be solved to conduct pairwise comparisons between solutions. The authors noted that alternatives compared by the DM should be selected carefully so that they can be ranked consistently, unless conflicting constraints may be produced. Consequently, there will be no solution for the resulting linear programming problem, i.e., this latter would be infeasible. The authors implemented an algorithm for identifying the inconsistent preference statements. This algorithm identifies the minimum sets of preference statements that, if removed, would result in a feasible solution to the linear programming instance. However, this algorithm has an exponential time complexity.

2.2.2 Deb et al. [25] Work: The Progressively Interactive EMO Algorithm (PI-EMOA)

The authors proposed a preference-based-MOEA based on the concept of value function. Every few τ generations, the DM is provided with a sample of η solutions and is asked to rank these solutions from the best to the worst where the incomparability between solutions is allowed. This step is termed "*DM call*." Based on this preference information, an optimization problem is formulated and solved to find a suitable value function which optimally captures DM's preference information by maximizing the value function value between ranked points. From this iteration till the next DM call, the derived value function is utilized to drive the MOEA in: (1) modifying the domination principle which directly affects MOEA's convergence and diversity preserving operators, thereby guiding the search toward the preferred solutions and (2) determining the termination criterion of the overall procedure.

During the preference elicitation step (i.e., the DM call), the DM is provided with a sample of η points and for each pair of alternatives (x, y), he/she can precise if x is preferred to y $\left(\text{denoted } P_x \succ P_y\right)$ or x and y are incomparable $\left(\text{denoted } P_x \equiv P_y\right)$. For the biobjective case, the authors proposed the following value function structure:

$$V(f_1, f_2) = (f_1 + k_1 f_2 + l_1)(f_2 + k_2 f_1 + l_2) \tag{14}$$

where f_1 and f_2 are the considered objective functions and k_1, k_2, l_1, and l_2 are unknown parameters and should be determined from the DM's preference information. For this purpose, the following value function optimization problem (VFOP) should be solved:

$$\begin{cases} \text{Max } \varepsilon \\ V \text{ is nonnegative at every point } P_x; \\ V \text{ is strictly increasing at every point } P_x; \\ V(P_x) - V(P_y) \geq \varepsilon, \text{ for all pairs}(x, y)\text{staisfying } P_x \succ P_y; \\ \left| V(P_x) - V(P_y) \right| \leq \delta_V, \text{ for all pairs}(x, y)\text{staisfying } P_x \equiv P_y; \\ \varepsilon > 0, \delta_V = 0.1\,\varepsilon. \end{cases} \tag{15}$$

We remark that the value function V is considered to be the product of two linear functions $S_1 = f_1 + k_1 f_2 + l_1 : \mathfrak{R}^2 \rightarrow \mathfrak{R}$ and $S_2 = f_2 + k_2 f_1 + l_2 : \mathfrak{R}^2 \rightarrow \mathfrak{R}$. A little thought reveals that the above optimization problem (15) attempts to find a value function for which the minimum difference in the value function values between the ordered pairs of points is maximal. The interested reader is invited to refer to the original paper in order to find the VFOP for the general M-objective case.

Once the value function has been built, the conventional dominance principle is modified in order to focus the search on preferred solutions. Let V be the value function found from the most recent decision-making interaction. Let V_2 be the value function value for the second best member (P_2 defined previously) from the sample of η points. For the maximization case, any two feasible solutions x and y can be compared with their objective function values by using the following modified domination criteria:

- If both solutions have a value function value less than V_2, then the two points are compared based on the usual Pareto dominance principle;
- If both solutions have a value function value more than V_2, then the two points are compared based on the usual Pareto dominance principle;
- If one has a value function value more than V_2 and the other has a value function value less than V_2, then the former dominates the latter.

Figure 5 illustrates a confrontation between the value function-based dominance dominated region and the Pareto dominance one for the biobjective maximization case. This figure presents the region dominated by two points A and B. The value function contour having a value V_2 is shown by the curved line. The point A lies in the region in which the value function is smaller than V_2. The region dominated by point A is shaded. This dominated area is identical to that which can be obtained using the Pareto dominance principle. However, the point B lies in the region in which the value function is larger than V_2. For this point, the dominated region is different from that which would be obtained using the usual domination principle. In addition to the usual region of dominance, the dominated region includes all points having a smaller value function value than V_2.

Once the value function V is determined, the MOEA is driven by it in the next τ generations. The value function V can also be used for

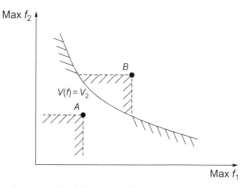

Figure 5 Dominated region for: (1) Pareto dominance with solution A and (2) value function-based dominance with solution B.

determining whether the overall optimization procedure should be terminated or not. To implement the idea, the best and second best points P_1
and P_2 from the given set of η points are firstly identified based on the
DM's preference. The constructed value function can provide information
about whether any new point P is better than the current best solution P_1
with respect to the value function. Thus, a single-objective search is performed along the gradient of the value function (∇V) from P_1 in order
to create better preferred solutions than P_1. This principle is used to develop
a termination criterion by solving the following achievement scalarizing
function (ASF) problem for $P_1 = z^b$:

$$
\text{Max} \quad \min_{m=1}^{M} \left(\frac{f_m(x) - z_m^b}{\frac{\partial V}{\partial f_m}} \right) + \rho \sum_{m=1}^{M} \frac{f_m(x) - z_m^b}{\frac{\partial V}{\partial f_m}} \tag{16}
$$

The second term with a small ρ ($=10^{-10}$ used in this work) prevents the
solution to converge to a weak Pareto optimal point. Any single-objective
optimization method (e.g., the sequential quadratic programming (SQP)
method [26]) can be used for solving the above problem and the intermediate solutions $(z^i, i = 1, 2, \ldots)$ can be recorded. If at any intermediate point,
the Euclidean distance between z^i from P_1 is larger than a termination
parameter d_s, the ASF optimization task is stopped and the MOEA search
is resumed. In this case, we replace P_1 with z^i. Figure 6A depicts this scenario
for the biobjective maximization case. If at the end of the SQP run, the final
SQP solution (say, z^T) is not greater than d_s distance away from P_1, the
MOEA is terminated and z^T is declared as the final preferred solution. This
situation indicates that based on the current value function, there exist no

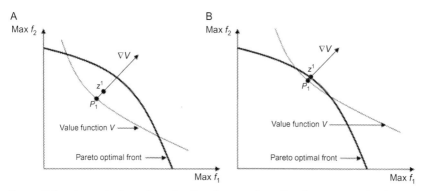

Figure 6 Local search along the value function gradient direction as a termination criterion: (A) success of the search and (B) failure of the search.

solution in the search space which will provide a significantly better objective vector than P_1. Hence, the optimization run is terminated. Figure 6B shows such a situation, for the two-objective maximization case, warranting a termination of the PI-EMOA.

The PI-EMOA has shown its effectiveness on two- to five-objective test problems in providing the preferred point corresponding to a DM-emulated utility function. However, the authors have not handled the case in which the DM judges some of the η points to be incomparable and the role of the δ_V parameter is not studied in the value function construction. Moreover, the authors noted that there are some cases which may occur in which the building of a value function satisfying all DM's preferences is not possible.

2.2.3 Köksalan and Karahan [27] Work: The Interactive Territory Defining Evolutionary Algorithm

The interactive Territory Defining Evolutionary Algorithm (iTDEA) is a preference-based interactive version of the Territory Defining Evolutionary Algorithm (TDEA) [28]. The TDEA is a new MOEA that approximates the whole Pareto front by using the concept of territory. This MOEA is a steady-state algorithm that maintains two populations: (1) the archive population that consists of individuals that are nondominated relative to the population at hand and (2) the regular population that contains both dominated and nondominated individuals. When updating the archive population, a territory around the individual closest to the offspring is defined and the offspring is rejected if it violates this territory. The territory defining property of TDEA eliminates the need for an explicit diversity operator, resulting in a fast operation while always keeping a diverse set of individuals in the archive population. The concept of territory is illustrated in Figure 7A. The territory region is highlighted with gray color. The territory

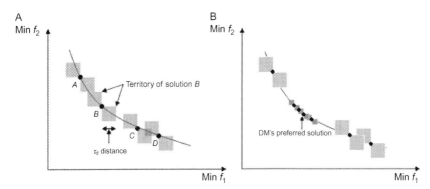

Figure 7 The territory effect with: (A) TDEA and (B) iTDEA.

of a particular solution x corresponds to the region with a distance τ_d from $f(x)$ in each objective among the region that neither dominates nor is dominated by $f(x)$. Mathematically, the territory of $f(x)$ is defined as the following hypervolume:

$$T(f(x)) = \{f(y) \in \mathfrak{R}^M \mid |f_m(x) - f_m(y)| < \tau_d \forall m = 1, \ldots, M \text{ and } \exists f_m(x) - f_m(y) < 0$$
$$\text{for at least one } m \text{ and } \exists f_m(x) - f_m(y) > 0 \text{ for at least one } m\}$$

(17)

The authors proposed a strategy to choose a convenient τ_d value. The authors modified the TDEA in order to handle DM's preferences and focus the search on the preferred part of the front. The DM is supplied with a sample of diversified solutions and is invited to select the best one from his/her own perspective. In order to concentrate the search toward the preferred solution, the authors suggest shrinking the territories of the individuals falling near the preferred solution. This can be achieved by simply using a smaller τ_d for such offspring in the archive evaluation stage. This maintains more individuals in this region in the archive population, leading to a higher resolution and better approximation. Meanwhile, individuals located elsewhere are evaluated using a larger τ_d. This leads to less population density in the regions that are less desirable to the DM. An illustration of this mechanism is shown by Fig. 7B. The iTDEA has demonstrated its effectiveness in providing a biased distribution of the supplied nondominated solution set where the distribution is denser near the DM's preferred solution. However, the authors noted that filtering the population to provide the potential sample to the DM from which he/she picks his/her preferred solution may mislead the algorithm in the first interactions. They suggest increasing the number of solutions to present to the DM; however, this number should have a limit.

2.2.4 Battiti and Passerini [29] Work: The Brain-Computer Evolutionary Multiobjective Optimization Algorithm

The authors suggested a preference-based MOEA characterized by its ability to learn an arbitrary utility function from a human DM who expresses his/her preferences between couples of selected solutions. The used method to build a flexible preference model, possibly highly nonlinear, is based on the concept of support vector machine (SVM) [30]. The objective of the learning process is the approximated construction of a utility function U to be optimized by the DM, who is also the source of learning signals. The function U to be optimized is not completely unknown, such as in a black-box context [31], but is to be modeled based on the DM's ranking of candidate solutions. Preference models are built from the DM input by using a SVM-based ranking method (cf. the original paper for the mathematical description of this method). The functional form of the preference function is not fixed *a priori* by a well-defined ASF, such as in the weighted-sum or Chebyshev approaches [32], but is itself learnt during the process in a reactive fashion. The authors noted that SVM-based ranking has a number of desirable properties making it a suitable candidate for learning the DM's preferences. First, it accepts supervision in terms of pairwise preferences, a much more affordable request for a human DM than a quantitative quality score. Second, it is well grounded on learning theory; its trading-off data fitting and complexity of the learned hypothesis allows to effectively dealing with noisy observations, a situation which is quite likely to occur when receiving feedback from a human DM with only partial knowledge on the domain at hand. Third, the ability to implicitly project data onto a higher dimensional feature space via the kernel trick [33] provides the needed flexibility in order to best approximate the underlying preference model of the specific user.

The basic functioning of Brain-Computer Evolutionary Multiobjective Optimization Algorithm (BC-EMOA) can be summarized as follows. Objective vectors are passed to the DM who ranks them and returns the ordered list as feedback. This feedback is converted into *pairwise constraints* for the SVM-based ranking procedure. After training, the predicted utility function U is employed to guide the search toward the ROI. From the multiobjective decision-making perspective, the main contribution of this method is its ability to function without any *a priori* assumptions on the shape of the DM's utility function. The methodology of reactive search optimization [34], based on the paradigm of learning while optimizing, is adopted in two directions: (1) the progressive tuning of a preference model following a DM's interactive evaluation and (2) the automated adaptation of the model form to one which is most appropriate, in a cross-validated manner, to the data collected during the interaction. The method is robust as it can potentially withstand incomplete, imprecise, and even contradictory feedback by the DM. The BC-EMOA is a generic formulation which can be implemented on top of any MOEA. In this study, the authors adopted the NSGA-II [35]. NSGA-II runs in its original formulation, including the crowded-comparison operator for guaranteeing a sufficiently diversified population, for gen_1 generations. After that, the preference model is trained according to the DM's feedback and the ordering of the new population and the selection criterion of the binary tournament selection operator are performed based on the actual utility function value. Additionally, the crowding mechanism is switched-off at this point as the goal is directing the generation of new individuals toward the ROI. The BC-EMOA has demonstrated its effectiveness in guiding the search toward the DM's most preferred solution on some selected Deb–Thiele–Laumans–Zitzler (DTLZ) problems [36] in addition to some instances of the 0/1 multiobjective knapsack problem [37]. However, the authors noted that the gen_1 parameter value should allow a reasonable coverage to the Pareto front in order not to miss portions possibly containing the DM's preferred solutions; it should thus be of the same order of the number of generations for a plain MOEA run on the same problem. This step seems to be computationally costly. Additionally, after gen_1 generations, the crowding mechanism is turned-off and the population is guided toward a certain region of the search space based on the utility function which can reduce population diversity significantly and encourage the premature convergence to occur especially on multimodal MOPs. This problematic is omitted by the authors.

2.2.5 Fowler et al. [38] Work: The Cone-Dominance-Based Approach

The authors exploited the notion of preference convex polyhedral cones [39] in order to integrate DM's preferences in a MOEA. Periodically, the DM is provided with a sample of η solutions and is invited to specify the best alternative in addition to the worst one from his/her own perspective. These two selected solutions are then used to form a convex polyhedral cone. The cone defines a convex set of solutions (shaded region in Fig. 8B) that is inferior not only to the cone vertex (point A in Fig. 8B) but also to solutions residing within the cone (gray region in Fig. 8B). Since the designed algorithm is interactive, all defined cones are retained during the overall optimization run whether or not the population members from which they are derived are still surviving. Figure 8 illustrates graphically the concept of convex polyhedral

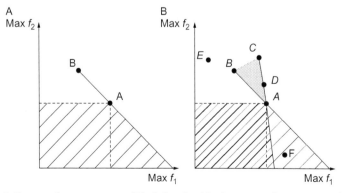

Figure 8 Two preference cones: (A) defined with the two solutions A and B and (B) defined with the three solutions A, B, and C (inspired by Ramesh et al. [39]).

cone for the biobjective maximization case for: (a) the case of two solutions (B is preferred to A) and (b) the case of three solutions (B is preferred to A and C is preferred to A). For the case of $\eta = 2$ (cf. Fig. 8A), the convex cone corresponds to the line segment AB and has solution A as vertex. Accordingly, every solution that is dominated by the cone (shaded region in Fig. 8A) is less preferred to solution A, and hence to every solution belonging to the line segment AB. These solutions are considered to be inferior and are to be discouraged in the selection process of the MOEA. For the case of $\eta = 3 > 2$ (cf. Fig. 8B), the preference cone corresponds to a convex polyhedral set. In this case, any population member can have one of the following four possible locations: (1) under the cone (like solution F), (2) in the cone (like solution D), (3) outside the cone (like solution E), or (4) being the cone's vertex (like solution A). The DM's preference information is applied by placing solution v before solution u if v is within the cone and u is the cone's vertex. The three-point cone in Fig. 8B is composed from the union of two two-point cones defined by the two preference relations: (1) solution B is preferred to solution A (the corresponding shaded area is drawn with thin lines) and (2) solution C is preferred to solution A (the corresponding shaded area is drawn with bold lines). Solutions under the cone (shaded area) like F are considered to be dominated by the cone. We say that they are cone dominated. Solution D is considered to be superior to solution A since D belongs to the cone and A is the cone's vertex. It is important to note that every solution from the gray region defined by points A, B, and C is considered to be superior to the cone's vertex A and subsequently preferred to every point belonging to the shaded region.

The cone-dominance principle is used in parent selection and replacement mechanisms. The designed preference-based MOEA has been assessed on the multiobjective 0/1 knapsack problem with 2, 3, and 4 objectives. The computational experiments have shown that it is possible to obtain solutions with a reasonable number of DM interactions that are very near to or equal to the best found by a similar algorithm that is operating with perfect knowledge of the user's preference function. However, the authors noted that investigating the effect of DM's preferences inconsistencies is still a direction for future research. Moreover, there is no control over the ROI extent.

2.2.6 Branke et al. [40] Work: The Necessary Preference-Enhanced Evolutionary Multiobjective Optimizer

The necessary preference-enhanced evolutionary multiobjective optimizer (NEMO) algorithm is the result of the combination of NSGA-II [35] and the robust ordinal regression (ROR) [41] within an interactive procedure. In ROR, the DM is presented with a small set of alternatives and can express his/her preferences by specifying a holistic preference of one alternative over another or comparing intensities of preferences between pairs of alternatives. ROR then identifies the whole set of additive value functions compatible with the preference information given by the DM. This allows comparing any pair of alternatives in a simple and intuitive way. The authors noted that, usually, among the many sets of parameters of a preference model representing the preference information, only one specific set is used to give a recommendation on a set of alternatives. For example, among many value functions representing pairwise comparisons of some alternatives made by the DM, only one value function is finally used to recommend the best choice, or sorting, or ranking of alternatives. Since the choice of one among many sets of parameters compatible with the preference information is rather arbitrary, ROR has been recently proposed with the aim of taking into account all the sets of parameters compatible with the preference information given by the DM [42,43]. The ROR approach extends the simple ordinal regression by taking into account not a single instance of the preference model compatible with DM's preference information but the whole set of compatible instances of the preference model. As a result of considering the whole set of compatible instances of the preference model, one gets two kinds of results with respect to each pair of alternatives x and y:

- *necessary preference relation* $(x \succsim^N y)$, if and only if x is at least as good as y according to all instances of the preference model compatible with the preference information (i.e., x is at least as good as y for all compatible value functions);

- *possible preference relation* $(x \succsim^P y)$, if and only if x is at least as good as y according to at least one instance of the preference model compatible with the preference information (i.e., x is at least as good as y for at least one compatible value function).

The reader is invited to refer to the original paper in order to explore the computational issues and details of the ROR approach. Since, NEMO, is a modified version of NSGA-II, we give the modifications performed to this latter as follows:

- the Pareto dominance relation is replaced by the necessary preference relation in the nondominated sorting;

- the crowding distance is substituted by a distance calculated by taking into account the multidimensional scaling given by the most representative value function among the whole set of compatible value functions. The most representative value function corresponds to the value function which maximizes the difference of scores between alternatives related by preference in the necessary preference relation-based ranking [44].

The NEMO algorithm has demonstrated its ability to bias the search toward the ROI interactively. However, the algorithm was tested only on two biobjective test problems. Consequently, a more thorough empirical analysis on a variety of test problems with more than two-objective functions is necessary. Moreover, there is no control over the ROI spread.

2.3 Objective Ranking-Based Approaches

2.3.1 Jin and Sendhoff [45] Work

The authors turned fuzzy preferences into weight intervals which were incorporated into a MOEA using random weighted aggregation (RWA) and dynamic weighted aggregation (DWA) techniques [46]. This was achieved by setting the upper and lower bounds to the weight perturbations. In fact, the DM is invited to make pairwise comparisons on the set of objectives by using linguistic statements such as "objective f_2 is much more important than objective f_1." The authors developed a method that converts these fuzzy preferences into interval-based weights where each weight indicates the importance of the relative objective. This approach converts the MOP into a SOP by weighted aggregation, but varies the weights dynamically during the run within the relevant boundaries.

For the RWA, assuming that each individual i has it own weight combination $(w_1^i(t), w_2^i(t))$ in generation t for the biobjective case, then the MOEA is able to find different Pareto optimal solutions. The weight combinations need to be distributed uniformly and randomly among the individuals in each generation as follows:

$$w_1^i(t) = \text{random}(P)/P \tag{18}$$

$$w_2^i(t) = 1 - w_1^i(t) \tag{19}$$

where P is the population size and random is function that generates a uniformly distributed random number between 0 and P.

For the DWA, all the individuals have the same weight combination which is changed gradually in each generation. The change of the weights is realized as follows assuming a biobjective case:

$$w_1(t) = |\sin(2\pi t/F)| \tag{20}$$

$$w_2(t) = 1 - w_1(t) \tag{21}$$

The weights will change from 0 to 1 periodically from generation to another. The change frequency can be adjusted by the F parameter.

In both RWA- and DWA-based EMO approaches, the weight varies in the interval [0,1] in order to approximate the whole Pareto front. However, in order to take the DM's preferences into account, the weight of each objective f_m is varied in the interval $[w_m^{min}, w_m^{max}]$ where the boundaries of the latter interval are obtained from the conversion of the DM's fuzzy preferences. In this way, the search process is guided toward the ROI. The designed weighted-sum-based algorithms support incomparability between solutions and provide the user with a control over the focus extent. While DWA facilitates retention of compromise solutions in the nonconvex parts of the nondominated front, the lack of explicit diversity preservation and inferior performance in high-dimensional problems constitute significant drawbacks of the approach [46]. Arriving at the upper and lower bounds of weights for higher dimensional problems is also difficult.

2.3.2 Cvetkovic and Parmee [47] Work: The Weighted-Dominance Relation-Based Approach

The authors proposed the integration of DM's fuzzy preferences into MOEAs by converting linguistic variables into weights. The DM is invited to make pairwise comparisons between the MOP's objectives by using some linguistic labels such as "more important," "much less important," and "do not care." As the number of objectives increases, the number of pairwise comparisons becomes a tedious task for the DM. The use of transitive relations was therefore proposed to reduce the number of pairwise comparisons required from the DM [47]. The reader is invited to confer to the original paper to explore the details of the mechanism converting the linguistic terms to weights. Based on the obtained weight vector expressing the relative importance for each objective, a new weight-based dominance relation is designed. This relation is called weighted-dominance relation and is expressed by:

$$ x \preceq_w y \Leftrightarrow \sum_{m=1,\,...,\,M,\,f_m(x) \leq f_m(y)}^{M} w_m \geq \tau \tag{22} $$

with a strict inequality for at least one objective. $x \preceq_w y$ means that solution x is preferred to solution y based on weighted-dominance and τ is a user-defined parameter expressing the minimum required level of dominance. The main drawback of this dominance relation is that it only considers the number of improvements of one solution with respect to another one and it ignores the amount of each improvement. Additionally, the control of the guidance is difficult and there is no clear interest to use such an approach in an interactive way. In a more recent study, Rachmawati [48] have discussed the effects produced by the obtained values for the weighting coefficients. The weighted-dominance relation preserves Pareto dominance relation and also allows incomparability when τ is set such that $\tau \geq \min_{m=1,\ldots,M} w_m$. However, the weighted-dominance has a serious drawback illustrated in the following for a biobjective MOP. Without loss of generality, we assume that $w_1 > w_2$. For biobjective problems, three scenarios with respect to different values of τ exist. The dominated and nondominated regions of the objective space around a candidate solution in the three scenarios are as follows:

- $\tau \geq w_1$: In this scenario, the weighted-dominance is equivalent to the Pareto dominance.
- $\tau \leq w_2$: In this scenario, the weighted-dominance includes all solutions nondominated in terms of the Pareto dominance relation. In an MOEA implementing weighted Pareto dominance with this setting, there will be no nondominated solution according to the weighted-dominance unless a candidate solution that strongly Pareto dominates all other solutions in the population is present. If this latter does not exist in the population, the MOEA degenerates into a random search.
- $w_2 \leq \tau \leq w_1$: In this scenario, the weighted-dominance includes solutions nondominated in terms of the Pareto dominance relation with inferior f_2 values. In an MOEA implementing weighted-dominance with this setting, the solution in the best nondominated front that also corresponds to the smallest f_2 value dominates all other solutions. Unless the archiving policy allows inclusion of weakly dominated solutions, only the extreme solution is retained in each generation. With an archival policy that allows dominated solutions with respect to the weighted dominance, the archive includes solutions other than the extreme solution that corresponds to the best secondary niching criterion. Preference is only incorporated in the search in as much as the inclusion of the extreme solution corresponding to the smallest attainment f_1 into the archive is guaranteed. However, even in general-purpose MOEAs using the Pareto dominance relation, the inclusion of extreme solutions in the archive is always guaranteed.

2.3.3 Rachmawati and Srinivasan [49] Work

In this approach, the DM is invited to express his/her preferences in the form of relative importance of objectives without using any weighting coefficient. In fact, the DM is invited to specify a total or partial order on the set of objectives. For each pair of objectives (f_m, f_n), the DM can express one of the following statements: (1) objective f_m is preferred to objective f_n (denoted $f_m Prf_n$), (2) f_m and f_n are equally important (denoted $f_m If_n$), or (3) f_m and f_n are incomparable (denoted $f_m Q f_n$). An elicitation algorithm is provided to assist the DM in constructing a coherent overall preference. Besides elicitation of *a priori* preference, an interactive facility is also furnished to enable modification of overall preference while the search progresses. We note that the default preference relation between pairs of objectives is the incomparability relation. If incomparability is the only preference relation considered by the DM, the whole Pareto front is ret-urned as a general-purpose MOEA.

A way of consistently characterizing the preferred solutions for a given preference profile irrespective of the geometry of the Pareto front is desir-able. This consistency is instrumental to an effective articulation of prefer-ence by the DM. Even if the geometrical attributes of the actual Pareto front are unknown *a priori*, a consistent characterization equips the DM with some information of the solutions he/she may expect for any given preference profile. To achieve this consistency, the functional mapping from prefer-ences expressed in the preference structure P_F (i.e., the group of binary rela-tions that can be defined on the set of objective pairs) to the Pareto front is defined in terms of a prototype nondominated front. The selected prototype front is linear, continuous and defined in the interval $[0,1]$. Let the prototype front be described by $\widetilde{F} = \left[\widetilde{f}_1, \widetilde{f}_2\right]$, then $\widetilde{f}_1 + \widetilde{f}_2 = 1$. An illustration of the prototype front and a mapping from the actual front is given in Fig. 9. The choice of the linear front is motivated partly by its simplicity and its scal-ability with the number of objectives. Simplicity helps the DM in formulat-ing his/her preference in terms of binary relations in P_F. The scaling of the preference model and its functional mapping to the M-objective case are also addressed in this study [49].

To accommodate the three binary preference relations defined in P_F, the prototype front is divided into three nonoverlapping segments of identical length as depicted by Fig. 9. The linear front in this figure is the prototype front while the curve is a normalized concave Pareto front associated with an actual MOP. The first portion plotted as squares is desired when $f_m Pr f_n$ is asserted. The second and third portions, marked by asterisks and triangles, respectively, are the desired subsets of the front when $f_m If_n$ and $f_n Prf_m$ are asserted, respectively. We recall that the preference assertion $f_m Q f_n$ corre-sponds to the entire span of the prototype Pareto front. Mathematically,

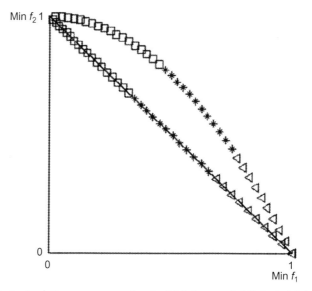

Figure 9 Desired solutions corresponding to $f_1 Prf_2$ (squares), $f_1 If_2$ (asterisks), and $f_2 Prf_1$ (triangles). *From Ref. [49].*

the desired subsets of the Pareto front could be characterized by the following inequalities:

$$f_1 Pf_2 \Leftrightarrow 2\widetilde{f}_1 \le \widetilde{f}_2 \tag{23}$$

$$f_1 If_2 \Leftrightarrow \widetilde{f}_1 \le \widetilde{f}_2 \le 4\widetilde{f}_1 \tag{24}$$

where $\widetilde{f}_1$ and $\widetilde{f}_2$ correspond to the prototype objective space and Pareto front. The choice of the coefficients 2 and 4 in the above inequalities follows from equal division of the prototype front into three nonoverlapping subsets. Other values may of course be used if other ways of dividing the prototype front is deemed necessary or desirable. In this approach, equal and nonoverlapping division is adopted as it is deemed most intuitive for the general case.

The authors proposed three versions of the NSGA-II where DM's preferences are incorporated as follows:

– *Inclusion of preference information as constraints*: To incorporate preference, the inequalities (23) and (24) are applied to the current population and/or archive where normalization is done with respect to the extrema of the best nondominated front. In this particular strategy, the ROI, as defined by inequalities derived from the partial ranking of solutions, is considered as the feasible region. The following rule is applied when comparing a pair of solutions (x, y) in the population and/or the archive:

```
If (( V(x) > 0) and ( V(y) >0)) Then
    If ( V(x) <V(y)) Then
        x ≺pref y
    Else If ( V(y) <V(x)) Then
        y ≺pref x
    End If
Else
    If ( x ≾ y) Then
        x ≺pref y
    Else If (y ≾ x) Then
        y ≺pref x
    End If
End If
```

The function $V(x)$ in the above rule denotes a measure of constraint violation of solution x, which is taken to be the maximum magnitude of the violation of all inequalities describing the desired region. The expression $x \prec_{pref} y$ indicates that solution x is preferred to solution y.

- *Inclusion of preference information as rank penalty*: Pareto ranking introduces a complete order to the partially ordered objective space by means of existing dominance relation between solution pairs in the set. Here, incompatibility with the preference-based inequalities incurs a penalty in the Pareto rank of a solution. As Pareto rank is usually defined as integers, the penalty imposed is one. The strategy works only with MOEAs that implement Pareto ranking. Pareto dominance is preserved in NSGA-II by performing the ranking from the best nondominated layer such that nondominated solutions satisfying preference-based inequalities are assigned rank 1 (subset 1), nondominated solutions not satisfying preference inequalities are assigned rank 2 (subset 2) along with solutions which satisfy preference inequalities and are nondominated with solutions in subset 2, and so on until the population is filled. In this manner, the search is guided based on DM's preferences.

- *Inclusion of preference in the crowding distance computation*: Satisfaction of the preference inequalities leads a multiple of the actual crowding distance of a solution to be considered as the crowding distance, i.e., if a solution satisfies the inequalities then $CrowdingDistance = Factor \times ActualCrowdingDistance$ with *Factor* is larger than one, whereas dissatisfaction with inequalities corresponds to factor equals one. The multiplication factor is the biasing strength of this approach. This strategy is applicable to any MOEA that implements crowding in the computation of the fitness. The three NSGA-II versions were assessed on two- to six-objective test functions. The constraint-based approach and the rank penalty-based approach have demonstrated their abilities to provide a ROI based on DM's preferences. The crowding-based approach has shown its effectiveness in biasing the nondominated solution distribution toward the preferred Pareto front subset. However, there is no control over the ROI spread.

2.4 Reference Point-Based Approaches
2.4.1 Fonseca and Fleming [50,51] Work
This work is probably the first attempt to incorporate DM's preference information in EMO. The authors model DM's preferences as a goal to be achieved (i.e., a reference point). The main idea, in this study, is to give higher priority to objectives that do not satisfy the goal. Assuming a goal $g = (g_1, ..., g_M)$ and two-objective vectors $u = (u_1, ..., u_M)$ and $v = (v_1, ..., v_M)$ to be compared, there exist three cases:

- *Case 1*: u meets $M - k$ goals (i.e., $M - k$ of the specified goal components) which can be expressed as follows:

$$\exists k = 1, ..., M - 1 : \forall i = 1, ..., k; \ \ \forall j = k+1, ..., M (u_i > g_i) \wedge (u_j \leq g_j) \quad (25)$$

The expression (25) assumes a convenient permutation of the objectives.

- *Case 2*: u does not meet any goal which can be expressed as follows:

$$\forall i = 1, ..., M (u_i > g_i) \quad (26)$$

- *Case 3*: u meet all the goals which can be expressed as follows:

$$\forall i = 1, ..., M (u_i \leq g_i) \quad (27)$$

In case 1 (cf. (25)), u meets the goals $k + 1, ..., M$ and therefore it is considered to be preferred to v if it Pareto dominates v with respect to its k components. For the case where all of the k components of u are equal to those of v, u is preferred to v if it Pareto dominates v with respect to the remaining $M - k$ components or if the remaining $M - k$ components of v does not meet their goals. Analytically, u is preferred to v (denoted $u \prec_p v$) if and only if:

$$\begin{aligned} &\left(u_{(1, ..., k)} \preceq v_{(1, ..., k)} \right) \vee \\ &\left\{ \left(u_{(1, ..., k)} = v_{(1, ..., k)} \right) \wedge \left[\left(u_{(k+1, ..., M)} \preceq v_{(k+1, ..., M)} \right) \right. \right. \\ &\left. \left. \vee \neg \left(v_{(k+1, ..., M)} \leq g_{(k+1, ..., M)} \right) \right] \right\} \end{aligned} \quad (28)$$

In case 2 (cf. (26)), u does not satisfy any goal, then u is preferred to v if and only if u Pareto dominates v, i.e.:

$$u \preceq v \tag{29}$$

In case 3 (cf. (27)), u meet all the goals which means that it is a satisfactory, though not necessarily optimal solution. Then, u is preferred to v if and only if u Pareto dominates v or v is not a satisfactory solution, i.e.:

$$(u \preceq v) \vee \neg(v \leq g) \tag{30}$$

This approach can be used *a priori* or interactively. The authors also proposed an expert system ensuring the task of supplying goals since setting an appropriate goal is not a trivial task. However, if the goal has been set so ambitious that there is no solution which can reach the goal in even a single objective, the goal has no effect on the search, and simply the whole Pareto front is returned. Consequently, we can say that the obtained results heavily depend on the position of the goal in the objective space. Moreover, the spread of the obtained ROI cannot be controlled and the proposed approach does not consider this issue.

2.4.2 Tan et al. [52,53] Work

The authors proposed a variant of the Pareto dominance incorporating goal and priority information. In the first stage, the ranking scheme prefers objective vectors fulfilling all criteria and ranks those vectors according to MOGA Pareto dominance-based sorting [50]. Among the remaining solutions, the objective vector u dominates the objective vector v if and only if u dominates v with respect to the criteria in which u does not fulfil the goal $g = (g_1, ..., g_M)$ (as in Ref. [50]), or if $|u - g| \prec |v - g|$ (where $|u - g|$ denotes the vector composed with the absolute values of the differences between the objectives values of the solution v and the goal g). The latter expression corresponds to a *mirroring* of the objective vector along the axis of the fulfilled criteria. Analytically, u is preferred to v (denoted $u\pi_g v$) if and only if:

(1) u and v both satisfy all the goals and $u \preceq v$; or

(2) u and v both does not satisfy all the goals and $\bar{u} \preceq \bar{v}$ or $|u - g| \preceq |v - g|$, where $\bar{u}$ and $\bar{v}$ corresponds to the vectors composed with the components that do not fulfil the goals of u and v, respectively.

The main drawback of this approach is that this kind of dominance is intransitive, i.e., it may lead to the case, where x is preferred to y and y is preferred to z, but x and z are considered to be equivalent. The main advantages of this approach is the possibility to consider multiple goals by the use of *AND* and *OR* connectives.

2.4.3 Deb et al. [8] Work: The Reference Point-Based NSGA-II (R-NSGA-II)

R-NSGA-II is a modified version of NSGA-II that focuses the search on the ROIs according to a user-provided reference point set. The reference points are used to guide the search toward the preferred parts of the Pareto front. In fact, the crowding distance of NSGA-II is modified as follows. For each reference point, the normalized Euclidean distance of each solution of the front is calculated and the solutions are sorted in ascending order of distance. The closest solution from the reference point is assigned a rank of one; the second nearest solution is assigned a rank of two and so on. After such computations are performed for all reference points, the crowding distance of a certain solution is equal to the minimum of its assigned ranks. In this way, solutions closest to all reference points are assigned the smallest crowding distance of one. The solutions having next-to-smallest Euclidean distance to all reference points are assigned the next-to-smallest crowding distance of two, and so on. Thereafter, solutions with smaller crowding distances are preferred in the tournament selection and in forming the new population from the combined population of parents and children. In order to control the extent of the obtained solutions, all solutions having a sum of normalized difference in objective values of ε or less between them are grouped. A randomly picked solution from each group is retained and the rest of all group members are assigned a large crowding distance in order to discourage them to remain in the race. The above procedure provides an equal emphasis of solutions closest to each reference point, thereby allowing multiple ROIs to be found simultaneously in a single simulation run. R-NSGA-II has demonstrated good results on two- to five-objective test problems. However, there were difficulties when using a single reference point since diversity is not well maintained. Moreover, the ε clearing parameter setting is not trivial.

2.4.4 Deb and Kumar [54] Work: The Reference Direction-Based Approach

The authors combined the reference direction method [55] with NSGA-II. The reference direction method allows the DM to set a starting point and a reference point such that the difference of the two defines the reference direction. First, a set of point $r(t)$ $(t = 1, 2, \dots)$ are marked on the given reference direction. Then, for each point $r(t)$, we compute the ASF value $s(z, r, w)$ for a chosen weight vector w and for each population member z. Thereafter, the individual z^* having the smallest value of s is declared to lie on the first nondominated front by assigning it the rank of one. This procedure is continued for each point r and the corresponding population member for the minimum s is included in the first nondominated front. Thereafter, these chosen population members are temporarily discarded from the population and the above procedure is repeated. The next set of minimum s solutions is then declared to form the second nondominated front. This procedure is repeated till all population members are classified into nondominated frontiers. Thereafter, the crowding distance procedure is repeated with the classified population members as usual. This hybrid method has the ability to find Pareto optimal solutions corresponding to several reference points along the reference direction. Several preferences could be modeled by various reference directions and the hybrid algorithm found for each reference direction its corresponding ROI. The authors noted that the population size in such a NSGA-II version should be at least two or three times the number of points considered along the reference direction. The multiplicity is needed to ensure that the search is adequately guided toward the corresponding efficient point. The reference direction approach has demonstrated good results in tackling two- to 10-objective MOPs. However, the population diversity degradation that can be yielded when using a single reference direction remains a significant matter since this approach does not include a clearing mechanism such as the R-NSGA-II one.

2.4.5 Deb and Kumar [56] Work: The LBS-Based Approach

The authors combined the LBS method [57] with NSGA-II. In the LBS method, the DM has to specify three preference parameters for each objective which is quite demanding on the part of the DM. In order to reduce the DM's load, the authors use only the veto preference parameter (cf. Eq. (34)). Once, the middle point is obtained (cf. Fig. 10), the feasible direction of the largest improvement of each objective is determined. The best feasible point in each direction satisfying the outranking criterion is determined. These points are then projected on the Pareto optimal front by solving an augmented form of Wierzbicki's ASF. This results in the best feasible point in each direction satisfying the outranking criterion and Pareto optimality. The authors hybridized NSGA-II and LBS method. The DM is asked to supply an aspiration point (i.e., a reference point) and a reservation point. The hybrid algorithm is as follows:

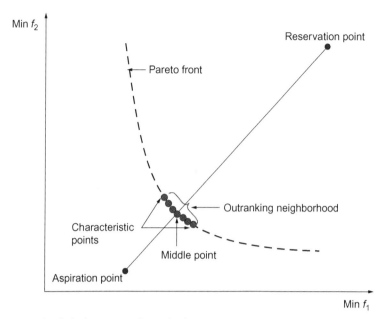

Figure 10 The light beam search method.

(1) Nondominated sorting is performed for the whole population,
(2) For each front, each solution from the front is assigned a crowding rank:

(a) Crowding distance cd of each solution x is computed as:

$$cd(x) = \max_{m=1,\ldots,M} \left\{ \lambda_m \left(f_m(x) - z_m^a \right) \right\} + \rho \sum_{m=1}^{M} \left(f_m(x) - z_m^a \right) \quad (31)$$

where $z^a = \left[z_1^a, \ldots, z_M^a \right]$ is the aspiration point, $\Lambda = [\lambda_1, \ldots, \lambda_M]$ is the weighting coefficient vector $(\lambda_m > 0 \;\; \forall m = 1, \ldots, M)$ and ρ is a sufficient small positive number (called augmentation coefficient which is fixed to 10^{-6} here). The weighting vector can be defined by the aspiration point z^a and the reservation one z^r (where $z_m^a < z_m^r \;\; \forall m = 1, \ldots, M$) as follows:

$$\lambda_m = \frac{1}{z_m^r - z_m^a} \quad (32)$$

(b) Solution with least cd value is the middle point z^c (cf. Fig. 10) and it is assigned the highest crowding rank.
(c) For all solutions x outranking z^c (cf. Eq. (34)), the maximum difference in objective value with z^c is determined:

$$\phi(x) = \max_{m=1,\dots,M} \left(f_m(x) - z_m^c \right) \tag{33}$$

Based upon the $\phi(x)$ value, a crowding rank is assigned to each solution. Solutions with lesser $\phi(x)$ are assigned higher ranks and vice versa.

(d) The remaining solutions, that do not outrank z^c, are assigned lesser crowding ranks so they are discouraged during the selection process.

In the case of multiple light beams, a crowding rank corresponding to each light beam is first determined for each solution. Then, the minimum rank for all light beams is assigned as the final crowding rank of the considered solution.

(3) In order to obtain a uniform distribution in the lighted regions, no two-objective vectors apart by less than an ε distance are preferred in the same manner as the clearing procedure of R-NSGA-II.

The modified outranking relation used in this work is:

$$\begin{cases} f(x)\, S z^c & \text{if } t_v\left(f(x), z^c \right) = 0 \\ t_v(f(x), z^c) = \operatorname{card}\left\{ m : f_m(x) - z_m^c \geq \text{veto}_m, \quad m = 1, \dots, M \right\} \end{cases} \tag{34}$$

The objective vector $f(x)$ outranks z^c (denoted $f(x)\, S z^c$) means that $f(x)$ is at least as good as z^c. As both solutions belong to the same nondominated front, if $f(x)$ is worse than z^c in some objectives, the amount of deterioration of $f(x)$ over z^c must not exceed the corresponding provided veto thresholds (veto_m, $m = 1, \dots, M$).

This hybrid algorithm has demonstrated its ability to find the part of the Pareto optimal region illuminated by the light beam emanating from the reservation point to the aspiration point with a span controlled by the veto thresholds. The simulation results have shown good results when applying this approach on a suite of benchmarks. However, providing the veto thresholds is not an easy task for the human DM. Further efforts are needed to study how to help the DM to elicit such parameters.

2.4.6 Allmendinger et al. [58] Work: The Reference Point-Based Particle Swam Optimization Using a Steady-State Approach

The authors hybridized the particle swarm optimization (PSO) meta-heuristic [59] with the reference point method [60]. The authors used a steady-state approach where an offspring is generated one at a time. A replacement strategy is often employed to compare the offspring with its parents. The offspring only replaces a weaker parent (i.e., dominated by its child). Note that this procedure results in a population size that is constant during the entire run of the algorithm. There is no notion of generation. The velocity is set randomly to be within the variable ranges. The DM is invited to supply one or more reference point(s). The population is divided into equal sized clusters each focusing on one reference point. The main loop is described as follows. Do the following for each particle x in each cluster until a stopping criterion is met:

(1) Choose a particle randomly from the current cluster as the global best particle $p^g = [p_1^g, ..., p_M^g]$;

(2) Produce an offspring based on x, p^g, and p^b, where $p^b = [p_1^b, ..., p_M^b]$ is the best position found by the particle x so far during the optimization process;

(3) If the generated offspring Pareto dominates x/p^g then it replaces it, else if the offspring is nondominated with respect to both x and p^g then the two particles closest to the reference point are kept and the farthest particle is deleted.

Reference point-based particle swam optimization using a steady-state approach (RPSO-SS) uses also an ε-clearing mechanism like R-NSGA-II in order to preserve population diversity and to allow the DM to control the ROI extent. The experimental study has mentioned good results in solving two- and three-objective test problems. However, there were difficulties when solving highly multimodal problems such ZDT4.

In the same study, the authors proposed an extended selection strategy. In fact, the original selection strategy will not keep an offspring in the population that is farther than x and p^g from the reference point. The new replacement strategy extends the replacement strategy of the basic RPSO-SS and provides the offspring with the opportunity to replace particles other than x or p^g. Thus, a randomly selected particle y is compared to the offspring and it is replaced if it is dominated by the offspring or it is nondominated regarding the offspring but it is farther than the offspring from the reference point. Additionally, instead of using a single randomly selected particle as a p^g, the new sampling-based selection mechanism selects Np^g particles randomly. Among these particles, the one with the shortest Euclidean distance to the reference point is chosen as p^g. The obtained results have demonstrated the larger the Np^g value is, the better the convergence is.

2.4.7 Wickramasinghe and Li [61] Work

The authors hybridized the nondominated sorting PSO (NSPSO) [62] and the MaxiMin PSO (MMPSO) [63] with the reference point method. The

NSPSO has the same sorting and diversity preserving mechanisms of NSGA-II. In fact, from a population of size N, an offspring population of size N is created. After that, a nondominated sorting is performed on the merged population of size $2N$ in order to classify it into several nondominated fronts. Once nondomination ranks are assigned, the crowding distance assignment is performed front-wise. The leaders p^g are then selected from the set of top 10% least crowded solutions from the first nondominated front. In MMPSO, the fitness of particle x is given by the maximum of the minimum values between x and all other particles y from the population P and is given by:

$$\text{fitness}(x) = \max_{m=1,\dots,M; y \in P\{x\}} \left\{ \min \left\{ f_m(x) - f_m(y) \right\} \right\} \tag{35}$$

The particles having a fitness values less than zero are considered as nondominated and constitute the first nondominated front. The total number of individuals that move to the next generation will consist of all individuals in the first nondominated set. If the nondominated set size is less than desired, then dominated individuals are chosen randomly to fill the vacant positions. A particle will choose a leader (global best), randomly from the top 10% of least crowded particles in the nondominated front. In both reference point-based PSO algorithms, the leader selection strategy is modified. In NSPSO, a particle chooses its leader from the potential set corresponding to the top 10% closest particles to the reference point picked from the first nondominated front. In MMPSO, a particle will choose random values from all dimensions of the set of potential leaders and produce a new leader. An ε-clearing mechanism is included in both NSPSO and MMPSO in the same way as R-NSGA-II in order to control the ROI spread. The two PSO algorithms have demonstrated their ability to provide several ROIs near the user-provided reference points with a controlled spread defined by the user-specified ε parameter. However, NSPSO and MMPSO effectiveness depends on the population size since the potential set size depends on the population size.

2.4.8 Molina et al. [64] Work: The g-dominance

The authors suggested a new kind of dominance, called g-dominance, where solutions satisfying all aspiration levels and solutions fulfilling none of the aspiration levels are preferred over solutions satisfying some aspiration levels. The authors noted that the g-dominance has three merits: (1) it can be incorporated in several metaheuristics, (2) although the preferences are modeled as a reference point, the search process works without using any ASF, and (3)

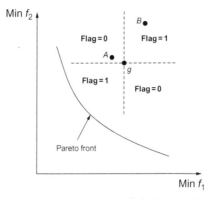

Figure 11 The g-dominance: nonpreservation of the Pareto dominance order.

it can be used in an interactive way. Formally, assuming $g = (g_1, ..., g_M)$ to be a reference point, each solution x is assigned a flag as follows:

$$\text{Flag}_g(x) = \begin{cases} 1 & \text{if } f_m(x) \leq g_m \ \forall m = 1, ..., M \\ 1 & \text{if } f_m(x) \geq g_m \ \forall m = 1, ..., M \\ 0 & \text{otherwise} \end{cases} \tag{36}$$

Given two distinct solutions x and y, x is said to g-dominate y if and only if:

$$\text{Flag}_g(x) > \text{Flag}_g(y) \quad \text{or} \quad \text{Flag}_g(x) = \text{Flag}_g(y) \ \text{and} \ f(x) \preceq f(y) \tag{37}$$

The main disadvantage of this approach is that it does not preserve the order induced by the Pareto dominance relation. Hence, a dominated solution which satisfies none of the goals may be preferred to a solution that dominates it and which fulfills some of the goals. Figure 11 illustrates this case. Solution A Pareto dominates B, however solution B g-dominates solution A. This fact discourages convergence toward the Pareto optimal front.

2.4.9 Thiele et al. [65] Work: The Preference-Based Evolutionary Algorithm

The authors combined IBEA [20] with the reference point method. The obtained method is called the Preference-based IBEA and denoted Preference-Based Evolutionary Algorithm (PBEA). In IBEA the fitness function of a particular solution x is given by:

$$\text{fitness}(x) = \sum_{y \in P \setminus \{x\}} \left(-e^{-I(y, x)/\kappa} \right) \tag{38}$$

where κ is a scaling factor [20]. The fitness of x expresses the loss in quality if solution x is removed from the population, i.e., the marginal contribution of x in terms of approximation quality. The quality indicator used in IBEA is the additive binary ε-indicator I_{ε^+} which is a Pareto compliant indicator (i.e., Pareto dominance preserving) [18] and is expressed as follows:

$$I_{\varepsilon^+}(x, y) = \min_{\varepsilon} \{ f_m(x) - \varepsilon \le f_m(y) \quad \forall m = 1, \ldots, M \} \tag{39}$$

In order to take DM's preferences into account, the authors modified (39) as follows:

$$I_p(x, y) = I_{\varepsilon^+}(x, y) / s(g, f(x), \delta_{\text{PBEA}}) \tag{40}$$

where

$$s(g, f(x), \delta_{\text{PBEA}}) = s(g, f(x)) + \delta_{\text{PBEA}} - \min_{y \in P} \{ s(g, f(y)) \} \tag{41}$$

δ_{PBEA} is called the specificity parameter and allows the DM to control the spread of the obtained ROI and $s(g, f(x))$ is the ASF of solution x. The main advantages of this approach are that the used $I_p(x, y)$ binary quality indicator is Pareto dominance preserving and the approach can be used interactively with more than one reference point. However, the authors noted that adjusting the specificity parameter is not an easy task and such topic is for further investigation.

2.4.10 Bechikh et al. [66] Work: The r-Dominance

The r-dominance (reference-solution-based dominance) takes its origins from the hybridization between the Pareto dominance principle and the reference point method. The key feature of this preference-based dominance relation is to prefer solutions that are closer to the reference point (DM's preferences) while preserving the order induced by the Pareto dominance [66,67]. In order to determine the closeness of a certain solution to the reference point, the following ASF, called the weighted Euclidean distance [8], is used:

$$\text{Dist}(x, g) = \sqrt{\sum_{i=1}^{M} w_i \left(\frac{f_i(x) - f_i(g)}{f_i^{\max} - f_i^{\min}} \right)^2}, \quad w_i \in]0, 1[, \sum_{i=1}^{M} w_i = 1 \tag{42}$$

where x is the considered solution, g is the user-specified reference point, $f_i^{\max}$ is the upper bound of the ith objective value, $f_i^{\min}$ is the lower bound of the ith objective value, and w_i is the weight associated with the ith objective. It should be noted that the ASF (40) can be used when solving nonconvex MOPs [8]. Our choice is justified by the fact that the weighted Euclidean distance gathers more information about the closeness of a certain solution to the reference point than the ASF proposed by Wierzbicki (4) especially when the number of objectives increases [67]. The r-dominance is defined as follows:

Definition 2.1

r-Dominance

Assuming a population of individuals P, a reference vector g and a weight vector w, a solution x is said to r dominate a solution y (denoted $x \prec_r y$) if one of the following statements holds true:

(1) x dominates y in the Pareto sense,
(2) x and y are Pareto-equivalent and $D(x,y,g) < -\delta$, where $\delta \in [0,1]$ and:

$$D(x, y, g) = \frac{\text{Dist}(x, g) - \text{Dist}(y, g)}{\text{Dist}_{max} - \text{Dist}_{min}} \tag{43}$$

$$\text{Dist}_{max} = \text{Max}_{z \in P} \text{Dist}(z, g) \tag{44}$$

$$\text{Dist}_{min} = \text{Min}_{z \in P} \text{Dist}(z, g) \tag{45}$$

δ is termed as the *non-r-dominance threshold*.

The main idea behind the r-dominance relation is to create a *strict partial order* between Pareto-equivalent solutions. Hence, the r-dominance has the ability to differentiate between nondominated solutions in a partial manner based on the user-supplied aspiration level vector. This fact not only makes the r-dominance selection pressure "*stronger*" than the Pareto dominance one, but also it integrates the DM's preferences in the selection process. After substituting the Pareto dominance with the r-dominance in the NSGA-II algorithm with an adaptive management of the δ parameter, the resulting preference-based MOEA, named r-NSGA-II (reference-solution-based NSGA-II), has demonstrated its ability to:

(1) easily guide the search toward the ROI(s) independently of the reference point position in the search space;
(2) control the ROI spread by means of the δ parameter;
(3) be executed interactively which facilitates the DM's task and develops his/her acquired knowledge about the considered MOP;
(4) handle some many-objective instances of the DTLZ problems (i.e., DTLZ problem instances involving up to 10-objective functions); and

(5) provide competitive and better results then those furnished by three recently proposed reference point-based MOEAs, i.e., g-NSGA-II, PBEA, and R-NSGA-II (which are previously discussed in this section).

We note that r-NSGA-II has faced difficulties when solving highly multimodal problems such as ZDT4 [68]. These difficulties seem to be due to the diversity reduction induced by the progressive focus of the population individuals on a particular region of the objective space (i.e., ROI). Thus, it is important to design some strategies allowing escaping from local optima when resolving such type of problems. Moreover, although the spread control parameter δ belongs to [0,1], the appropriate setting of this parameter is not easy in real world applications.

2.4.11 López Jaimes et al. [69] Work: The Chebyshev Preference Relation-Based Approach

The authors hybridized NSGA-II with an ASF based on the Chebyshev distance, which computes the distance separating a particular objective vector z from a reference point g capturing the DM's preference information in the form of desired values for each objective function. The ASF is expressed as follows:

$$s(z, g, \lambda) = \max_{i=1,\ldots,M} \{\lambda_i(z_i - g_i)\} + \rho \sum_{i=1}^{M} \lambda_i(z_i - g_i) \qquad (46)$$

where ρ is an augmentation coefficient sufficiently small and $\lambda = [\lambda_1, \ldots, \lambda_M]$ such that:

$$\lambda_i = \frac{1}{z_i^{\text{nad}} - z_i^{**}} \qquad (47)$$

where z_i^{nad} is the ith component of the nadir point and z_i^{**} is the ith component of the utopian point.

The basic idea of the Chebyshev preference relation is to combine the Pareto dominance relation and the ASF (46) to compare solutions in the objective function space. First, $s(z, g, \lambda)$ is computed for each solution z. Then, the objective space is divided into two regions. One region defines the ROI and contains those solutions with an ASF value less or equal to $(s^{\min} + \delta)$ where $s^{\min} = \min_{z \in Z} s(z, g, \lambda)$ and δ is a threshold that determines the ROI spread.

Figure 12 shows the ROI space defined by means of the ASF. If both solutions under comparison reside in the ROI space than they are compared using the usual Pareto dominance. However, when at least one solution resides outside the ROI space then the two solutions are compared using their ASF values and the solution with the least ASF value is preferred. The Chebyshev preference relation is defined as follows:

Definition 2.2

Chebyshev Preference Relation

An objective vector z^1 is preferred to and objective vector z^2 with respect to the Chebyshev relation $\left(z^1 \preceq_{\text{Cheby}} z^2\right)$ if and only if:

(1)

$$s\left(z^1, g, \lambda\right) < s\left(z^2, g, \lambda\right) \wedge \left[z^1 \notin R(g, \delta) \vee z^2 \notin R(g, \delta)\right];$$

or

(2)

$$z^1 \preceq z^2 \wedge \left[z^1, z^2 \in R(g, \lambda)\right].$$

where $R(g, \lambda) = \{z \mid s(z, g, \lambda) < s^{\min} + \delta\}$ is the ROI space with respect to the user-supplied reference point g.

The Pareto dominance is replaced with the Chebyshev preference relation in NSGA-II. The resulting algorithm has demonstrated its ability to guide the search interactively toward the ROI on two- to six-objective airfoil design problem. Additionally, the ROI breadth can be controlled with the δ parameter. However, the setting of such parameter seems to be not trivial especially in real world problems.

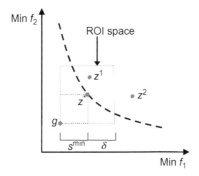

Figure 12 Illustration of the Chebyshev preference relation.

2.5 Trade-Off-Based Approaches

2.5.1 *Branke* et al. *[16] Work: The G-MOEA*

The authors proposed a variant of the Pareto dominance relation that focuses the search toward the preferred part of the front based on trade-off information provided by the DM. In fact, the DM is invited to provide, for each pair of objectives, maximally acceptable trade-offs. For example, for the biobjective case, the DM could specify that an improvement by one unit in objective f_2 is worth a degradation of objective f_1 by at most c_{12} unit. Similarly, a gain in objective f_1 by one unit is worth a degradation of objective f_2 by at most c_{21} unit. This trade-off information is then used to modify the dominance relation as follows:

$$x \preceq_t y \Leftrightarrow \left(f_1(x) + c_{12} f_2(x) \leq f_1(y) + c_{12} f_2(y)\right)$$
$$\wedge \left(c_{21} f_1(x) + f_2(x) \leq c_{21} f_1(y) + f_2(y)\right) \tag{48}$$

where $x \preceq_t y$ means that x is preferred to y based on the designed trade-off-based dominance relation. Figure 13 shows the effect produced by the new dominance relation in the objective space. In fact, when compared to the original dominance relation, a particular solution now dominates a larger region. With this dominance scheme, only a part of the Pareto optimal front remains nondominated. This corresponds to the ROI. However, since this approach implicitly assumes linear utility functions, it may not be possible for G-MOEA to focus on all parts of concave Pareto optimal front. Moreover, this approach is restricted to the biobjective case.

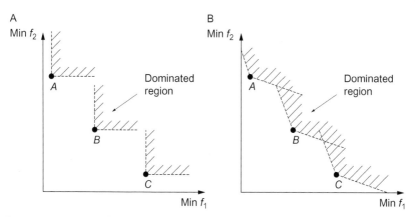

Figure 13 Dominated region for: (A) Pareto dominance and (B) trade-off-based dominance.

2.6 Outranking-Based Approaches

2.6.1 *Fernandez* et al. *[70] Work: The Nonoutranking Sorting Genetic Algorithm*

The authors exploited the outranking concept [71] in order to integrate DM's preferences in NSGA-II. For each objective function f_m, a relational system of preferences (Pr_m, I_m) is designed where Pr means preference and I means indifference. For each objective vector component pair $(f_m(x), f_m(y))$, one and only one of the three following statements holds:

(1)

$$f_m(x),\ \mathrm{Pr}f_m(y)$$

(2)

$$f_m(y)\,\mathrm{Pr}f_m(x),\quad or$$

(3)

$$f_m(x)\mathit{I}f_m(y).$$

This formulation allows indifference thresholds in order to model some kinds of imprecise one-dimensional preferences. It should be noticed that the considered relational system of preferences is more general than the usual formulations which consider only true criteria (i.e., $f_m(x) \neq f_m(y)$ implies nonindifference). Without loss of generality, the following is supposed:

$$f_m(x)Pr \Rightarrow f_m(x) > f_m(y)f_m(y) \tag{49}$$

For each pair $(f(x), f(y))$, the DM, assisted by the decision analyst, creates a fuzzy predicate modeling the truth degree of the predicate "$f(x)$ is at least as good as $f(y)$." The authors adopted the outranking approach based on ELECTRE methods [72]. Assuming $u = f(x)$ and $v = f(y)$, the proposition "u outranks v" which means "u seems at least as good as v" holds if and only if the coalition of criteria in agreement with this proposition is strong enough and there is no important coalition discordant with it. It can be expressed by the following logical equivalence:

$$uSv \Leftrightarrow C(u,v) \wedge \neg D(u,v) \tag{50}$$

where $C(u,v)$ is the predicate about the strength of the concordance coalition and $D(u,v)$ is the predicate about the strength of the discordance coalition. Let $c(u,v)$ and $d(u,v)$ denote the truth degrees of the predicates $C(u,v)$ and $D(u,v)$, respectively. From (50), the truth degree of "uSv" can be calculated as in ELECTRE-III method:

$$\sigma(u, v) = c(u, v) \times N(d(u, v)) \qquad (51)$$

where $N(d(u, v))$ denotes the truth degree of the nondiscordance predicate. As in the earlier versions in ELECTRE methods, the following is assumed:

$$c(u, v) = \sum_{m \in C_{u,v}} w_m \qquad (52)$$

where $C_{u,v} = \{m \in \{1, ..., M\} | u_m Prv_m \vee u_m Iv_m\}$ and w_m is the objective weight such that $\sum_{m=1}^{M} w_m = 1$.

Let $D_{u,v} = \{m \in \{1, ..., M\} | v_m Pru_m\}$ be the discordance coalition with "uSv." The discordance intensity is measured in comparison with a veto threshold ve_m which corresponds to the maximum difference $(v_m - u_m)$ compatible with $\sigma(u, v) > 0$. Following Mousseau and Dias [73], the authors used a simplification of the original formulation of the discordance indices in the ELECTRE-III method which is given by:

$$N(d(u, v)) = \min_{m \in D_{u,v}} [1 - d_m(u, v)] \qquad (53)$$

$$d_m(u, v) = \begin{cases} 1 & \text{iff } \nabla_m \geq ve_m \\ (\nabla_m - dth_m)/(ve_m - dth_m) & \text{iff } dth_m < \nabla_m < ve_m \\ 0 & \text{iff } \nabla_m \leq dth_m \end{cases} \qquad (54)$$

where $\nabla m = v_m - u_m$ and dth_m is a discordance threshold (cf. Fig. 14).

The λ-cut $\sigma(u, v) \geq \lambda$ defines a crisp outranking relation "uSv." Credible outranking statements are obtained with $\lambda = 0.75$ (strong outranking) and even with $\lambda = 0.67$ (weak outranking). Additionally, according to Ostanello [74], $\sigma(u, v) \approx 0.5$ is defined as a doubtful outranking and $\sigma(u, v) < 0.5$ means a definitive no outranking. According to Roy [71], a presumed preference favoring u over v is expressed by:

$$(uSv) \wedge \neg(vSu) \Leftrightarrow (\sigma(u, v) \geq \lambda) \wedge (\sigma(v, u) < \lambda) \qquad (55)$$

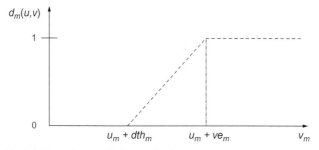

Figure 14 Partial discordance relation $d_m(u,v)$.

Following Fernandez *et al.* [75], the existence of a threshold $\beta > 0$ is assumed such that if $(\sigma(u, v) \geq \lambda)$ and $(\sigma(v, u) \leq (\sigma(u, v) - \beta))$, then there is an asymmetric preference relation favoring u which is denoted by: $uPr(\lambda, \beta)v$. The authors concretized this preference relation as follows. $uPr(\lambda, \beta)v$ if one of the following statements holds:

(1) u Pareto dominates v,

(2) $\sigma(u, v) \geq 0.67 \wedge \sigma(v, u) < 0.5$, or

(3) $(\sigma(u, v) \geq 0.67) \wedge (0.5 \leq \sigma(v, u) < 0.67) \wedge ((\sigma(u, v) - \sigma(v, u)) \geq \phi)$

where φ is a strictly outranking parameter whose value might depend on the number of criteria. It is assumed that φ should be greater than $(0.67-0.5) = 0.17$.

In the following, the basic definitions adopted in this work are presented:

Definition 2.3

Outranking relation

An objective vector u strictly outranks an objective vector v if and only if u $Pr(\lambda, \beta)$ v.

Definition 2.4

Nonstrictly outranked objective vector

An objective vector u is said to be nonstrictly outranked if and only if there does not exist another objective vector v that outranks u.

Definition 2.5

Strictly outranking set

For an objective vector u, the strictly outranking set is defined as:

$$S_o(u) = \{v \text{ belonging to the objective space} | vPr(\lambda, \beta)u\} \qquad (56)$$

The cardinality of this set is denoted $\text{card}(S_o)$ which is an integer function depending of the objective vector u.

Definition 2.6

Weakness of an objective vector

The weakness of an objective vector u in an objective vector set A is:

$$W(u) = \text{card}(\{v \in A | (\sigma(v, u) > \sigma(u, v)) \wedge (\sigma(v, u) \geq 0.5)\}) \qquad (57)$$

Definition 2.7

Strength of an objective vector

The strength of an objective vector u in an objective vector set A is:

$$S_t(u) = \text{card}(\{v \in A | (\sigma(u, v) > \sigma(v, u)) \wedge (\sigma(u, v) \geq 0.5)\}) \qquad (58)$$

The Nonoutranking Sorting Genetic Algorithm (NOSGA) works with nonstrictly outranked solutions instead of nondominated ones. The selection process is similar to NSGA-II one but it extracts nonstrictly out-ranked individuals, solutions having the same card(S_o) value, to classify the population into different nonstrictly outranked fronts. It should be noted that the first front may have card(S_o) different of zero. Since the MOEA searches for the ROI and not an approximation of the whole Pareto front, the crowding distance criterion is replaced by the weakness measure W. That is, when two individuals with equal card(S_o) are compared, the least weak is preferred. NOSGA selective pressure depends on σ values in the current population. The authors noted that when no veto condition is held, $\sigma(u, v)$ is replaced by the strength S_t of the concordance coalition. The NOSGA performance assessment was done on several instances of four-to nine-objective knapsack problem. The NOSGA has demonstrated its superiority over NSGA-II in providing nonoutranked solutions in a privileged zone of the Pareto front. Moreover, the NOSGA is shown to be less sensitive to the increase of the number of objectives than NSGA-II. The main crux of this study is that the NOSGA was not confronted to any preference-based MOEA. Such confrontation is required for more validation.

In a more recent study [76], the same authors proposed an enhanced version of NOSGA, called NOSGA-II, which augments the selective pressure toward the preferred solutions. This is achieved by considering other binary preference relations in the preferential system in addition to the strict preference relation and the indifference one. These relations are the following:

— *Weak preference*: It corresponds to the existence of clear and positive reasons in favor of *u* over *v*, but that are not sufficient to justify strict preference.

— *Incomparability*: None of the situations of indifference, strict preference nor weak preference predominates. That is, the absence of clear and positive reasons that justify any of these relations.

— *K-preference*: It corresponds to the existence of clear and positive reasons that justify strict preference in favor of one (identified) of the two objects or incomparability between the two objects, but with no significant division established between the situations of strict preference and incomparability.

The authors reported that the NOSGA-II outperforms the NSGA-II and the NOSGA on a real world instance of the multiobjective knapsack problem.

2.7 DF-Based Approaches

2.7.1 Wagner and Trautmann [77] Work: The Desirability Function-Based SMS-EMOA (DF-SMS-EMOA)

The authors proposed a preference-based version of the SMS-EMOA [78], which combines nondominated sorting with hypervolume-based selection.

In fact, in each generation, the last (worst) considered nondominated front is pruned by removing the individual having the least contribution in terms of hypervolume. For each objective function, the DM is invited to express his/her preferences by supplying two thresholds which represent: (1) an AS and (2) a MI. These thresholds serve as parameters to the DF of the corresponding objective function. The concept of desirability was introduced by Harrington [79] in the context of multiobjective industrial quality control. DFs map the values of the objectives to desirabilities, i.e., values on a unitless scale in the domain [0,1]. The mapping is based on preference information regarding exemplary objective values (i.e., the two thresholds AS and MI). We note that in addition to supplying AS and MI, the DM specifies a desirability value for each threshold in the domain [0,1]. The preferences are specified under the assumption that the smaller the difference between the actual desirability and the maximum value of one is, the better the quality of the solution in the corresponding objective is. In general, any DF: $f(x) \rightarrow$ [0,1] describing the desirability of different regions in the objective space can be defined as a DF. Figure 15 presents an example of a realization of Harrington's DF [79]. The main idea of Desirability Function-based S Metric Selection-based Evolutionary Multiobjective Optimization Algorithm (DF-SMS-EMOA) is to convert the objective functions of the original MOP into DFs and then optimizing these DFs instead of the original objectives. We recall that desirabilities are to be maximized. The DF-SMS-EMOA has demonstrated its ability to bias the search toward the DM's preferred region on the biobjective ZDT test functions and the five-objective turning process problem [80]. However, there is no control over the ROI spread.

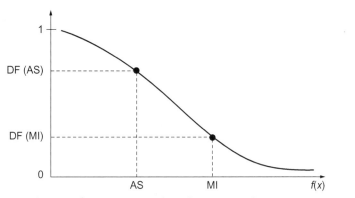

Figure 15 A realization of Harrington's DF based on DM's preferences: (AS, DF(AS)) and (MI, DF(MI)).

3. DISCUSSION

3.1 From MOEAs to Preference-Based MOEAs

If a single solution is to be selected from the Pareto front of a MOP at some point during the optimization process, the DM has to reveal his/her preferences. Specifying these preferences *a priori*, i.e., before alternatives are known, often means to ask too much from the DM. On the other hand, searching for all nondominated solutions, as most MOEAs do, may result in: (1) wasting computational efforts to find solutions that are clearly undesired by the DM and (2) complicating the DM's task when selecting the final preferred alternative from a huge set of solutions. In the previous section, we presented a review of the most prominent preference-based MOEAs, which allow avoiding the two above cited shortcomings of general-purpose MOEAs. Table 1 presents a synthetic comparison of preference-based

Table 1 Comparison of Preference-Based MOEAs (Inspired by Branke [12])

| References | General Criteria | | Pros and Cons Criteria | | | | |
	Modification	Influence	MROI	SC	PDP	DP	SCAD
Weights							
[13]	Crowding operator	Distribution	N	N	Y	N	N
[15]	Crowding operator	Distribution	N	Y	Y	N	Y
[17]	Quality indicator	Distribution	N	N	Y	N	Y
Ranking some candidate solutions							
[24]	Dominance	Region	N	N	Y	N	N
[25]	Dominance	Region	N	N	Y	N	Y
[27]	Dominance	Distribution	N	Y	Y	N	N
[29]	Crowding operator	Region	N	N	Y	Y	Y
[38]	Dominance	Region	N	N	Y	N	Y
[40]	Dominance + crowding distance	Distribution	N	N	Y	N	N
Ranking objectives							
[45]	Objectives aggregation	Distribution	N	N	N	Y	N
[47]	Dominance	Distribution	N	Y	N	N	N

Continued

Table 1 Comparison of Preference-Based MOEAs (Inspired by Branke [12])—cont'd

	General Criteria		Pros and Cons Criteria				
References	Modification	Influence	MROI	SC	PDP	DP	SCAD
[49]	(1) Dominance	Region	N	N	N	N	Y
	(2) Solution sorting	Region	N	N	Y	N	Y
	mechanism	Distribution	N	N	Y	N	Y
	(3) Crowding operator						
Reference point							
[50]	Dominance	Region	N	N	Y	N	N
[52,53]	Dominance	Region	Y	N	N	N	Y
[8]	Crowding operator	Region	Y	Y	Y	Y	Y
[58]	Leader selection strategy	Region	Y	Y	Y	Y	N
[61]	Leader selection strategy	Region	Y	Y	Y	Y	N
[64]	Dominance	Region	Y	N	N	Y	N
[65]	Quality indicator	Region	Y	Y	Y	N	Y
[66]	Dominance	Region	Y	Y	Y	N	Y
[69]	Dominance	Region	Y	Y	Y	N	Y
Reference direction (reference point + reservation point)							
[54]	Solution sorting mechanism	Region	Y	Y	Y	Y	Y
Reference direction and some preference thresholds							
Deb and Kumar [56]	Crowding operator	Region	Y	Y	Y	Y	Y
Trade-offs between objectives							
[16]	Objective functions	Region	N	N	Y	Y	N
Outranking parameters							
[70]	Dominance	Region	N	N	Y	N	Y
[76]	Dominance	Region	N	N	Y	N	Y
Desirability thresholds							
[77]	Objective functions	Region	Y	N	Y	N	Y

MROI means multiple ROIs, SC means spread control, PDP means Pareto dominance preservation, DP means diversity problems, and SCAD means SCAlability Demonstration with respect to the number of objectives. For pros and cons criteria, "Y" means yes and "N" means no.

MOEAs. The works are classified based on the type of the DM's preferences and are listed in a chronological order for each category in order to illustrate the evolution scheme of each class of algorithms. We remark that most of these works are published after 2006. Additionally, we see that from 2009, there is an increasing emphasis on the topic of including DM's preferences in EMO. Table 1 lists several comparison criteria that are classified into two main classes: (1) general criteria that are discussed in this subsection and (2) pros and cons criteria that will be discussed in Section 3.3. The general criteria are: (1) *modification* which indicates the modified part of the MOEA and (2) *influence* which indicates whether the result is a bounded region of the Pareto optimal front or just a biased distribution.

According to the algorithmic details of the different search methods provided in Section 2, we remark that most preference-based MOEAs are modified versions of general-purpose MOEAs. This observation is emphasized by the column *modification* in Table 1, where we see that the most frequently modified part of the MOEA is the dominance relation. In fact, several preference-based dominance relations were proposed such as the *r*-dominance, the *g*-dominance, the trade-off-based dominance, and so forth. When the Pareto dominance is replaced by such dominance relations, the search process is guided toward the ROI according to the DM's preferences. Based on the column *influence*, we see that most preference-based MOEAs aim at providing a bounded ROI rather than a biased distribution of nondominated solutions.

3.2 Preference Modeling Tools

From the preference modeling tools cited in this table, it is difficult for the DM to precisely state his/her preferences in *a priori* way, e.g., how could the DM specify the aspiration/reservation levels while he/she does not know the range of each objective function? A simple way to handle this difficulty is to run the MOEA for some small number of generations and then provide the DM with some solutions such as the ideal point and the nadir one. In this way, the DM builds an idea about the ranges of the different objectives, which facilitates the task of supplying aspiration/reservation levels. This fact has motivated researchers to design some EMO-based techniques for estimating the nadir point which plays a crucial role in the discovery of the objective ranges [81,82]. Such techniques have demonstrated their ability in finding the nadir point quickly and reliably on high dimension MOPs. When modeling preferences as weights, it is difficult to control the guidance of the search process toward the ROI. In fact, with the increase of the number of objectives, it is difficult to verify whether the MOEA's provided approximation really replies to the DM's specified weights. For this reason, using weights in an interactive manner is not really so attractive. Modeling preferences as trade-offs between objectives is a complicated task especially when the number of objectives increases. Consequently, using such an approach interactively augments the demanded effort from the DM. Ranking a sample of solutions seems to be an interesting way to elicit DM's preferences. However, how to select solutions to build such a sample is still an open question for further research. For example, in the BC-EMOA [29], the authors noted that the evolutionary process should be run for a certain number of generations, that is, of the same order of a plain MOEA run on the same problem, in order to ensure a reasonable coverage of the whole Pareto front and eventually not to miss portions containing some possibly preferred solutions. This fact makes BC-EMOA behave like a general-purpose MOEA where the entire Pareto front is firstly approximated and then the DM's preferences are used to select the final alternative to realize. Consequently, we do not really see the advantages of articulating DM's preferences within the MOEA. Furthermore, the computational complexity is increased. Using outranking relations in *a priori* way seems to be interesting. However, the DM should be assisted by the decision analyst (an expert) to set appropriate outranking parameters [83]. Objective ranking is also an interesting way to model DM's preferences. However, the preference update mechanism should be controlled in order to ensure preference consistency as noted by Rachmawati and Srinivasan [49]. Desirability thresholds seem to allow a straightforward specification of the DM's preferences. We note that the concepts of desirability thresholds and aspiration/reservation levels seem to be so similar.

Among all the used preference modeling tools, it seems to be that the most natural and precise way to express DM's preferences is the reference point (e.g., the DM would like to achieve 20 units in the first objective and 15 units in the second objective). In this way, DM's preferences could guide the search toward the ROI precisely and interactively without demanding a great effort from the DM even if the number of objectives M increases. Indeed, the reference point could be drawn on the same plot of the MOEA's population whatever is the number of objectives M (by using the 2D/3D plots for the two-/three-dimensional cases and the parallel coordinates plots for higher dimension cases). This fact facilitates not only the verification of the guidance of the population but also the update of the reference point. These statements are emphasized by the results presented in Table 1 since the reference point is the most used DM's preference information structure.

3.3 Pros and Cons

Table 1 lists a set of criteria that allow illustrating the pros and cons of the different approaches:

- *MROI*: "Y" value means that the algorithm offers the DM the ability to obtain more than one ROI. Usually, at the beginning of the evolutionary process, the DM does not have any idea about the search space. This fact can make the DM doubtful when expressing his/her preferences. Hence, with the option multiple regions of interest (MROI), the DM can guide the search toward multiple ROIs and then he/she focuses the MOEA's population on the final desired ROI during the interactive run. The MROI option represents an advantage for the MOEA, since it allows the DM to learn about the search space and consequently about his/her preferences during the interactive optimization process which facilitates the task of preference updating and adjusting.

- *SC*: "Y" value means that the algorithm allows the DM to control the spread of the obtained ROI whether being represented by: (1) a bounded region or (2) a biased distribution. The option spread control (SC) represents an advantage for the MOEA because if the algorithm does not allow controlling the ROI extent, the obtained results can be ambiguous for the DM. For example, in the NEMO algorithm [40] which does not allow controlling the ROI spread, the extent of the focus on the desired region is influenced by the number of generations. The larger this latter is, the stronger the focus is and consequently the smaller the ROI spread is. If the DM obtains a significantly different spread after each interaction, he/she can be misled not only while updating his/her preferences but also while deciding between stopping and continuing the interactive run. It is important to note that there is no general rule to set *a priori* a precise value for the spread control parameter. The researchers provide, in their studies, some values that can guide the DM in setting such a parameter. These values are obtained by *trial and error* (i.e., after several experiments). Hence, it is up to the DM to find *interactively* the spread control value that fits his/her preferences (e.g., [8,15,65], etc.).

- *PDP*: "Y" value means that the preference-based guidance mechanism of the related MOEA preserves the order induced by the Pareto dominance relation, i.e., a dominated solution with respect to the Pareto dominance relation cannot be preferred to a solution that dominates it. This fact preserves elitism [2]. In fact, the Pareto dominance preservation (PDP) criterion has been mentioned in the survey of Coello Coello [5]. If the preference-based MOEA allow contradicting the Pareto dominance order, then serious convergence problems can occur.

- *DP*: "*Y*" value means that the algorithm has some diversity problems (DPs), which represents an inconvenient for the MOEA. In fact, guiding the search process toward a particular region of the search space at the beginning of the search process may cause a reduction in the population phenotypic diversity. For this reason, when designing a preference-based MOEA, it is of particular interest to conceive a diversity mechanism that allows preserving the population diversity. For example, this was achieved in r–NSGA-II (cf. Section 2.4) by an adaptive management of the δ parameter that controls the ROI spread. This adaptive management makes the population converging gradually and progressively from one generation to another toward the desired region in such a way, at the end of the optimization process, we obtain a well-bounded ROI without facing any DP during the MOEA run.

- *SCAD*: "*Y*" value means that the scalability of the proposed approach with respect to the number of objectives is demonstrated in the original paper of the algorithm. The emerging field of many-objective optimization [84] has recently attracted a lot of researchers. One of the proposed approaches to handle such type of problems is to incorporate DM's preferences in the evolutionary process in order to explore only the desired portion of the Pareto front. With the increase of the number of objectives, the Pareto dominance becomes ineffective when comparing between solutions. Consequently, researchers have used DM's preferences as an additional criterion to distinguish between the population individuals and focus the search toward the optimal ROI of a many-objective problem.

4. CONCLUSIONS AND FUTURE RESEARCH PATHS

In this chapter, we have surveyed the most prominent preference-based MOEAs. Since these search methods are mostly variations of already existing general-purpose MOEAs, we have furnished the necessary algorithmic details of each described work so that the reader could understand how researchers have incorporated the DM's preferences in MOEAs. The main goal of preference incorporation in EMO is to summarize the Pareto front into a ROI, which is in turn a subset of the Pareto frontier, from which the DM selects the solution to realize; thereby facilitating the decision-making task. From the conceptual details provided in this chapter, we have detected several guidelines to pursue when designing preference-based MOEAs. First, the preference-based selection mechanism should preserve the order induced by the Pareto dominance relation otherwise convergence will be deteriorated by the acceptance of dominated solutions instead of dominating ones. For example, in Ref. [67], the r-dominance, which is a Pareto dominance preserving relation, is demonstrated to be superior to the g-dominance relation since this latter may favor dominated solutions over dominating ones. The Pareto preservation could be established by designing the preference-based selection mechanism so that it is: (1) complete with the Pareto dominance (i.e., if solution x Pareto dominates solution y then solution x should be preferred to solution y) and (2) compatible with the non Pareto dominance (i.e., if solution x is preferred to solution y then solution y does not Pareto dominate solution x). Second, the preference-based MOEA should preserve sufficiently the population diversity since guiding the search toward a particular region in the search space at the beginning of the evolutionary process may reduce the population diversity. Consequently, the search process may stagnate and the premature convergence phenomenon could occur. For example, Deb *et al.* [8] have suggested not only the use of the ε-clearing mechanism but also the preservation of the extreme solutions of the best nondominated front in order to preserve diversity. Third, the designer should minimize the DM's burden when specifying his/her preferences. This depends on the preference information structure. For example, when solving an M-objective problem with $M > 2$, it is so easier to specify a reference point than to specify acceptable trade-offs between pairs of objectives. Fourth, for the two- and three-objective cases, obtaining a biased distribution focusing on the preferred region may be interesting in order to have a rough idea about the entire front, which is valuable information. However, when the number of objectives exceeds three ($M \geq 4$), the dimensionality of the Pareto front augments dramatically and obtaining a rough idea about the Pareto front becomes very computationally expensive [85]. Hence, it is interesting to allow the DM to direct the search toward multiple ROIs whether being represented by: (1) bounded regions or (2) biased distributions. In fact, the DM could be doubtful about his/her preferences especially at the beginning of the MOEA run. By providing him/her the MROI option (cf. Table 1), the DM can learn about the search space and thereby this problem could be resolved. Fifth, the designer should provide the DM with the ability to control the ROI spread by means of a particular parameter so that, during an interactive run of the MOEA on the considered MOP, the DM obtains approximately the same ROI spread after each interaction. Moreover, the ROI extent should be controlled because the focus of the population on the desired region heavily depends on the termination criterion since the population is guided *gradually* toward a particular region in the search space from one generation to another, which may cause a DP especially with the increase of the number of objectives.

Although several works were conducted in the direction of preference incorporation in MOEAs, several research issues still remain to be addressed. In the following, we describe some of them:

- *Fuzzy preferences*: Usually, the DM would like to express his/her preferences by means of linguistic terms. Consequently, it seems to be interesting to the EMO community to integrate fuzzy preferences within MOEAs.
- *Group decision making*: A real aspect which has been omitted so far in the research on integrating preferences in EMO would be the decision making in the presence of several DMs trying to find a consensus decision all participants are willed to agree on. In fact, most preference-based MOEAs assume the uniqueness of the DM. Very few of these algorithms consider the hypothesis that there exists more than one DM by injecting several reference points in the MOEA each corresponding to a particular DM then the algorithm provides an average ROI [86]. However, this mechanism does not resolve the problem since most DMs are still dissatisfied [87]. Consequently, it is important to aggregate the conflicting DM's preferences before the beginning of the evolutionary process with the aim of maximizing the consensus between the different DMs while minimizing their dissatisfaction rates. This issue seems to be also a very challenging task due to Arrow's Impossibility Theorem [88]. It is worth noting that outranking relations seem to be very interesting to handle group preference aggregation in EMO [89].
- *Preference elicitation*: An important issue in preference-based algorithms is how to interact with the DM(s) and how to guide the DM(s) during the interaction in order to elicit his/her or their preferences in a consistent manner. Indeed, after each interaction, the DM is provided with a representation of the obtained solution set according to a particular visualization technique that should provide a clear picture of the results to the DM. The preference update seems to be not so difficult when solving a bi-/triobjective MOP [90]. However, when the number of objectives

exceeds three, both the visualization and the preference update become difficult. For example, when solving a 10-objective MOP interactively, the DM faces difficulty when settling his/her preferences (e.g., a reference point) after each interaction since the human cognitive load is limited [91]. Besides, the DM's interactive preference statements may be intransitive [92]. Consequently, the preference update is not trivial at all and the difficulty of such a task augments with the increase of the number of objectives. For all these reasons, there is a clear need to develop advanced techniques that assist the DMs when visualizing, evaluating, and comparing alternatives characterized by multiple attributes according to his/her wishes. This fact will further encourage the DMs to use interactive preference-based MOEAs when solving many-objective problems. Another important issue in interactive preference-based multiobjective optimization is the number of DM's calls. Recently, Pedro and Takahashi [93] proposed a neural network-based decision maker (called NN-DM) that corresponds to an artificial DM that learns the human DM's preferences obtained via queries where each query corresponds to a comparison between two solutions and the user specifies which one is more preferred. The NN-DM is shown to be able to build an utility function-based model for the human DM's preferences so that no more queries are required from the user. Once this preference model is adjusted, it can be used inside the interactive optimization process in order to guide the search toward the ROI without the need of more information from the human DM. This work seems to be very interesting and it opens several challenging research perspectives.

- *Stopping criteria for preference update and MOEA run*: We remark from the algorithmic details of the different discussed works that there is not a clear rule for setting the stopping criteria (e.g., number of generations) of the MOEA run from one DM call to another. In fact, when the MOEA run should be interrupted in order to allow the DM to update his/her preferences? Additionally, there is no a clear rule for setting the stopping criteria of the overall interactive optimization process.

- *Diversity preserving techniques*: As mentioned previously, driving the search toward a particular region in the search space, at the beginning of the evolutionary process, may cause a lack of population diversity. Consequently, the search process may stagnate in local optima especially when solving multimodal problems such as ZDT4 [68]. Hence, the designer should take care of this problem by conceiving diversity preserving techniques for preference-based MOEAs.

- *Implicit preferences*: Das [94] noted that from practical experience, the DM usually picks a point in the middle of the surface where the Pareto front bulges out the most. This particular region of the front is called knee region and is of particular interest in practical situations [95,96]. In fact knee regions are composed with solutions presenting the maximal trade-offs between the different objectives. Solutions residing in knee regions are characterized by the fact that a small improvement in either objective will cause a large deterioration in at least another one which makes moving in either direction not attractive. Thus, in the absence of explicit DM's preferences (e.g., weights, reference points, trade-offs, etc.), knee regions are considered to represent the DM's preferences themselves [97]. Consequently, in this case, knee regions are implicitly the ROIs. It is seems to be interesting to further focus on this issue and to propose some preference-based MOEAs for knee regions discovery such as the parallel local weighted-sum optimization method [98] and the Knee-region-based R-NSGA-II [99].
- *Many-objective optimization*: As noted in the previous section, most MOEAs' selection mechanisms become ineffective with the increase of the number objectives. Since the DM is not interested with the whole Pareto front, researchers have suggested the articulation of the DM's preferences as a way to handle many-objective problems [69]. Hence, it is interesting to further investigate the effectiveness and efficiency of preference-based MOEAs in solving many-objective problems.
- *Robustness*: In optimization studies including multiobjective optimization, the main focus is placed on finding the global optimum or global Pareto optimal solutions, representing the best possible objective values. However, in practice, users may not always be interested in finding the so-called global best solutions, particularly when these solutions are quite sensitive to the variable perturbations which cannot be avoided in practice. In such cases, practitioners are interested in finding the robust solutions which are less sensitive to small perturbations in variables [100]. Hence, it is interesting to search for the *robust ROI*.
- *Noisy objective functions*: The uncertainty of environment represents an additional challenge to multiobjective optimization practitioners especially in real world applications. One can distinguish between noisy fitness/objective functions on the one hand and noise in the variables on the other hand. The latter corresponds to the problematic of robustness that we have just discussed in this section. The former problematic has been tackled recently, by Trautmann and Mehnen [101], by using a

preference-based MOEA based on the concept of DFs. Consequently, it is seems to be a challenging topic to further study the usefulness of preference incorporation in EMO in handling MOPs with noisy objective functions.

− *Application to real world MOPs*: We conclude, from the described works in this chapter, that most researchers have assessed their preference-based MOEAs on academic benchmarks such as the ZDT suite [68] and DTLZ one [36]. For this reason, the researchers are encouraged to apply these algorithms to handle real world problems in an attempt to further valorize the preference-based EMO research field [102].

REFERENCES

[1] C.A. Coello coello, G.B. Lamont, D.A. Van veldhuizen, Evolutionary Algorithms for Solving Multi-Objective Problems, second ed., Springer, New York, USA, 2007.

[2] K. Deb, Multi-Objective Optimization Using Evolutionary Algorithms, John Wiley and Sons Ltd., New York, USA, 2001

[3] L. Huang, A.S.M. Masud, Multiple Objective Decision Making: Theory and Applications, Springer, New York, USA, 1979, Lecture Notes in Economics and Mathematical Systems.

[4] K. Miettinen, Nonlinear Multiobjective Optimization, Kluwer Academic Publishers, Boston, USA, 1999.

[5] C.A. Coello Coello, An updated survey of GA-based multiobjective optimization techniques, ACM Comput. Surv. 32 (2) (2000) 109–143.

[6] A. Zhou, B.-Y. Qu, H. Li, S.-Z. Zhao, P.N. Suganthan, Q. Zhang, Multiobjective evolutionary algorithms: a survey of the state of the art, Swarm Evol. Comput. 1 (1) (2011) 32–49.

[7] S.F. Adra, I. Griffin, P.J. Fleming, A comparative study of progressive preference articulation techniques for multiobjective optimisation, in: Proceedings of the 4th International Conference on Evolutionary Multi-criterion Optimization (EMO'07), Springer, Matsushima, Japan, 2007, pp. 908–921.

[8] K. Deb, J. Sundar, U. Bhaskara, S. Chaudhuri, Reference point based multi-objective optimization using evolutionary algorithms, Int. J. Comput. Intell. Res. 2 (3) (2006) 273–286.

[9] A.P. Wierzbicki, Reference point approaches and objective ranking, in: J. Branke, K. Deb, K. Miettinen, R. Slowinski (Eds.), Practical Approaches to Multi-Objective Optimization, Dagstuhl Seminar Proceedings, 2007, pp. 1862–4405.

[10] C.A. Coello Coello, Handling preference in evolutionary multiobjective optimization: a survey, in: Proceedings of IEEE Congress on Evolutionary Computation (CEC'00), IEEE, San Diego, CA, USA, 2000, pp. 30–37.

[11] L. Rachmawati, D. Srinivasan, Preference incorporation in multi-objective evolutionary algorithms: a survey, in: In IEEE Congress on Evolutionary Computation (CEC'06), IEEE, Vancouver, BC, Canada, 2006, pp. 3385–3391.

[12] J. Branke, Consideration of partial user preferences in evolutionary multiobjective optimization, in: J. Branke, K. Deb, K. Miettinen, R. Slowinski (Eds.), Multiobjective Optimization—Interactive and Evolutionary Approaches, Springer, Berlin, Heidelberg, 2008, pp. 157–178.

[13] K. Deb, Multi-objective evolutionary algorithms: introducing bias among Pareto optimal solutions: KanGAL Report 99002, Indian Institute of Technology, Kanpur, India, 1999.

[14] N. Srinivas, K. Deb, Multiobjective optimization using nondominated sorting in genetic algorithms, Evol. Comput. 2 (3) (1994) 221–248.

[15] J. Branke, K. Deb, Integrating user preferences into evolutionary multi-objective optimization, in: Y. Jin (Ed.), Knowledge Incorporation in Evolutionary Computation, Springer, Berlin, Heidelberg, 2004, pp. 461–478.

[16] J. Branke, T. Kaussler, H. Schmeck, Guidance in evolutionary multi-objective optimization, Adv. Eng. Softw. 32 (6) (2001) 499–507.

[17] E. Zitzler, D. Brockhoff, L. Thiele, The hypervolume indicator revisited: on the design of Pareto-compliant indicators via weighted integration, in: Proceedings of the 4th International Conference on Evolutionary Multi-criterion Optimization (EMO'07), Springer, Matsushima, Japan, 2007, pp. 862–876.

[18] E. Zitzler, L. Thiele, M. Laumanns, C.M. Fonseca, G. Grunert da Fonseca, Performance assessment of multiobjective optimizers: an analysis and review, IEEE Trans. Evol. Comput. 7 (2) (2003) 117–132.

[19] E. Zitzler, L. Thiele, Multiobjective evolutionary algorithms: a comparative case study and the strength Pareto approach, IEEE Trans. Evol. Comput. 3 (4) (1999) 257–271.

[20] E. Zitzler, S. Künzli, Indicator-based selection in multiobjective search, in: Proceedings of the 8th International Conference on Parallel Problem Solving from Nature (PPSN VIII), Springer, Birmingham, UK, 2004, pp. 832–842.

[21] M. Fleischer, The measure of Pareto optima: applications to multi-objective metaheuristics, in: Proceedings of the 2nd International Conference on Evolutionary Multi-Criterion Optimization (EMO'03), Springer, Faro, Portugal, 2003, pp. 519–533.

[22] V.G. Da Fonseca, C.M. Fonseca, A.O. Hall, Inferential performance assessment of stochastic optimisers and the attainment function, in: Proceedings of the 1st International Conference on Evolutionary Multi-Criterion Optimization (EMO'01), Springer, Zurich, Switzerland, 2001, pp. 213–225.

[23] A. Auger, J. Bader, D. Brockhoff, E. Zitzler, Articulating user preferences in many-objective problems by sampling the weighted hypervolume, in: Proceedings of the 11th Genetic and Evolutionary Computation Conference (GECCO'09), ACM, Montreal, Canada, 2009, pp. 555–562.

[24] G.W. Greenwood, X.S. Hu, J.C. D'ambrosio, Fitness functions for multiple objective optimization problems: combining preferences with Pareto rankings, in: R.K. Belew, M.D. Vose (Eds.), Foundations of Genetic Algorithms, Morgan Kaufmann, San Francisco, CA, USA, 1997, pp. 437–455.

[25] K. Deb, A. Sinha, P. Korhonen, J. Wallenius, An interactive evolutionary multi-objective optimization method based on progressively approximated value functions, IEEE Trans. Evol. Comput. 14 (5) (2010) 723–739.

[26] R.B. Wilson, A simplicial algorithm for concave programming, PhD thesis, Graduate School of Business Administration, Harvard University, USA, 1963.

[27] M. Köksalan, I. Karahan, An interactive territory defining evolutionary algorithm: iTDEA, IEEE Trans. Evol. Comput. 14 (5) (2010) 702–722.

[28] I. Karahan, M. Köksalan, A territory defining multiobjective evolutionary algorithm and preference incorporation, IEEE Trans. Evol. Comput. 14 (4) (2010) 636–664.

[29] R. Battiti, A. Passerini, Brain–computer evolutionary multiobjective optimization: a genetic algorithm adapting to the decision maker, IEEE Trans. Evol. Comput. 14 (5) (2010) 671–687.

[30] W.W. Cohen, R.E. Schapire, Y. Singer, Learning to order things, J. Artif. Intell. Res. 10 (1) (1999) 243–270.

[31] D. Jones, A taxonomy of global optimization methods based on response surfaces, J. Glob. Optim. 21 (4) (2001) 345–383.

[32] Q. Zhang, H. Li, MOEA/D: a multiobjective evolutionary algorithm based on decomposition, IEEE Trans. Evol. Comput. 11 (6) (2007) 712–731.

[33] J. Shawe-Taylor, N. Cristianini, Kernel Methods for Pattern Analysis, Cambridge University Press, New York, USA, 2004.

[34] R. Battiti, M. Brunato, F. Massica, Reactive search and intelligent optimization, Operations Research/Computer Science Interfaces Series, vol. 45, Springer-Verlag, Berlin, Heidelberg, 2008.

[35] K. Deb, A. Pratap, S. Agarwal, T. Meyarivan, A fast and elitist multiobjective genetic algorithm: NSGA-II, IEEE Trans. Evol. Comput. 6 (2) (2002) 182–197.

[36] K. Deb, L. Thiele, M. Laumanns, E. Zitzler, Scalable multiobjective optimization test problems, in: Proceedings of IEEE Congress on Evolutionary Computation (CEC'02), IEEE, Hawaii, USA, 2002, pp. 825–830.

[37] S. Martello, P. Toth, Knapsack Problems: Algorithms and Computer Implementations, John Wiley and Sons, Ltd, New York, USA, 1990.

[38] J.W. Fowler, E.S. Gel, M. Köksalan, P. Korhonen, J.L. Marquis, J. Wallenius, Interactive evolutionary multi-objective optimization for quasi-concave preference functions, Eur. J. Oper. Res. 206 (2) (2010) 417–425.

[39] R. Ramesh, M.H. Karwan, S. Zionts, Theory of convex cones in multicriteria decision making, Ann. Oper. Res. 16 (1) (1988) 131–147.

[40] J. Branke, S. Greco, R. Slowinski, P. Zielniewski, Interactive evolutionary multiobjective optimization driven by robust ordinal regression, Bull. Polish Acad. Sci. 58 (3) (2010) 347–358.

[41] S. Greco, R. Slowiński, J. Figueira, V. Mousseau, Robust ordinal regression, in: M. Ehrgott, J. Figueira, S. Greco (Eds.), Trends in Multiple Criteria Decision Analysis, Springer, Berlin, Heidelberg, 2010, pp. 241–283.

[42] J. Figueira, S. Greco, R. Slowiński, Building a set of additive value functions representing a reference preorder and intensities of preference: GRIP method, Eur. J. Oper. Res. 195 (2) (2009) 460–486.

[43] S. Greco, V. Mousseau, R. Slowiński, Ordinal regression revisited: multiple criteria ranking with a set of additive value functions, Eur. J. Oper. Res. 191 (2) (2008) 415–435.

[44] J. Figueira, S. Greco, R. Slowiński, Identifying the "most representative" value function among all compatible value functions in the GRIP method, in: Proceedings of the 68th Meeting of the EURO Working Group on MCDA, CD-ROM, 2008.

[45] Y.C. Jin, B. Sendhoff, Incorporation of fuzzy preferences into evolutionary multiobjective optimization, in: Proceedings of the 4th Asia-Pacific Conference on Simulated Evolution and Learning, Nanyang, Singapore, 2002, pp. 26–30.

[46] Y. Jin, T. Okabe, B. Sendhoff, Adapting weighted aggregation for multiobjective evolution strategies, in: Proceedings of the 1st International Conference on Evolutionary Multicriterion Optimization (EMO'01), Springer, Zurich, Switzerland, 2001, pp. 96–110.

[47] D. Cvetkovic, I.C. Parmee, Preferences and their application in evolutionary multiobjective optimisation, IEEE Trans. Evol. Comput. 6 (1) (2002) 42–57.

[48] L. Rachmawati, Incorporating decision maker preference in multi-objective evolutionary algorithms, PhD thesis, National University of Singapore, Singapore, 2008.

[49] L. Rachmawati, D. Srinivasan, Incorporating the notion of relative importance of objectives in evolutionary multiobjective optimization, IEEE Trans. Evol. Comput. 14 (4) (2010) 530–546.

[50] C.M. Fonseca, P.J. Fleming, Genetic algorithms for multi-objective optimization: formulation, discussion and generalization, in: Proceedings of the 5th International Conference on Genetic Algorithms (ICGA'93), Morgan Kaufmann, Urbana-Champaign, IL, USA, 1993, pp. 416–423.

[51] C.M. Fonseca, P.J. Fleming, Multiobjective optimization and multiple constraint handling with evolutionary algorithms-Part I: a unified formulation, IEEE Trans. Syst. Man Cybernet. A 28 (1) (1998) 26–37.

[52] K.C. Tan, E.F. Khor, T.H. Lee, An evolutionary algorithm with advanced goal and priority specification for multi-objective optimization, J. Artif. Intell. Res. 18 (1) (2003) 183–215.

[53] K.C. Tan, T.H. Lee, E.F. Khor, Evolutionary algorithms with goal and priority information for multi-objective optimization, in: Proceedings of IEEE Congress on Evolutionary Computation (CEC'99), Washington, DC, USA, 1999, pp. 106–113.

[54] K. Deb, A. Kumar, Interactive evolutionary multi-objective optimization and decision making using reference direction method, in: Proceedings of the 9th Genetic and Evolutionary Computation Conference (GECCO'07), ACM, London, UK, 2007, pp. 781–788.

[55] P. Korhonen, J. Laasko, A visual interactive method for solving the multiple criteria problem, Eur. J. Oper. Res. 24 (2) (1986) 277–287.

[56] K. Deb, A. Kumar, Light beam search based multi-objective optimization using evolutionary algorithms, in: Proceedings of IEEE Congress on Evolutionary Computation (CEC'07), IEEE, Singapore, 2007, pp. 2125–2132.

[57] A. Jaszkiewicz, R. Slowinski, The light beam search approach—an overview of methodology and applications, Eur. J. Oper. Res. 113 (2) (1999) 300–314.

[58] R. Allmendinger, X. Li, J. Branke, Reference point-based particle swarm optimization using a steady-state approach, in: Proceedings of the 7th International Conference on Simulated Evolution and Learning (SEAL'08), Springer, Melbourne, Australia, 2008, pp. 200–209.

[59] J. Kennedy, R.C. Eberhart, Particle swarm optimization, in: Proceedings of the 3rd IEEE International Conference on Neural Networks (ICNN'95), IEEE, Perth, Australia, 1995, pp. 1942–1948.

[60] A.P. Wierzbicki, The use of reference objectives in multiobjective optimization, in: G. Fandel, T. Gal (Eds.), Multiple Criteria Decision Making Theory and Applications, Springer, Berlin, Heidelberg, 1980, pp. 468–486.

[61] W.R.M.U.K. Wickramasinghe, X. Li, Integrating user preferences with particle swarms for multi-objective optimization, in: Proceedings of the 10th Genetic and Evolutionary Computation COnference (GECCO'08), ACM, Atlanta, Georgia, USA, 2008, pp. 745–752.

[62] X. Li, A non-dominated sorting particle swarm optimizer for multiobjective optimization, in: Proceedings of the 5th Genetic and Evolutionary Computation Conference (GECCO'03), ACM, Chicago, IL, USA, 2003, pp. 37–48.

[63] X. Li, Better spread and convergence: particle swarm multiobjective optimization using the maximin fitness function, in: Proceedings of the 6th Genetic and Evolutionary Computation COnference (GECCO'04), ACM, Seattle, WA, USA, 2004, pp. 117–128.

[64] J. Molina, L.V. Santana-Quintero, A.G. Hernández-Díaz, C.A. Coello Coello, R. Caballero, g-dominance: reference point based dominance for multiobjective metaheuristics, Eur. J. Oper. Res. 197 (2) (2009) 685–692.

[65] L. Thiele, K. Miettinen, P. Korhonen, J. Molina, A preference-based evolutionary algorithm for multiobjective optimization, Evol. Comput. 17 (3) (2009) 411–436.

[66] S. Bechikh, L. Ben Said, K. Ghédira, The r-dominance: a new dominance relation for preference-based evolutionary multi-objective optimization: Technical report No. BS-2010-001, 2010), SOIE Research Unit, High Institute of Management of Tunis, University of Tunis, Tunisia, January, 2010. https://sites.google.com/site/slimbechikh/technical_reports/Technical_Report_BS-2010-001.pdf.

[67] L. Ben Said, S. Bechikh, K. Ghédira, The r-dominance: a new dominance relation for interactive evolutionary multi-criteria decision making, IEEE Trans. Evol. Comput. 14 (5) (2010) 801–818.

[68] E. Zitzler, K. Deb, L. Thiele, Comparison of multiobjective evolutionary algorithms: empirical results, Evol. Comput. 8 (2) (2000) 173–195.

[69] A. López Jaimes, A. Arias Montaño, C.A. Coello Coello, Preference incorporation to solve many-objective airfoil design problems, in: Proceedings of IEEE Congress on Evolutionary Computation (CEC'11), IEEE, New Orleans, 2011, pp. 1605–1612.

[70] E. Fernandez, E. Lopez, S. Bernal, C.A. Coello Coello, J. Navarro, Evolutionary multiobjective optimization using an outranking-based dominance generalization, Comput. Oper. Res. 37 (2) (2010) 390–395.

[71] B. Roy, Multicriteria Methodology for Decision Aiding, Kluwer Academic Publishers, Dordrecht, The Netherlands, 1996.

[72] B. Roy, The outranking approach and the foundations of ELECTRE methods, in: - C.A. Bana e Costa (Ed.), Reading in Multiple Criteria Decision Aid, Springer, Berlin, Heidelberg, 1990, pp. 155–183.

[73] V. Mousseau, L.C. Dias, Valued outranking relations in ELECTRE providing manageable disaggregation procedures, Eur. J. Oper. Res. 156 (2) (2004) 467–482.

[74] A. Ostanello, Outranking methods, in: B. Fandel, G. Spronk, J. Matarazzo (Eds.), in: Proceedings of the 1st International Summer School on Multiple Criteria Decision Making Methods, Applications and Software, vol. 1, Springer, Acireale, Italy, 1983, pp. 41–60.

[75] E. Fernandez, N. Cancela, R. Olmedo, Deriving a final ranking from fuzzy preferences: an approach compatible with the principle of correspondence, Math. Comput. Model. 47 (3) (2008) 218–234.

[76] E. Fernandez, E. Lopez, F. Lopez, C.A. Coello Coello, Increasing selective pressure towards the best compromise in evolutionary multiobjective optimization: the extended NOSGA method, Inf. Sci. 181 (1) (2011) 44–56.

[77] T. Wagner, H. Trautmann, Integration of preferences in hypervolume-based multiobjective evolutionary algorithms by means of desirability functions, IEEE Trans. Evol. Comput. 14 (5) (2010) 688–701.

[78] N. Beume, B. Naujoks, M. Emmerich, SMS-EMOA: multiobjective selection based on dominated hypervolume, Eur. J. Oper. Res. 181 (3) (2007) 1653–1669.

[79] J. Harrington, The desirability function, Indus. Qual. Control 21 (10) (1965) 494–498.

[80] D. Biermann, K. Weinert, T. Wagner, Model-based optimization revisited: toward real-world processes, in: Proceedings of IEEE Congress on Evolutionary Computation (CEC'08), IEEE, Atlanta, Georgia, USA, 2008, pp. 2980–2987.

[81] S. Bechikh, L. Ben Said, K. Ghédira, Estimating nadir point in multi-objective optimization using mobile reference points, in: Proceedings of IEEE Congress on Evolutionary Computation (CEC'10), IEEE, Barcelona, Spain, 2010, pp. 2129–2137.

[82] K. Deb, K. Miettinen, A review of nadir point estimation procedures using evolutionary approaches: a tale of dimensionality reduction: KanGAL report number 2008004, Kanpur Genetic Algorithms Laboratory (KanGAL), Indian Institute of Technology Kanpur, India, 2008. http://www.iitk.ac.in/kangal/papers/k2008004.pdf.

[83] L.C. Dias, V. Mousseau, Inferring Electre's veto-related parameters from outranking examples, Eur. J. Oper. Res. 170 (1) (2006) 172–191.

[84] E.J. Hughes, Evolutionary many-objective optimization: many once or one many? in: Proceedings of IEEE Congress Evolutionary Computation (CEC'05), IEEE, Edinburgh, UK, 2005, pp. 222–227.

[85] A. López Jaimes, C.A. Coello Coello, J.E. Urías Barrientos, Online objective reduction to deal with many-objective problems, in: Proceedings of the 5th International

Conference on Evolutionary Multi-criterion Optimization (EMO'09), Springer, Nantes, France, 2009, pp. 423–437.

[86] J. Pfeiffer, U. Golle, F. Rothlauf, Reference point based multiobjective evolutionary algorithms for group decisions, in: Proceedings of Genetic and Evolutionary Computation COnference (GECCO'08), ACM, Georgia, Atlanta, USA, 2008, pp. 697–704.

[87] S. Bechikh, L. Ben Said, K. Ghédira, Negotiating decision makers' reference points for group preference-based evolutionary multi-objective optimization, in: Proceedings of the 11th IEEE International Conference on Hybrid Intelligent Systems (IEEE HIS'11), IEEE, Melaka, Malaysia, 2011, pp. 377–382.

[88] K.J. Arrow, Social Choice and Individual Values, John Wiley and Sons, Ltd., New York, USA, 1951.

[89] S. Greco, M. Kadzinski, V. Mousseau, R. Slowinski, Robust ordinal regression for multiple criteria group decision: UTA^{GMS}-GROUP and $UTADIS^{GMS}$-GROUP, Decis. Support. Syst. 52 (3) (2012) 549–561.

[90] A. Lotov, K. Miettinen, Visualizing the Pareto frontier, in: J. Branke, K. Deb, K. Miettinen, R. Slowinski (Eds.), Multiobjective Optimization—Interactive and Evolutionary Approaches, Springer, Berlin, Heidelberg, 2008, pp. 213–243.

[91] P. Korhonen, J. Wallenius, Visualization in the multiple objective decision-making framework, in: J. Branke, K. Deb, K. Miettinen, R. Slowinski (Eds.), Multiobjective Optimization—Interactive and Evolutionary Approaches, Springer, Berlin, Heidelberg, 2008, pp. 195–212.

[92] S. French, Decision Theory: An Introduction to the Mathematics of Rationality, Halsted Press, New York, USA, 1986.

[93] L.R. Pedro, H.C.R. Takahashi, Decision-maker preference modeling in interactive multiobjective optimization, in: Proceedings of the 7th International Conference on Evolutionary Multi-criterion Optimization (EMO'13), Springer, Sheffield, UK, 2013, pp. 811–824.

[94] I. Das, On characterizing the knee of the Pareto curve based on normal-boundary intersection, Struct. Optim. 18 (2–3) (1999) 107–115.

[95] J. Branke, K. Deb, H. Dierolf, M. Osswald, Finding knees in multiobjective optimization, in: Proceedings of the 8th International Conference on Parallel Problem Solving from Nature (PPSN VIII), Springer, Birmingham, UK, 2004, pp. 722–731.

[96] K. Deb, S. Gupta, Understanding knee points in bicriteria problems and their implications as preferred solution principles, Eng. Optim. 43 (2011) 1175–1204. , online first, Taylor & Francis. http://www.tandfonline.com/doi/abs/10.1080/0305215X.2010.548863.

[97] S. Bechikh, L. Ben Said, K. Ghédira, Searching for knee regions of the Pareto front using mobile reference points, Soft Comput. Fusion Found. Methodol. Appl. 15 (9) (2011) 1807–1823.

[98] L. Rachmawati, D. Srinivasan, Multiobjective evolutionary algorithm with controllable focus on the knees of the Pareto front, IEEE Trans. Evol. Comput. 13 (4) (2009) 810–824.

[99] S. Bechikh, L. Ben Said, K. Ghédira, Searching for knee regions in multi-objective optimization using mobile reference points, in: Proceeding of the 25th ACM Symposium on Applied Computing (ACM SAC'10—Best Paper Award), ACM, Sierre, Switzerland, 2010, pp. 1118–1125.

[100] K. Deb, S. Gupta, Introducing robustness in multi-objective optimization, Evol. Comput. 14 (4) (2006) 463–494.

[101] H. Trautmann, B. Mehnen, Preference-based Pareto optimization in certain and noisy environments, Eng. Optim. 41 (1) (2008) 23–38.

[102] S. Bechikh, L. Ben Said, K. Ghédira, Group preference-based evolutionary multi-objective optimization with non-equally important decision makers: application to the portfolio selection problem, Int. J. Comput. Inform. Syst. Indus. Manage. Appl. 5 (1) (2013) 278–288.

ABOUT THE AUTHORS

Slim Bechikh received the B.Sc. degree in computer science applied to management and the M.Sc. degree in modeling from the University of Tunis, Tunisia, in 2006 and 2008, respectively. He also obtained the Ph.D. degree in computer science applied to management from University of Tunis in January 2013. He worked, for 4 years, as an attached researcher within the Optimization Strategies and Intelligent Computing Lab (SOIE), Tunisia. Now, he is a postdoctoral researcher at the SBSE@Michigan, University of Michigan, Dearborn Campus. His research interests include multicriteria decision making, evolutionary computation, multiagent systems, portfolio optimization, and search-based software engineering. Since 2008, he published several papers in well-ranked journals and conferences. Moreover, he obtained the best paper award of the ACM Symposium on Applied Computing 2010 in Switzerland among more than three hundreds participants. Since 2010, he serves as reviewer for several conferences such as ACM SAC and GECCO and various journals such as Soft Computing and IJITDM.

Marouane Kessentini is a tenure-track assistant professor at University of Michigan, Dearborn campus. He is the founder of the research group: Search-based Software Engineering@Michigan. He holds a Ph.D. in Computer Science, University of Montreal (Canada), 2012. His research interests include the application of artificial intelligence techniques to software engineering (search-based software engineering), software testing, model-driven engineering, software quality, and reengineering. He has published around 50 papers in conferences, workshops, books, and journals including three best paper awards. He has served as program-committee/organization member in several conferences and journals.

Lamjed Ben Said received the B.S. degree in computer science applied to management from the High Institute of Management of Tunis, University of Tunis, Tunis, Tunisia, in 1998, and the M.S. and Ph.D. degrees in computer science from the University of Paris VI, Paris, France, in 1999 and 2003, respectively. He was a Research Fellow for 3 years at France Telecom, Research and Development, Paris, France. He is currently an Associate Professor with the High Institute of Management of Tunis, University of Tunis. He is currently also the director of the High Institute of Management of Tunis, University of Tunis. His research interests include multiagent systems, multicriteria decision making, evolutionary computation, supply chain management, and behavioral economics.

Khaled Ghédira received the B.E. degree in hydraulics from École Nationale Supérieure d'Électronique, d'Électrotechnique, d'Informatique, d'Hydraulique, et des Télécommunications, Toulouse, France, in 1983, the B.E. degree in computer science and applied mathematics from École nationale supérieure d'informatique et mathématiques appliquées de Grenoble, Grenoble, France, in 1986, and the M.S. and Ph.D. degrees in artificial intelligence from École Nationale de la Statistique et de l'Administration Économique, Malakoff, France, in 1990 and 1993, respectively. He also received the Habilitation à Diriger des Recherches degree in computer science from the National School of Computer Studies, Ecole Nationale des Sciences de L'informatique, Tunis, Tunisia, in 1999. He was a Research Fellow with the Institute of Computer Science and Artificial Intelligence, Neuchâtel, Switzerland, and a Consultant with British Telecom, London, UK. He is currently a Professor of artificial intelligence with the High Institute of Management of Tunis, University of Tunis, Tunis, Tunisia. He is currently also the President of the Tunisian Association of Artificial Intelligence. He has authored and coauthored more than 180 international journals and conference research papers. He has written one text book on combinatorial optimization. His research interests include multiagent systems, constraint satisfaction problems, combinatorial optimization, supply chain management, multicriteria decision making, and metaheuristics.

AUTHOR INDEX

Note: Page numbers followed by "*f*" indicate figures and "*t*" indicate tables.

SUBJECT INDEX

Note: Page numbers followed by "*f*" indicate figures and "*t*" indicate tables.

CONTENTS OF VOLUMES IN THIS SERIES

Printed in the United States
By Bookmasters